Thomas E. Patterson

INFORMING THE NEWS

Thomas E. Patterson is Bradlee Professor of Government and the Press and teaches at the Joan Shorenstein Center on the Press, Politics and Public Policy at Harvard University's John F. Kennedy School of Government. His book *The Vanishing Voter* looks at the causes and consequences of electoral participation. His earlier book on the media's political role, *Out of Order*, received the American Political Science Association's Graber Award as the best book of the decade in political communication. His first book, *The Unseeing Eye*, was named by the American Association for Public Opinion Research as one of the fifty most influential books on public opinion in the past half century. His research has been funded by the Ford, Markle, Smith Richardson, Pew, Knight, Carnegie, and National Science foundations.

ALSO BY THOMAS E. PATTERSON

The Unseeing Eye

Out of Order

The Vanishing Voter:
Public Involvement in an Age of Uncertainty

INFORMING THE NEWS

INFORMING THE NEWS

The Need for Knowledge-Based Journalism

Thomas E. Patterson

Vintage Books
A Division of Random House LLC | New York

A VINTAGE ORIGINAL, OCTOBER 2013

Library of Congress Cataloging-in-Publication Data:
Patterson, Thomas E.
Informing the news: the need for knowledge-based journalism / by Thomas E. Patterson.
pages cm
ISBN 978-0-345-80660-4 (pbk.)
1. Journalism—Study and teaching—United States. I. Title.
PN4788.P38 2013 070.4071—dc23 2013009242

Book design by Heather Kelly

www.vintagebooks.com

Printed in the United States of America
10 9 8 7 6 5 4 3 2 1

FOR LORIE

In an exact sense the present crisis in Western democracy is a crisis in journalism.

—Walter Lippmann,
Liberty and the News, 1920

CONTENTS

ACKNOWLEDGMENTS

Journalists cannot meet democracy's needs unless they become "knowledge professionals" who have "mastery not only of technique but also of content." This idea, put forth by Dr. Vartan Gregorian, president of the Carnegie Corporation of New York, marked the beginning of the Carnegie-Knight Initiative, from which this book stems.

Vartan's vision caught the attention of Hodding Carter III, the president and CEO of the John S. and James L. Knight Foundation. In 2005, they announced the Carnegie-Knight Initiative for the purpose of strengthening journalism education and practice. Journalism education was the starting point. Four top journalism schools—those at Columbia, Northwestern, the University of California–Berkeley, and the University of Southern California, as well as Harvard University's Shorenstein Center on the Press, Politics and Public Policy—were asked to rethink how journalism students were being trained. Two years later, the journalism programs at Arizona State, Maryland, Missouri, Nebraska, North Carolina, Syracuse, and Texas were added to the initiative. These twelve institutions spent much of the past decade developing ways to bring knowledge more fully into journalism training.

This book focuses more on journalism practice than on journalism education. Nevertheless, my participation in the initiative and belief in its goals are what led to the writing of this book. Special thanks are due to Vartan Gregorian and to Alberto Ibargüen, who succeeded Hodding Carter as Knight's president and CEO shortly after the initiative started. Vartan and Alberto did more than put institutional funds into the initiative. They put their energy and ideas into it. So did Susan King, Carnegie's vice president of external affairs, and Eric Newton, Knight's vice president for the journalism program. Without Susan's and Eric's steady influence, the initiative would have had much less power and direction. Carnegie's Ambika Kapur helped all of us, foundation officers and scholars alike, by organizing the initiative's activities.

I also want to thank all those who served as dean at the participating institutions during the six years of the Carnegie-Knight Initiative: Chris Callahan of Arizona State University; Orville Schell and Neil Henry of the University of California–Berkeley; Nicholas Lemann of Columbia University; Tom Kunkel and Kevin Klose of the University of Maryland; Dean Mills of the University of Missouri–Columbia; Gary Kebbel and Will Norton of the University of Nebraska; Loren Ghiglione and John Lavine of Northwestern University; David Rubin and Lorraine Branham of Syracuse University; Jean Folkerts and Susan King of the University of North Carolina at Chapel Hill; Geoffrey Cowan and Ernest Wilson of the University of Southern California; and Roderick Hart of the University of Texas at Austin. Their insights on journalism influenced my thinking on the subject, although I'm sure they would take exception to some—perhaps many—of the arguments put forth in this book.

Thanks also to Alex Jones, my colleague at the Shorenstein Center, who is the center's director and served from the start as coordinator of the initiative's task force, which had the lead role on research and policy issues. Alex's contribution goes beyond his service to the initiative. His friendship and advice are treasured, in my personal as well as professional life. The Shorenstein Center's Nancy Palmer protected my writing time and was my constant reader. I knew a chapter was nearing completion when she returned it with only a suggestion or two. For the final draft, the center's John Wihbey weighed in. Kristina Mastropasqua of the center was my research assistant, as were graduate students Will Cole, Melissa Galvez, and Hanna Siegel. They did the work cheerfully, and well.

If the activities of the Carnegie-Knight Initiative are the source of the book, the century-old writings of journalist Walter Lippmann have been its guide. I have tried to honor Lippmann's contribution by citing him regularly, by consciously modeling some of my arguments after his, by starting each chapter with a quote from his writings, and by adopting Lippmann's signature use of numbers to head chapter sections.

The largest group that could have been acknowledged is the hundreds of scholars and journalists whose work informed my analysis. Their identities are revealed in the book's footnotes. Their contributions bolster my claim that journalism can and should become a knowledge-based profession.

The shortest list in these acknowledgments consists of one individual, my wife, Lorie Conway. I owe her my heartfelt thanks. The weekends and evenings I spent hunched over the keyboard imposed unreasonably on our time together. The fact that she is a journalist by training and a former Nieman Fellow at Harvard might explain her patience. I know better. Her support was unconditional, and her suggestions helped me unravel the many puzzles that arose while developing the case for knowledge-based journalism. The preparation of the book would not have been anywhere near as manageable or as enjoyable without her at my side.

Thomas E. Patterson
Harvard University
Cambridge, Massachusetts
January 30, 2013

INFORMING THE NEWS

INTRODUCTION

The Corruption of Information

Incompetence and aimlessness, corruption and disloyalty, panic and ultimate disaster, must come to any people which is denied access to the facts. No one can manage anything on pap. Neither can a people.[1]

—Walter Lippmann

As the possibility of invading Iraq was being debated in Washington, pollsters were busy asking Americans for their opinions. A slim majority expressed support for an invasion if President George W. Bush thought it necessary.[2] But Americans' willingness to go to war depended on what they believed was true of Iraq. Contrary to fact, most Americans thought Iraq was aligned with al-Qaeda, the terrorist group that had attacked the United States on September 11, 2001. Some Americans even believed Iraqi pilots had flown the planes that slammed into the World Trade Center towers and the Pentagon.[3]

Citizens with mistaken beliefs were twice as likely as other Americans to favor an invasion of Iraq.[4] They might also have had other reasons for wanting to rid the world of Saddam Hussein. He had repeatedly thwarted UN inspections of his weapons systems and had killed tens of thousands of his own people. Nevertheless, the notion that Hussein was aligned with al-Qaeda was pure fiction.

Fox News viewers were the most misinformed. Two-thirds of them perceived a "clear link" between Saddam Hussein and al-Qaeda, a research finding that journalists at rival news outlets found amusing.[5] A more sober look at the evidence would have tempered their response. Fox viewers were not the only ones with a false sense of reality. Roughly half of ABC, CBS, CNN, and NBC viewers wrongly thought that Iraq and al-Qaeda were collaborators, as did two in five newspaper readers.[6]

Warped understandings are hardly new. When fluoride was added to the nation's water supply a half century ago, some Americans claimed it was a communist plot to poison the nation's youth.[7] In a seminal 1964 *Harper's Magazine* article, the historian Richard Hofstadter described such thinking as "the paranoid style." "No other word," Hofstadter wrote, "adequately evokes the sense of heated exaggeration, suspiciousness, and conspiratorial fantasy that I have in mind."[8]

The crazed anticommunists of postwar America have their counterparts today. Can anything except the "paranoid style" explain the conspiracy theorists who claim Barack Obama funneled money to extremist Muslim groups in an effort to sabotage American interests[9] or who say George W. Bush knew in advance of the September 11 terrorist plot and chose not to stop it?[10] Yet paranoia cannot explain today's astonishing misinformation level. As Hofstadter defined it, the "paranoid style" describes the thinking of the delusional few, whereas it is easy today to find issues on which tens of millions of Americans have far-fetched ideas. At one point in the 2009–2010 health care reform debate, for instance, half of the American public falsely believed the legislation included "death panels"—government-appointed committees with the power to deny medical treatment to old folks.[11]

It is a short step from misinformation to mischief, as we have seen repeatedly in recent policy debates. It is nearly impossible to have sensible public deliberation when large numbers of people are out of touch with reality.[12] Without agreement on the facts, arguments have no foundation from which to build.[13] Recent debates on everything from foreign policy to the federal budget have fractured or sputtered because of a factual deficit.[14]

What's going on here? Why are Americans mired in misinformation? Several factors are at work, but changes in communication top the list. Americans have been ill-served by the intermediaries—the journalists, politicians, talk show hosts, pundits, and bloggers—that claim to be their trusted guides.

Journalists are our chief sense-makers. Journalists are other things, too, but we need them mostly to help us understand the world of public affairs beyond our direct experience. That's not to say that journalists bear the full burden of keeping us informed. If they are to be charged with that responsibility, they will fail. They cannot make up for glaring defects in the work of others, including our educators and political leaders.[15] Yet, as journalist Walter Lippmann noted, democracy falters "if there is no steady supply of trustworthy and relevant news."[16]

Journalists are failing to deliver it. A 2006 Carnegie Corporation report concluded that "the quality of journalism is losing ground in the drive for profit, diminished objectivity, and the spread of the 'entertainment virus.' "[17] The public certainly recognizes the problem. In a 2012 Gallup poll, a mere 8 percent of respondents said they had a "great deal" of confidence in the news media's ability to report "the news fully, accurately, and fairly." More than seven times that number 60 percent in all—said they had little or no confidence in the press.[18] That's a dramatic comedown from a few decades ago, when a majority of Americans trusted what the press was telling them.[19]

Some journalists dismiss criticisms of their work, saying that the public is "shooting the messenger"—blaming the press for what's being reported, whereas it ought to be aiming its fire at others.[20] There's some truth to their claim. Yet most journalists are keenly aware that they are contributing to the problem. A Pew Research Center survey found that journalists thought reporting had become "shallower," "increasingly sloppy," and "too timid."[21] A subsequent Pew survey found that 68 percent of reporters believed that "bottom-line pressure is hurting journalism," up from 41 percent a decade earlier. Six in ten of those surveyed said that journalism is headed "in the wrong direction."[22]

Nevertheless, journalists are the best hope for something better. Talk show hosts, bloggers, political activists, politicians, and commentators cannot be trusted to protect the facts. Many in their ranks are conscientious and public minded, but others willfully twist the facts for partisan or personal gain. They have concocted most of the half-truths and lies foisted on the American public.

Some observers say journalists are less relevant today, given the increase in information sources and the greater ease with which people can share information.[23] As I see it, citizens need journalists more than ever, precisely because there is so much information available, of such varying quality and relevance. The contribution of the reporter cannot be compared with that of the scholar or the policy analyst, much less that of the talk show host or blogger. Each has a place in our public life, but none of the others are equipped to do what journalists do. Journalists are in the daily business of making the unseen visible, of connecting us to the world beyond our direct experience. Public life is increasingly complex, and we need an ongoing source of timely and relevant information on the issues of the day. That's why we need journalists.

Yet, the claim that journalists are the public's indispensible source of information dissolves when reporters peddle hype and misinformation, which, as the first two chapters in this book will show, has too often been the case in recent years. There are plenty of conscientious journalists, but their efforts are diminished by what other reporters are doing. The costs of poor reporting are higher than many journalists might think, not only to our democracy but to their livelihoods. If the public concludes that the messages of journalists are no more valuable than those of other sources, the demand for news will go down.[24] The shift is already under way. Surveys over the past decade show a steady rise in the number of Americans who prefer to get their information from partisan bloggers, talk show hosts, and pundits.[25] In its 2013 "State of the News Media" report, the Project for Excellence in Journalism noted that nearly a third of American adults had stopped using a news source because they believed its reporting had declined in quality.[26]

Journalists have had crises of confidence in the past, most pointedly in the "yellow journalism" era of the early 1900s, when vanity, advertisers' clout, and market competition led to what one critic called "a shrieking, gaudy, sensation-loving, devil-may-care kind of journalism which lured the reader by any possible means."[27] The challenge of that earlier era was answered by separating the advertising and news departments and by devising a form of reporting—objective journalism—that sought to strip the news of unfounded opinion.[28]

What might be the answer this time? What might increase the trustworthiness of the news? Some observers believe that digital-era breakthroughs—citizen journalists, fact checkers, crowdsourcing, and the like—are the keys to a more reliable form of news. These developments can help, but they have major limits of their own.[29] A more promising possibility is what I will call "knowledge-based journalism." Today's journalists use reporting tools that were developed more than a century ago and were better suited to the demands of that age than to those of today, where manufactured consent, clever fabrications, and pumped-up claims are everyday assaults on the public's sense of reality.

In the chapters that follow, I identify the extent to which the public's information has been corrupted by its providers and how knowledge-based journalism can act as a corrective. I also provide tantalizing evidence that suggests knowledge-based journalism could solidify the audience for news. To be sure, knowledge-based journalism would not be a cure-all. Information corruption is deeply rooted in contemporary America. Too much money, power, and celebrity rest on it for it to be wished away. Nevertheless, knowledge-based journalism would provide the steady supply of trustworthy and relevant news that Americans now lack, but sorely need.

ONE

The Information Problem

All that the sharpest critics of democracy have alleged is true, if there is no steady supply of trustworthy and relevant news.[1]

—Walter Lippmann

1.

"The citizen performs the perilous business of government under the worst possible conditions."[2] Journalist Walter Lippmann wrote these words in 1922, a time when deafening factories, oversized families, and the grind of household chores sapped people's time and attention. A quiet moment with the evening paper was as close as most people came to a civic education. "For the newspaper in all literalness is the bible of democracy, the book out of which a people determines its conduct," Lippmann wrote. "It is the only serious book that most people read. It is the only book they read every day."[3]

Life today is much easier. Yet the same instrument—the media—that in Lippmann's time was a citizen's refuge has become a fool's paradise. Never before has the public had access to such a vast amount of public affairs information. Yet never before has so much of the information been untrustworthy or pointless. New York University's Neil Postman worried that in the media age we risk "amusing ourselves to death."[4] We now also risk deluding ourselves to no good end. On one issue after the next, many Americans' beliefs are so wildly at odds with reality that they could not possibly think sensibly about it. Numerous indicators reveal that the earth is warming from human activity and that the temperature rise is accelerating. Yet much of the public either flatly denies global warming or thinks that human activity is not a contributing factor.[5]

Ever since the first scientific opinion polls revealed that most Americans are at best marginally informed about politics, analysts have asked whether citizens are equipped to play the role democracy assigns them.[6] However, there is something worse than an inadequately informed public, and that's a misinformed public.[7] It's one thing when citizens don't know something, and realize it, which has always been a problem.[8] It's another thing when citizens don't know something, but think they know it, which is the new problem. It's the difference between ignorance and irrationality.[9] Whatever else one might conclude about self-government, it's at risk when citizens don't know what they're talking about.[10]

Our misinformation owes partly to psychological factors, including our tendency to see the world in ways that suit our desires. Such factors, however, can explain only the misinformation that has always been with us. The sharp rise in misinformation in recent years has a different source: our media. "They are making us dumb," says one observer.[11] It's worse than that. They are also making us wary. When fact bends to fiction, the predictable result is political distrust and polarization.[12]

2.

The sources of Americans' misinformation are many, one of which got its start when the Federal Communications Commission (FCC) rescinded the Fairness Doctrine in 1987. The Fairness Doctrine had discouraged the airing of partisan talk shows by requiring stations that did so to offer a balanced lineup of liberal and conservative programs. Once the requirement was eliminated, hundreds of stations launched talk shows of their choosing, the most successful of which had a conservative slant.[13] Within a few years, the highest-rated program, *The Rush Limbaugh Show,* had a weekly audience of twenty million listeners.[14] Limbaugh's success helped convince Rupert Murdoch to start a conservative alternative to the traditional TV networks in 1996.* Talk show host Bill O'Reilly was among Fox News' first hires. By 2001, O'Reilly had the highest-rated political talk show on cable, and Fox's total audience had surpassed that of its competitors, prompting CNN and MSNBC to hire talk show hosts of their own.

Radio and television talk shows now have a combined weekly audience in excess of fifty million Americans.[15] Although some talk shows provide a forum for thoughtful discussion, most only pretend to offer it.[16] Many talk show hosts traffic in what Nicholas Lemann, former dean of Columbia University's journalism school, calls "the corruption of information."[17] When Glenn Beck in an unguarded moment called himself a "rodeo clown," he put his finger on half the formula—showmanship—for a successful political talk show. Double-talk is the other half.[18] Said Beck of the Occupy Wall Street protesters: "Capi-

* Cable television news was not subject to the Fairness Doctrine and could have pursued a partisan model from the start. The first of the cable news outlets, CNN, adopted a policy of politically balanced news programming.

talists, if you think that you can play footsie with these people, you're wrong. They will come for you and drag you into the streets and kill you."[19]

The disinformation that spews from talk shows can be seen in the following examples, one from the right and one from the left. On July 16, 2009, Betsy McCaughey, the former lieutenant governor of New York, falsely claimed on *The Fred Thompson Show* that the health care reform bill under debate in Congress "would make it mandatory—absolutely require—that every five years people in Medicare have a required counseling session that will tell them how to end their life sooner."[20] From there, McCaughey's allegation snaked from one right-wing show to the next.[21] Beck called the legislation "euthanasia." "Sometimes for the common good," Beck said, "you just have to say, 'Hey, Grandpa, you've had a good life. Sucks to be you.' "[22]

If right-wing hosts rail endlessly against big government, their left-wing counterparts pretend to know what lurks in the dark corners of the conservative mind. In 2010, MSNBC's Keith Olbermann said that followers of the "Tea Klux Klan" (his label for the Tea Party) were driven by hatred of the nation's first black president, citing as proof the color of their skin. Olbermann asked: "Why are you surrounded by the largest crowd you will ever again see in your life that consists of nothing but people who look exactly like you?" About as close as Olbermann came to acknowledging the movement's deeper roots was a moment of mock humility: "I know if I could only listen to Lincoln about the better angels of our nature, I'd know that what we're seeing at the Tea Parties is, at its base, people who are afraid—terribly, painfully, cripplingly, blindingly afraid."[23]

Talk shows appeal to the like-minded.[24] Conservatives flock to right-wing hosts while liberals head for those on the left. Among Limbaugh and Beck listeners, self-identified conservatives outnumber self-identified liberals by more than fifteen to one.[25] The liberal talk show audience is not quite as one-sided, but conservatives account for only a fraction of it.[26]

As Harvard's Cass Sunstein has shown, exposure to one-sided arguments can lead people to adopt extreme political views.[27] It can also give them a warped sense of what the opposing side believes. The University of Pennsylvania's Kathleen Hall Jamieson and Joseph Cappella found, for example, that Limbaugh's listeners have a fairly accurate understanding of Republican positions but a distorted view of Democratic stands—the result of Limbaugh's habit of twisting Democratic positions and his listeners' eagerness to believe the worst about the Democrats.[28]

Political blogs have a similar effect, despite what their proponents say. In their 2005 book, *Blog!*, David Kline and Dan Burstein claimed that blogging is "the new paradigm of human communication"—a robust combination of information and discussion.[29] Blogs do bring information and discussion together, but usually in a narrow-minded way.[30] Most of them have intensely partisan followers who belittle or drive off those with opposing views.[31] Rare is the political blog in which people of differing opinions regularly convene, much less meet to sort out the facts.[32] And when blog users are directed to other blogs, they find additional people who think as they do. Nearly 90 percent of the links are to sites that promote the same ideology.[33]

Unlike during the broadcast era, when most Americans had a shared media reality, the Internet era is increasingly a time of separate realities—"cyber-ghettos," in the words of British scholar Peter Dahlgren.[34] "We're increasingly able to choose our information sources based on their tendency to back up whatever we already believe," says *Washington Post* columnist Ezra Klein. "We don't even have to hear the arguments from the other side, much less give them serious consideration."[35]

When people with strong but erroneous beliefs are given corrective facts, they find all sorts of reasons for rejecting them.[36] Leon Festinger, the founder of cognitive dissonance theory, was one of the first to describe the tendency. "A man with conviction is a hard man to change," wrote Festinger. "Tell him you disagree and he turns away. Show him facts and figures and he questions your sources. Appeal to logic and he fails to see your point. . . . [When] presented with evidence—unequivocal and undeniable evidence—that his belief is wrong, he will emerge not only unshaken but even more convinced of the truth of his beliefs than ever before."[37]

Festinger's claim is backed by scores of studies. In a 2005 experiment, for example, subjects were asked on a five-point scale ranging from "strongly agree" to "strongly disagree" whether it was likely that Iraq had had an active weapons program when the United States invaded in 2003.[38] Later in the experiment, the subjects were given a mock Associated Press (AP) story that included a recent statement by President George W. Bush on his Iraq policy: "There was a risk, a real risk, that Saddam Hussein would pass weapons or materials or information to terrorist networks, and in the world after September the 11th, that was a risk we could not afford to take." The mock story subsequently referred to the postinvasion investigation by U.S. intelligence agencies that found Iraq had destroyed all its WMDs well in advance of the American invasion. Later in the experiment, the subjects were again asked whether they thought Iraq had an active weapons program at the time of the invasion. On the retest, the opinions of every group of subjects except one shifted in the direction of the intelligence agencies' finding. Conservatives were the exception. They had become even more convinced that Iraq had had an active weapons program when the United States invaded. In the words of the researchers, conservatives had "moved in the 'wrong' direction."[39]

3.

"Blood on the floor" is how former *Los Angeles Times* editor John Carroll describes the talk show format.[40] He could have said somewhat the same of news reporting. To hear conservatives tell it, all the blood being spilled is theirs. Ever since 1968, when Edith Efron claimed in *The News Twisters* that the television networks had "clearly tried to defeat Mr. Nixon in his campaign for the Presidency of the United States,"[41] the notion that the press has a liberal bias has been an article of faith for conservatives.[42]

Decades of scholarly research, however, have failed to find what conservatives treat as gospel. Although examples of bias have been documented,* they are isolated cases rather than part of a systematic pattern. Researchers at the University of Connecticut examined fifty-nine separate bias studies in leading academic journals and found no consistent pattern of partisan bias in newspaper coverage, a slight but insignificant pattern of Democratic bias in television coverage, and a slight but insignificant pattern of Republican bias in magazine coverage.[43] In fact, the television-age president with the worst press coverage

---

* Partisan bias was found, for example, in news coverage of the 2008 presidential campaign. According to studies by the Center for Media and Public Affairs and the Project for Excellence in Journalism, for instance, the 2008 presidential election coverage was slanted heavily in Barack Obama's favor in his Democratic nominating race against Hillary Clinton and then again in his general election race against John McCain. When McCain went to Iraq during the campaign, few reporters followed. When Obama went to Europe, dozens went, including the network anchors. It is rare for a seated president to be featured on the cover of *Time* more than two or three times in a year. Obama appeared on *Time*'s cover six times during the campaign. In the opening stage of the Obama-Clinton race, Obama's coverage was three-to-one positive while Clinton's was three-to-two negative. In the 2012 presidential election, on the other hand, the press was highly critical of both Obama and Mitt Romney.

is a Democrat rather than a Republican. The Center for Media and Public Affairs found that Bill Clinton's negative coverage exceeded his positive coverage in every quarter of every year of his eight-year presidency—a dubious record that no president before or since has equaled.[44]

Clinton's coverage is an extreme example of the news media's real bias: its preference for the negative. Although the norms of American journalism dissuade reporters from taking sides in partisan debate, there is no rule that says they can't bash both sides.[45] News reporting turned sour during the Vietnam and Watergate era and has remained so ever since. In a 2010 interview on NPR's *On Point*, then editor of the *New York Times* Bill Keller blamed the rise of negativity on Fox News.[46] It actually started much earlier and the *Times* had a hand in it. In the two decades leading up to the founding of Fox News in 1996, negative coverage in the *Times* increased by a factor of three.[47]

Every president since Nixon has received reams of bad press.[48] Congress has fared no better. Press coverage of the institution has been steadily negative since the mid-1970s, regardless of which party controls Congress or how much or little is accomplished.[49] Year after year, nearly every high-level federal agency except the Department of Defense receives more negative than positive coverage.[50] "Journalism has slid from skepticism . . . toward cynicism," says *Time*'s Joe Klein. "It's gotten to the point where the toughest story . . . to write about a politician is a positive story."[51]

Critical journalism has been around for a long time. "There is but one way for a newspaper man to look at a politician, and that is down," said Pulitzer Prize–winning journalist Frank Simonds in 1917.[52] However, the muckrakers of the early twentieth century focused on activities worthy of criticism—the taking of bribes, the predatory practices of business trusts, the stuffing of ballots by party machines.[53] Modern-day reporters tear down politics and politicians for even the smallest of things.[54] Gaffes were nearly the headline of the day during the 2012 presidential campaign, many of which were taken out of context, as when Mitt Romney said, "I'm not concerned about the very poor," or when Barack Obama said, "The private sector is doing fine."[55] As political scientist Michael Robinson put it, journalists seem to have taken some motherly advice and turned it upside down: "If you don't have anything bad to say about someone, don't say anything at all."[56]

Journalists dismiss the notion that the news is too negative. "It's almost our role to be the bearer of bad news," said a veteran reporter.[57] Journalists also point out that Jefferson, Jackson, and Lincoln endured withering attacks and yet governed effectively.[58] This argument ignores a key distinction. Nineteenth-century newspapers were partisan outlets that lambasted one side while praising the other. In 1896, the *San Francisco Call* devoted 1,075 column inches of glowing photographs to the Republican ticket of McKinley-Hobart and only 11 inches to the Democrats, Bryan and Sewall.[59] San Francisco Democrats had their own oracle, the Hearst-owned *Examiner*, which touted Bryan as the savior of working men and blasted McKinley as a tool of moneyed interests. The partisan press of yesteryear was not in the business of tearing down the whole of politics. "With malice toward all" is how scholars Patricia Moy and Michael Pfau characterize today's journalists.[60]

Without doubt, a healthy dose of negativity is a good thing.[61] There's a lot of political puffery and manipulation that needs to be exposed, and the press would fail in its public responsibility by not doing so. Yet a constant barrage of criticism clouds people's thinking, as a 1995 survey by Harvard's Robert Blendon demonstrated. Respondents were asked whether the trends in inflation, unemployment, crime, and the federal budget deficit had been upward or downward in the past five years. Although there had been substantial improvement in each of these problem areas during the five-year period, two-thirds of the respondents in each case said things had gotten worse. After having heard repeatedly from reporters about government's failings, Americans had assumed the worst about its performance.[62]

Journalists in this instance were not trying to deceive the public. When they referred to policy trends, they usually cited them correctly.[63] However, the positive trends were buried in the news, which highlighted instead political failings and peccadilloes. According to *Congressional Quarterly*, which tracks the legislative process, President Clinton in 1993 had the highest congressional support score (88 percent) on legislative initiatives of any president since Lyndon Johnson in 1965.[64] Yet, according to a study by the Center for Media and Public Affairs,[65] more than 60 percent of news references to Clinton's policy accomplishments were negative.*

When it comes to economic policy, as scholarly studies have shown, "bad news" routinely trumps "good news."[66] A study

---

* Congress fared even worse in this period. The Democrat-controlled 103rd Congress (1993–1994) enacted a score of new programs but failed on health care reform and was described as "pathetically unproductive" by the *New York Times* in an October 8, 1994, editorial. According to Center for Media and Public Affairs data, the 103rd Congress's television coverage was nearly 70 percent negative. TV coverage of the Republican-controlled 104th Congress (1995–1996) was also nearly 70 percent negative, despite its historic first one hundred days, in which nearly all the planks in the GOP's Contract with America were enacted. In this case, Congress was criticized by the press for doing too much. (News coverage during the first half of the 1990s was not atypical. A Pew Research Center study of the 2012 presidential election, for example, found that negative statements about Obama and Romney outpaced positive ones by more than two to one in newspaper and television outlets. The ratio of negative to positive statements was even higher in journalists' Twitter feeds and blog postings.)

found, for example, that the economy is a front-page story when it's performing poorly and is relegated to the back pages when it's doing well.[67] Small wonder the public regularly underestimates the effectiveness of economic policy.[68] A Pew Research Center poll, for example, asked respondents whether the 2008 Troubled Assets Relief Program (TARP) had "helped prevent a more serious [economic] crisis" or "did not help." "Did not help" came out on top, even though TARP is widely credited with preventing an implosion of the financial sector in late 2008 and 2009.[69]

Americans also misjudged the effect of the $787 billion economic stimulus bill enacted in the early months of the Obama administration, which, according to the nonpartisan Congressional Budget Office (CBO), created and saved somewhere between two million and five million jobs.[70] Nevertheless, a CNN poll conducted a year after the bill's passage revealed that most Americans thought the government had willfully squandered hundreds of billions of dollars on the program. Nearly half of those surveyed claimed the government had wasted nearly all or most of the money while another quarter said it had wasted at least half the money.[71]

Public skepticism about government performance is also apparent from a 2010 University of Maryland survey that asked Americans about the impact of nearly a dozen public policies. Respondents greatly underestimated the effectiveness of *all* of them, leading the Maryland researchers to conclude: "False or misleading information is widespread in the general information environment."[72]

An irony of the press's critical tendency is that it abets the right wing. Although conservatives claim the press has a liberal bias, its negative focus reinforces their antigovernment message. For years on end, journalists have told the news audience that political leaders are not to be trusted and that the government is poorly run. The message has been so downbeat for so long that many Americans have taken it to heart.*

4.

As cable spread into American homes in the 1980s and 1990s, the audience for broadcast news and newspapers declined.[73] As the losses mounted, a theatrical style of news emerged that was designed to compete with cable entertainment. Critics called it "infotainment" and "news lite." Within the news business, it was commonly called "soft news" to distinguish it from traditional hard news (breaking events involving public figures, major issues, or significant disruptions to daily routines).[74] Former CBS anchor Walter Cronkite called soft news "one of the greatest blots on the recent record of television news."[75] NBC's Tom Brokaw defended it, saying that the networks would be committing "suicide" if they sat on their hands while their audiences slipped away.[76]

Whatever the justification, the news today is less substantial than it was during the broadcast era. Harvard University's Shorenstein Center on the Press, Politics and Public Policy conducted an exhaustive study of two decades of news coverage in a variety of news outlets. Included in the study were two national television networks (ABC and NBC), two mass-

* Negative news and perceptions of media bias are linked. Research has shown that negative news is perceived differently by those who oppose and those who support the politician being attacked. Opponents tend to see the criticism as valid whereas supporters tend to see it as unjustified and therefore biased. And unlike the perception of valid criticism, the perception of biased criticism tends to get people "to argue back" at the journalist and, eventually, to convince some of them—typically the strong partisans—that the press is thoroughly biased against their side.

circulation weekly newsmagazines (*Time* and *Newsweek*), three major newspapers (the *New York Times*, the *Washington Post*, and *USA Today*), and twenty-six local daily papers (for example, the *Dallas Morning News* and the *Minneapolis Star Tribune*). In every news outlet, soft news stories had increased in frequency over the course of the two decades. On average, celebrity profiles, hard-luck stories, good-luck tales, and other human interest stories had doubled during the period. Stories about dramatic incidents—crimes and disasters—had also doubled.[77] What Pulitzer Prize recipient Alex Jones calls "the iron core" of news—the news that aims "to hold government and those with power accountable"—had shrunk proportionally.[78]

Another study—this one of 154 local TV stations in fifty media markets over a five-year period—found that crimes and accidents received twice the coverage of public affairs. "Hook and hold" was the operative strategy. Local newscasts frequently opened with a sensational crime or accident story—sometimes several in a row without a commercial break—in order to "hook" the viewers. Teasers about soft news stories to be aired later in the newscast were used to "hold" the viewers. Civic affairs stories were jammed together in the middle of the telecast and given short shrift—two in five were thirty seconds or less in length.[79]

City hall was once a daily beat for local news outlets, but few of them now station a reporter there. Even fewer assign a reporter to the state capital.[80] As for congressional elections, they might as well be taking place in Canada. A study of Midwestern TV stations found that, although they ran dozens of candidate ads during their newscasts, they rarely aired stories on local congressional campaigns.[81] A study of California's TV stations found that on average they aired only a single story each on these local races.[82]

To be sure, soft news has old roots. One of America's highest-paid journalists in the 1830s was a veteran reporter brought over from London to write sensational stories about New York City's crime scene. In less than a year, he was the paper's co-owner.[83]

Nevertheless, the modern version of soft news is unlike anything that has gone before. The volume and tone are stupefying. In 2007, CNN gave the death of starlet Anna Nicole Smith a level of attention worthy of royalty. During the three weeks from the time of her death to her burial in the Bahamas, CNN devoted a fifth of its news time to the Smith story.[84] In 2010, the antics of Lindsay Lohan—a B-list actress by any standard—received a level of news coverage that would be the envy of a cabinet secretary. So would the name recognition she acquired. A poll revealed that Lohan was more widely known than all the cabinet members at the time except Hillary Clinton.[85]

If wayward and dead celebrities are the salad of soft news, crime is the main dish. Almost nothing can match the media frenzy that ensues when a sensational crime occurs. In 2011, CNN topped its Smith coverage with its reporting of Casey Anthony's Florida murder trial. In addition to live courtroom shots, CNN and its sister station HLN carried more than five hundred Anthony-based stories.[86] CNN even constructed a temporary two-story air-conditioned structure across from the courthouse so that its crews could work in comfort.[87]

The longest and most consequential of the media's crime sprees, however, occurred in the early 1990s. The binge was triggered by several high-profile cases, including the arrest of serial killer Joel Rifkin in New York, the trial of the parent-killing Menendez brothers, the kidnap and murder of twelve-year-old Polly Klaas in California, and a crazed gunman's shooting spree on a Long Island commuter train that killed six people and wounded nineteen. These running stories spawned a larger running story: the breakdown of law and order. Gang fights, drug busts, and other manifestations of a disorderly and dangerous society filled the headlines. Crime news tripled in the 1992–1994 period, overshadowing every other issue, including the economy, the Bosnian crisis, and the health care reform debate.[88] *Time* magazine's cover story of February 7, 1994, captured the frenzy: "Lock 'Em Up and Throw Away the Key: Outrage over Crime Has America Talking Tough."

The image of an America awash in murder and mayhem had a dramatic impact on public opinion.[89] At no time in the previous decade had even as many as one in ten Americans claimed that crime was the nation's most important problem. Yet in Gallup's August 1994 poll, an astonishing four in ten Americans called it the country's leading issue. Politicians, too, got caught up in the frenzy. Lawmakers rushed to enact harsh new sentencing policies and allocated more funds for prison construction than at any time in the nation's history. Within a decade, the United States had a larger proportion of its people behind bars than any other country in the world, higher even than Russia and Cuba and five times more per capita than China.[90]

The crime frenzy, however, was understandable only in terms of its media logic. Contrary to the impression conveyed by the news media, Justice Department statistics show that the crime rate, including the rate of violent crime, was falling—not rising—during the 1992–1994 period.[91] In 1994 alone, violent crime dropped by 4 percent from the previous year's level.[92]

Collective ignorance on the scale of Americans' fear of crime in the early 1990s is rare enough to be truly remarkable.[93] Yet the haphazard way in which Americans reached their opinions about crime is altogether ordinary. The world is far too complex to be traversed without mental shortcuts—what the linguist George Zipf called the "principle of least effort."[94] In most cases, our shortcuts serve our needs.[95] When selecting a bottle of wine, we listen to the store clerk rather than paging through back issues of *Wine Spectator*. When people are misinformed, however, their mental shortcuts send them to the wrong place.[96] Americans who believed that crime was rising sharply had a reason to want more prisons and longer sentences. The problem was not their deductive logic. The problem was their premise. They believed crime in America to be something it was not. "Cognoscenti of their own bamboozlement" is how sociologist Todd Gitlin describes such citizens.[97]

5.

If sensationalism is the hallmark of soft news, controversy has increasingly defined hard news.[98] "Unless something feels like a crisis," said a veteran broadcaster, "most journalists can't be bothered with it."[99] Journalists are also increasingly attracted to what the *Washington Post*'s Walter Pincus calls "the false gods of fame and fortune."[100] Ever since the Watergate scandal propelled reporters Bob Woodward and Carl Bernstein to national prominence, journalists have been on the lookout for what Columbia University's Michael Schudson calls "the story *behind* the story."[101]

Sometimes the story behind the story is so flimsy that it quickly deflates. After James Holmes murdered more than a dozen people in a Colorado theater at midnight on July 20, 2012, ABC News investigative reporter Brian Ross went on the air to say, "There's a Jim Holmes of Aurora, Colorado, page on the Colorado Tea Party site as well, talking about him joining the Tea Party last year. Now, we don't know if this is the same Jim Holmes. But it's Jim Holmes of Aurora, Colorado."[102] Ross's would-be scoop collapsed when it was pointed out that his "Jim Holmes" was at least twice as old as the shooter.

Wild speculation is not always so easily debunked. A case

in point is the mad cow stampede of 2004.[103] When the story broke that bovine spongiform encephalopathy—or "mad cow disease"—had been found in a cow in Washington State, reporters went looking for anything and everything—from the food supply to the blood supply—that might be endangered. When Department of Agriculture officials tried to dampen the speculation, journalists hinted they were conspiring with ranchers to downplay the problem. A sampling of newspaper headlines tells the story: "Mysterious Mad Cow–Like Disease Surfaces in Washington State," "Mad Cow Disease Raises Questions about Hamburger," "Mad Cow Raises Fears about Transfusions," "Threat to Food Supply Rising," "Mad Deer Disease—An Alarming Hazard for America's 12 Million Deer Hunters," "USDA Dithering Prompts Mad Cow Cover-Up Fears."[104]

Mad cow is a horrific disease. It eats away at the human brain, as reporters regularly reminded their audience. But what kind of risk does it pose? According to the Centers for Disease Control and Prevention, a total of three Americans have died from the disease during the past decade—one each in 2003, 2004, and 2006.[105] Each week, fifteen times as many Americans choke to death on food particles. The chances of dying from plain old food poisoning are about ten thousand times greater than the odds of dying from mad cow disease. Perhaps the alarmist news coverage in 2004 saved a life or two, but its unquestioned effect was to scare the bejesus out of the American consumer. It was estimated that beef and crop producers lost between $3.2 billion and $4.7 billion from the scare.[106]

In 2001, journalists took Americans on a different kind of hunt, searching for anything that might link Congressman Gary Condit to the disappearance of his intern Chandra Levy, with whom he had had an extramarital affair. Even though the D.C. police repeatedly told reporters, on the record and off, that Condit was not a suspect, the story's ingredients—power, sex, and mystery—made the chase irresistible.[107] What did Condit know that he was not telling? Did Condit have a hand in her disappearance? Over a period of four months, Condit was the target of hundreds of news stories before journalists abruptly ended the hunt. It was not that they stopped because charges against him had been dropped. They had never been filed. It was not that they stopped because Levy had been found. She was still missing.* Reality had intruded. The Condit frenzy ended at precisely 8:47 a.m. on September 11, 2001—the moment that the first hijacked plane slammed into the North Tower of the World Trade Center.

If journalists had not been preoccupied with the life of a backbench congressman, they might have acquired a better understanding of who was behind the terrorist attacks. Earlier that year, the U.S. Commission on National Security, headed by former senators Warren Rudman and Gary Hart, had issued a report predicting a "catastrophic attack" on American soil by international terrorists. The commission's evaluation was largely ignored, even by top news organizations.[108] CIA director George Tenet also issued a warning, saying at a Senate hearing in February 2001 that Osama bin Laden's "global network" was the "most immediate and serious" threat facing the country.[109] This alert, too, went largely unreported. The *New York Times*, for example, gave it only a few paragraphs in the middle of a page-eleven story headlined by Russia's efforts to revive itself as a great power.[110] In the year preceding the World Trade Center and Pentagon attacks, the al-Qaeda terrorist network

* Chandra Levy's remains were found in Washington, D.C.'s Rock Creek Park a year after her disappearance. Seven years later, an illegal immigrant from El Salvador was convicted of her murder. The police had identified him as a prime suspect early in the investigation but lacked sufficient evidence to arrest him at the time.

was mentioned by name only once on the evening newscasts of ABC, NBC, and CBS.[111]

In the early days after 9/11, the press was ill-prepared to help Americans understand the threat confronting them. Some journalists were candid enough to acknowledge the gaps in their analysis. Others plowed ahead, unmindful or uncaring that their assessments might be off the mark, a shortcoming not lost on Frank Rich of the *New York Times*. "From our flag-decorated TV screens," he wrote, three weeks after the attacks, "you would hardly know that the Taliban's internal opposition and would-be fellow freedom fighters, the ragtag Northern Alliance, is anathema to Pakistan, our other frail new ally. Or that Pakistan and its military, with its dozens of nuclear weapons, are riddled with bin Laden sympathizers."[112]

6.

The legendary publisher William Randolph Hearst once claimed that an "editor has no objection to facts if they are also novel. But he would prefer a novelty that is not a fact to a fact that is not a novelty."[113] No editor today would dare utter such a thought, but the point behind it—the need to attract an audience—is a constant concern in the news business.[114] Journalists' challenge is to take what's important and make it interesting, which would seem to mean starting with what's important and figuring it out from there. But that's not necessarily how it works. When editors were asked in a research study to rank a series of mock stories and say why they made their choices, they identified conflict, proximity, and timeliness as the major factors, leading communication scholar Doris Graber to note, "Conspicuously absent from their choice criteria was the story's overall significance."[115]

Few attributes in a news story are more highly prized by journalists than novelty.[116] During the 2000 presidential campaign, for instance, the revelation that George W. Bush had been arrested a quarter century earlier for drunken driving generated more coverage in the space of three days than did all of Bush's and Al Gore's foreign policy statements during the entire general election campaign.[117] It was an enticing story, coming as it did in the last week of a close race. Somewhere in the course of telling it, however, reporters placed a decades-old drinking episode ahead of the question of how the next president might conduct foreign policy. "There is," wrote communication scholar Murray Edelman, "a kind of Gresham's law of news prominence: dramatic incidents involving individuals in the limelight displace attention from the larger [issues]."[118]

The demand for novelty contributes to what *Newsweek*'s Meg Greenfield once called journalists' "chronic collective amnesia"—their eagerness to dump the old story in favor of the new.[119] Front-page stories in early 2006, for example, told of church bombings in the rural South and of Arab unrest over a Danish newspaper's publication of cartoons depicting the prophet Muhammad in terrorist garb. Suddenly, these issues disappeared from the front pages, though not because they had been resolved. They had been displaced by news out of Texas. Vice President Dick Cheney had just shot a hunting companion in the face.

Very little in the way of effective human communication occurs at high speed.[120] "The thing that has not speeded up," *Boston Globe* columnist Ellen Goodman explains, "is the capacity to actually think through something."[121] Nearly two decades ago, the *Atlantic*'s James Fallows said that news had devolved into "an endless stream of emergencies . . . of artificial intensity," the effect of which "is to make the week the fundamental unit of political measurement."[122] Since then, the pace has accelerated. "We are hostages to the non-stop, never-ending file-it-now, get-on-the-Web, get-on-the-radio, get-on-TV media environment," says the *New York Times*' Peter Baker.[123]

In *Warp Speed*, former journalists Bill Kovach and Tom Rosenstiel argue that the accelerated news cycle threatens the accuracy of reporting. "In the continuous news cycle," they write, "the press is increasingly oriented toward ferrying allegations rather than first ferreting out the truth."[124] In their haste to beat out competitors, for example, CNN and Fox News misreported the 2012 Supreme Court decision that upheld the health care reform bill enacted two years earlier. "Mandate Struck Down: High Court Finds Measure Unconstitutional" was how CNN headlined its story. "Supreme Court Finds Individual Healthcare Mandate Unconstitutional" was Fox's headline. Acting on the widespread assumption that the Supreme Court would overturn the legislation, CNN and Fox rushed their stories onto the air only minutes after the Court released to the press its lengthy and complex opinion.

Although CNN's and Fox's mishandling of the Court ruling was widely criticized by others in the press, some journalists believe that the public's interest in getting timely updates outweighs the occasional errors that result. The safeguard, they claim, is that errors will get spotted and then corrected in follow-up stories. "It gets fact checked, in effect, by the readers," a top editor says.[125] Studies indicate, however, that errors often go uncorrected, even when brought to an editor's attention.[126]

Reporting errors that enter people's heads often stay there, even in the face of subsequent corrections.[127] Once people accept something as fact, they tend to fend off information that would lead them to think otherwise.[128] When Representative Gabrielle Giffords was shot at a political gathering in Tucson in 2011, the hurried initial reports hinted that the gunman was a conservative fanatic who had been prodded into action by right-wing rhetoric. Sarah Palin's name got folded into the story when reporters discovered that her Web site contained a midterm election map showing the crosshairs of a rifle scope aimed at several Democratic districts, one of which was Giffords's.[129] A CNN poll taken within days of the shooting found that 35 percent of Americans believed Palin was partly or fully to blame for the shooting.[130] Her poll numbers, which had been trending upward, fell to their lowest level in two years, and didn't rebound even after it was reported that the assailant had a grudge against Giffords and had a history of mental problems but no history of right-wing activity.[131]

7.

Citizens can be faulted for their lack of attention, for their willingness to embrace thin portrayals, for their laziness in trying to resolve the contradictions between what they think and what they hear. In the final analysis, though, they suffer from a media system gone haywire. They are told they are in Kansas but are being led through Oz.

Writing in the 1960s, Pierre Salinger, press secretary to President John F. Kennedy, foresaw the destructive possibilities inherent in modern communication. "Perhaps in the long run," Salinger surmised, "we will find that the communications revolution has run away from us and that we have neither the ability nor the desire to adjust life and our practices to meet the challenges with which it has presented us." If this happens, Salinger said, the public "will ride from crisis to crisis, from crest to crest of 'happenings,' many of which are completely fabricated."[132]

Albert Camus observed that "one should never indulge in useless lamentations over an inescapable state of affairs."[133] Perhaps the corruption of information at the hands of today's communicators is precisely this type of situation. Perhaps the commercialism, personal ambition, and partisanship driving the factual distortions are too powerful to be blunted. For sure, the rabidly partisan talk show hosts and bloggers are beyond redemption. As British prime minister Stanley Baldwin said of the unscrupulous press barons of his era, they seek "power without responsibility—the prerogative of the harlot through the ages."[134] Nothing in their mode of operation dictates fidelity to the facts.

Nor can politicians be counted upon to guard the facts. Although politicians, unlike talk show hosts and bloggers, are accountable for the power they wield, their accountability is less to the facts than to the voters, some of whom prefer fabricated versions of reality to the real thing.

If there is to be a remedy, journalists are the logical choice. They claim to be "custodians of the facts"[135] and say that "accuracy" is the first principle of journalism.[136] Yet what they claim and what they do are all too often far apart. A decade ago, psychologist Howard Gardner and two of his Harvard colleagues conducted a comprehensive study of the relationship between professional norms and practices. Journalism emerged as a "massively misaligned" profession in the sense that its performance was out of line with its professed values, both in an absolute sense and in comparison with other professions.[137] Many of the journalists interviewed by Gardner and his colleagues said that their profession had drifted away from its public service mission. One of them said: "While the news can be entertaining, that's not our job, to be entertainers. Our job is to be informers."[138] A 2010 Pew survey of news executives yielded a similar finding. They felt the news was declining in quality and that factually inaccurate reporting was on the rise.[139] Their views echoed an earlier statement by the Committee of Concerned Journalists, a group of hundreds of U.S. journalists established in the late 1990s. "Many journalists feel a sense of lost purpose," wrote the committee. "There is even doubt about the meaning of news, doubt evident when serious journalistic organizations drift toward opinion, infotainment, and sensation."[140]

There is no quick fix for the shortcomings of today's journalism, nor are journalists necessarily thinking about solutions, preoccupied as they are with figuring out how to shore up their industry's eroding business model. But it will not serve them, or democracy, if they arrive at a business solution without also figuring out how to strengthen their reporting.

TWO

The Source Problem

There can be no liberty for a community that lacks the information by which to detect lies.[1]

—Walter Lippmann

1.

If journalists are neither as high-minded as their admirers claim nor as wily as their critics allege, they are less secure than their First Amendment protection would suggest.[2] The pillar of their profession—accuracy—is compromised by their dependence on high-ranking sources.

Public officials are journalists' prime source of news. As Leon Sigal wrote in *Reporters and Officials*, "Most news is not what has happened, but what someone says has happened."[3] The news, explains Michael Schudson, flows from the top down, "favoring high government officials over lower government officials, government officials over unofficial groups and . . . groups of any sort over unorganized citizens."[4] For a long period, this arrangement worked to journalists' advantage.[5] Although bullied by Senator Joseph McCarthy in the early 1950s,[6] they normally benefited from a close relationship with officials. It gave them credibility with their audience and a predictable source of news.

Nevertheless, the day has long passed when the relationship between reporters and officials was a healthy one. Changes within journalism and politics have placed these two groups on a collision course that has brought out the worst in both. National political reporting has become a two-ring partisan circus with citizens cast in the role of unwitting spectators, treated to a version of news that is as unsavory as it is deceptive.

2.

"The air was thick with lies, and the president was the lead liar," said Ben Bradlee, editor of the *Washington Post*.[7] It was the time of the Vietnam War and Watergate, and the deceptions of the Johnson and Nixon administrations had convinced reporters that politicians could not be trusted. If politicians were going to lie, journalists would challenge their every word and action.[8]

Newsweek's Meg Greenfield said journalists had been thinking that "the worst thing we could do . . . was [to] falsely accuse someone of wrongdoing." Now "the worst, the most embarrassing, humiliating thing is not that you accuse someone falsely but that you . . . fail to accuse someone of something he ought to be accused of."[9] Although some journalists were uneasy about questioning politicians at every turn,[10] most saw it as axiomatic.[11] The question was how to put it into practice, given that journalistic norms prevented reporters from challenging officials openly.[12] "If a [newsmaker] spouts fulsome bullshit all day," journalist Timothy Crouse said, "the formula [makes] it hard for [us] to say so."[13]

Investigative reporting was not a realistic alternative. Time-consuming and expensive, it was not a type of reporting that news organizations were equipped to do on a daily basis. Reporters needed an expedient alternative and by the late 1970s had devised it. When a politician said or did something newsworthy, journalists reached out to an opponent to attack it. The critical element was supplied not by careful investigation of whether a proposal was sound or sincere, but by seeking out an opponent who would rip it apart. "You go shopping" is how *Los Angeles Times* reporter Jack Nelson described the practice.[14] It was as ingenious in its safety as in its simplicity. It allowed the journalist to orchestrate the attack while staying out of the line of fire—politicians would do the dirty work of tearing each other down.

"He said, she said" reporting was abetted by a change in the style of journalism.[15] When broadcast networks introduced their thirty-minute picture-based newscasts in 1963, they found the newspaper style of reporting unsuited to television. The print style was descriptive—the journalist's job was to transport the audience to the scene of an event and tell it what had happened. However, television viewers didn't have to be told what they could see with their own eyes. Something different was needed, and the networks came up with an interpretive style based on story lines.[16] NBC's Reuven Frank instructed his correspondents: "Every news story should, without any sacrifice of probity or responsibility, display the attributes of fiction, of drama. It should have structure and conflict, problem and denouement, rising action and falling action, a beginning, a middle and an end."[17] Newspaper outlets, realizing that readers had little interest in descriptive accounts of events seen the night before on TV, soon followed suit.[18]

The new style cast the journalist in the role of expositor, which shifted control of the story from the newsmaker to the journalist. With the older, descriptive style, newsmakers had the upper hand. Their words were the central focus of the story, allowing them to control much of what was reported about them. "It is my job," veteran reporter Carl Leubsdorf said of the traditional style, "to report [the newsmaker's] words whether I agree with them or not."[19] With the new form, journalists selected the narrative theme and wove the pieces together, putting their own words at the center of the story.[20] In the early 1960s, speaking time on the evening newscasts had been divided almost evenly between journalists and newsmakers. By the 1990s, for every minute that newsmakers spoke on the evening news, the journalists who were covering them spoke for five minutes.[21] In newspapers, newsmakers were also being quoted less often and less fully—the average newspaper quote was only a third of its former length.[22]

With the new style, it was a simple matter for journalists to place political opponents side by side in the same story and to use battlefield metaphors—"took the first shot," "under fire," "shot back"—to make it appear as if the antagonists were engaged in actual debate rather than in one staged by the reporter.[23] In the words of the University of Virginia's Larry Sabato, reporters had taken "center stage in the process, creating the news as much as reporting it."[24] It was not long before charges and countercharges filled the airwaves. On the evening news, adversarial sound bites had come to outnumber conciliatory ones by a ratio of six to one.[25]

By the early 1990s, journalists no longer had to "go shopping" to find their assailants. The bipartisanship of the postwar era had faded, and a new breed of politician, less given to compromise, was emerging. Their kind had once been dismissed as oddballs and hotheads, but their blistering attacks made them good copy.[26] A University of Pennsylvania study found that members of Congress from the extreme wings of the parties were being quoted more often in the news while moderate party leaders were being quoted less often.[27] A Times Mirror survey found that 85 percent of the journalists covering the 1992 presidential primaries relished the candidacy of firebrand Pat Buchanan. Said one journalist: "He gives good sound bites. He's very quotable. Whether you're a print journalist or a broadcast reporter, he's a joy to cover."[28]

Critical journalism was not merely a means of cutting politicians down to size. It was a way for journalists to get ahead.[29] Although the reasoned voices in the Washington press corps could still be heard on the talk and interview shows, cable television had created more seats at the table and reserved them for reporters and pundits who savored a fight. In the view of the *Washington Post*'s David Broder, the press had spun out of control. "Cynicism is epidemic right now," he wrote. "It saps people's confidence in politics and public officials, and it erodes both the standing and standards of journalism."[30] The *New York Times*' Maureen Dowd saw it differently. The "raffish and rowdy" press, she wrote, had finally found the nerve to place politicians on twenty-four-hour watch.[31] "Wooing the press is an exercise roughly akin to picnicking with a tiger," she later wrote. "You might enjoy the meal, but the tiger always eats last."[32]

3.

Reporters are drawn to conflict, as is the news audience. "Everyone loves a fight" is how one scholar put it.[33] With "he said, she said" journalism, reporters don't have to wait for conflict to erupt. Fights can be arranged by soliciting opposing views and playing them against each other.[34] Fights can also be orchestrated through the old-fashioned process of selection, as political scientists Tim Groeling and Matthew Baum discovered in their study of newsmakers' appearances on *Meet the Press, Face the Nation,* and other Sunday morning interview programs. Although these newsmakers talk mostly about their policy goals and only occasionally attack their opponents, their attacks are what get reported on the Sunday night newscasts and in the Monday morning papers.[35]

To be sure, newsmakers are the ones doing the attacking. But journalists are the ones who decide which statements will make it into the news. A study of candidates' stump speeches found that journalists largely ignore the candidates' policy statements, which account for most of what they say, choosing instead to report the moments when they go on the attack.[36] Another study found that more than 80 percent of congressional sound bites in the area of foreign policy are attacks on the president's initiatives.[37] A third study found that the minority party in Congress is largely ignored by the press except when the other party controls the presidency. Then, as a prime source of attacks on the president, the minority party gets as much coverage as the majority party.[38]

At times, conflict seems nearly to be the point of the coverage. During the 2009–2010 health care reform debate, flash points like the "death panel" controversy so thoroughly dominated the coverage that key provisions of the bill, such as cost containment, escaped the public's attention.[39] High-profile issues are not the only ones to get such treatment. In a study of news coverage of the teaching of evolution in public schools, for example, Chris Mooney and Matthew Nisbet found that reporters "deemphasize the strong scientific case in favor of evolution and instead lend credence to the notion that a growing 'controversy' exists over [the validity of] evolutionary science."[40]

The greater the level of conflict, the bigger the story. The tendency is not absolute—there are plenty of times when cooperative efforts make news. Nevertheless, such developments typically take a backseat to conflict. Stem cell research, for example, seldom made headlines before 2001, even though breakthroughs in gene and bone marrow therapy were saving thousands of lives and promising to save millions more. Then, in 2001, politicians faced off over the issue of extracting stem cells from human embryos. In that year alone, the *New York Times* and the *Washington Post* carried 486 articles on stem cell research—more than they had published on the subject in the previous twenty-five years combined.[41]

For its part, cable television feasts on controversy. When an issue lacks conflict, cable shows invite guests who will fight over it anyway.[42] Sometimes, the host starts the fight. In late 2006, Chris Wallace, the host of *Fox News Sunday*, invited former president Bill Clinton to be his guest with the assurance that Clinton's global philanthropy would be a featured part of the interview. Wallace's fourth question revealed that he had something more provocative in mind. Said Wallace: "Why didn't you do more to put bin Laden and al-Qaeda out of business when you were president?" Clinton responded sharply, telling Wallace that his interview was a "conservative hit job." "I want to know," said Clinton, "how many people in the Bush administration you asked, 'Why didn't you do anything about the *Cole* [the navy ship attacked by terrorists in 2001]? Why did you fire Dick Clarke [the counterterrorism adviser who warned Bush of the likelihood of a pending attack on the scale of 9/11]?' "[43] Within a month of the Fox interview, CNN's Wolf Blitzer gave nearly the same treatment to Lynne Cheney, wife of former vice president Dick Cheney. Although the interview was ostensibly about a children's book she had written, Blitzer grilled her on her husband's role in authorizing the waterboarding of terrorism suspects.[44]

Few developments more clearly illustrate the press's zeal for conflict than the 2004 presidential campaign, when journalists spent weeks wading through distortions of John Kerry's war record of three decades earlier. The claims of the Swift Boat Veterans for Truth had been aired in locally televised ads and might have died there had reporters not turned them into front-page news. As the controversy grew, allegations about George W. Bush's National Guard service, which had been heavily aired in the previous election, got folded into the dispute. The controversy petered out only when CBS News overplayed its hand, unwittingly airing a charge based on a forged document. By then, the controversy had received enough news coverage to rank it among the most heavily reported issues of the 2004 campaign—this at a time when Americans were worried about weakness in the economy and the deteriorating war in Iraq.[45]

4.

As political scientist Lance Bennett notes, "power" rather than truthfulness is the operative standard of "he said, she said" reporting.[46] When a member of Congress tells a bald-faced lie and the journalist passes it along to the audience as a "he said, she said" controversy, what except deference to those in "power" explains the reporter's decision?[47] By conveying it, the reporter is complicit in the deception—the claim gets publicized and gains credibility as a result of being in the news.[48]

The *New York Times*' Jill Abramson says, "When you can name sources, you have a much more authoritative first draft of history than you do with one larded with anonymous sources."[49] True enough, if the named sources are playing it straight. In his weekly radio address of August 6, 2006, President Bush said that his tax cuts had "stimulated economic vitality and growth and it has helped increase revenues to the Treasury. The increased revenues and our spending restraint have led to good progress in reducing the federal deficit." Bush's claim was duly reported even though experienced reporters must have known it was false.* Bush's own Council of Economic Advisers had earlier announced that the tax cuts were not paying their way.[50]

Bill Kovach and Tom Rosenstiel argue that there is no excuse for reporters to transmit false claims without identifying them as such.[51] Yet it happens regularly, sometimes because the reporter doesn't have the time or knowledge to sort out the truth and sometimes because the reporter wants to avoid the appearance of taking sides.[52] Either way, the objective reporting model absolves journalists of their part in the deception.[53] As Stanford's Ted Glasser put it, objective reporting is "biased against the very idea of [journalistic] responsibility. . . . Objectivity requires only that reporters be accountable for how they report, not what they report."[54]

The objective reporting model, writer Gaye Tuchman says, is "a strategic ritual" that protects journalists "from the risks of their trade."[55] It's far less risky for the journalist to report "Senator Smith said . . ." than to pounce on Senator Smith for what was said.[56] The *Washington Post*'s Dana Milbank got frozen out of the White House press corps after writing a front-page article that carried the headline "For Bush, Facts Are Malleable."[57] Although some reporters are willing to jeopardize their access to high-ranking sources by challenging them openly, they are the exception. Says UCLA's John Zaller: "It would be more accurate to say that journalists are never afraid to say what other people [say] is true."[58]

No recent example illustrates the point more clearly than

* Reporters might have been forgiven the lapse if it had been the early 1980s and the Reagan tax cuts were at issue. Supply-side economics was relatively new then and poorly understood. Long before Bush took office, however, the adverse revenue effects of overly deep tax cuts were well known—a "crackpot theory" in the words of Reagan's onetime budget director David Stockman. Bush's tax cuts were deeper than Reagan's and were followed by meager economic growth and an exploding budget deficit.

the news coverage of the lead-up to the Iraq War. So much has been written on the subject that little needs to be said here except to note how skillfully the Bush White House steered the message. On the evening newscasts, administration officials were the most heavily quoted sources. The president alone accounted for roughly one in every six quotes. Democratic officeholders accounted for only 4 percent of the total number—and this figure includes those who backed the president's position. Antiwar protesters accounted for a mere 1 percent of the quoted statements—fewer even than those voiced by retired military officers. The most heavily quoted opponents of a U.S. invasion were Iraqi officials—the source least likely to sway an American audience.[59] Newspaper coverage was similarly one-sided. Fourteen months after the invasion—by which time the Iraq War had turned sour—the *New York Times* publicly apologized for the unsubstantiated claims that had driven much of its prewar coverage.[60] The *Washington Post*'s executive editor, Len Downie, also apologized for his paper's one-sided coverage, saying it "was a mistake on my part."[61]

5.

When attack journalism surfaced in the late 1970s, politicians were caught off guard. Why had the transgressions of the Johnson and Nixon administrations made *all* of them targets? "I feel like bait rather than a senior member of Congress," said Democratic congressman Jack Brooks.[62] GOP senator Alan Simpson's response was equally defensive: "You come out of a legislative conference and there's ten reporters standing around with their ears twitching. They don't want to know whether anything was resolved for the betterment of the United States. They want to know who got hammered, who tricked whom. . . . They're not interested in clarity. They're interested in confusion and controversy."[63]

Faced with an increasingly hostile press, politicians then did what they've always done. They adapted. If journalists had changed the rules, they would learn to play by the new rules. They had done so in the 1960s, when pictures began to drive television journalism. If pictures were what the networks wanted, pictures were what the networks would get. Image making—"it's not what you say, it's how you say it"—became the operative rule.[64] However, the new game—the "he said, she said" game—was not about imagery. It was about words. And with the rise of party polarization, it was closer to word combat than to wordplay. "Warfare among elites, waged . . . in the name of causes, not compromises" is how Harvard's Richard Neustadt described the temper of the new brand of politics.[65]

Most politicians are not themselves experts in communication strategy, but their media advisers are.* They have taught politicians the importance of staying on message, no matter how simplistic it sounds or how misleading it may be.[66] "The cure for propaganda is more propaganda" is how Edward Bernays, the founder of modern public relations, described the tactic.[67] Politicians have also been instructed in their choice of words.[68] Opposition to taxes on large inheritances, for

---

* Although nothing in politicians' communication strategies is truly new, the sophistication level today is far beyond what was true even a few decades ago. Applied psychology and social science methods have taken strategic communication to an unprecedented level, as has the increase in the number of communication specialists. According to Robert McChesney and John Nichols in their book *The Death and Life of American Journalism*, there were roughly as many journalists as there were public relations specialists in 1980. Since then, the number of journalists has declined while the number in PR has increased. By 2000, there were twice as many PR specialists as there were journalists, and today there are three times as many.

instance, rises sharply when politicians describe them pejoratively as "death taxes" rather than by their traditional label, "estate taxes."[69] Politicians have also been trained to find and exploit their opponents' weak spots. "Find the wart; make the wart stand for the whole" is how one analyst put it.[70] Politicians have also been taught that every issue is part of the larger competition for power. "The line between campaigning and governing has all but disappeared," Thomas Mann and Norman Ornstein write.[71] Politicians have also been schooled in how to use talk shows, cable, and the Internet to amplify their messages.[72] Republican lawmakers, for example, didn't have to go far to obtain extra fuel for their attacks on the 2010 health care reform bill. Fox News was twenty times more likely than other networks to use the terms "socialism" and "Obamacare" in referring to the bill.[73]

As politicians were folding these lessons into their communication strategies, a final question remained. Would journalists give voice to the clever labeling and mind-numbing repetition? Or would they expose them as gimmicks? As it turned out, journalists were inclined to do both of these things, which was good enough for the politicians. It meant they could achieve their main goal—getting their message into the flow of news.

Few examples illustrate more clearly the success of such efforts than the Bush administration's skill at managing how its use of waterboarding was characterized by the press. A study of three leading newspapers—the *New York Times*, the *Los Angeles Times*, and the *Wall Street Journal*—found that each of them had described waterboarding as torture during the period preceding the American wars in Afghanistan and Iraq. They had called it torture when applied by the Japanese during World War II, by the Chinese communists during the Korean War, and by the North Vietnamese during the Vietnam War. It was described this way in well over 80 percent of their newspaper stories prior to September 11, 2001. However, when it was discovered in 2005 that the U.S. government had used waterboarding to interrogate Islamic militants, these very same newspapers applied the label devised by the Bush administration: "enhanced interrogation technique." Fewer than 5 percent of the waterboarding references in these newspapers described the practice as a form of torture.[74]

Political leaders are not the only ones who've figured out how to manipulate the communication process. Early in the race for the 2008 Democratic presidential nomination, a blogger claimed that "researchers connected to Senator [Hillary] Clinton" had discovered that Barack Obama had attended a Muslim madrassa in Indonesia as a boy. The allegation quickly spread to talk shows and then to the news media. The attack on Obama was debunked within a few days, but the rumor that Clinton had orchestrated the dirty trick continued to circulate. More than a week after the story broke, ABC News ran an article on the front page of its Web site titled "Madrassa Madness: Was Hillary Behind Obama Smear?" As it happened, the allegation had been concocted by the conservative blogger who first posted it.[75] Commenting on the incident in the *Columbia Journalism Review*, Paul McLeary said: "It doesn't take a respected news organization to run a big-time smear campaign—all it takes is for the rest of the media to repeat the story, while neglecting to follow it up with their own reporting."[76]

6.

The proportion of saints to sinners among politicians is probably not much different from the proportion in the general population, or among journalists for that matter. What's different about politicians is their role. They are in the business of having to sell their ideas, which means that they'll mold the facts to fit their goals. Any leader who stands idly by while others define what's at stake in an issue is inviting defeat. The power to define an issue at the outset can be half the battle.[77] Every leader, as Lippmann noted, "is in some degree a censor" and "is in some degree a propagandist."[78]

Some politicians are better than others at crafting persuasive arguments but spin has been a political tactic since ancient Greece. "The political orator," Aristotle wrote, "aims at establishing the expediency or the harmfulness of a proposed course of action; if he urges its acceptance, he does so on the ground that it will do good; if he urges its rejection, he does so on the ground that it will do harm."[79] In his 2012 book, *The Righteous Mind,* psychologist Jonathan Haidt illustrates the point by describing the role of a hypothetical White House press secretary: "No matter how bad the policy, the secretary will find some way to praise or defend it. Sometimes you'll hear an awkward pause as the secretary searches for the right words, but what you'll never hear is: 'Hey, that's a great point! Maybe we should rethink this policy.' "[80]

Journalists criticize politicians for spinning their messages and dodging the tough issues. Citizens also find fault with these tactics. Yet journalists and citizens alike punish politicians who speak candidly or play the game poorly.* In

---

* Although journalists censure politicians for acting strategically, they save some of their sharpest criticisms for those who fail to play the game well. Examples from presidential election coverage include the campaign efforts of Walter Mondale, Michael Dukakis, Bob Dole, Al Gore, Howard Dean, John McCain, and Mitt Romney. When Dukakis in 1988 was savaged by deceptive advertising that pictured him as soft on crime, his refusal to respond in kind was taken as a sign of weakness. During an interview as the campaign was drawing to a close, NBC's Tom Brokaw asked Dukakis: "You said this is a campaign not about ideology. It's about competence. What about the competence of your campaign?"

the 1984 presidential campaign, Democratic nominee Walter Mondale stuck his neck out by saying that he would raise taxes in an effort to bring the spiraling federal deficit under control. "Let's tell the truth," said Mondale in his acceptance speech at the Democratic National Convention. "Mr. Reagan will raise taxes, and so will I. He won't tell you. I just did." Rather than plaudits, Mondale's stance garnered him a slew of unfavorable headlines.[81] "Reagan Ridicules Mondale 'Realism' "[82] and "Presidential Aide Scoffs at Mondale Tax Pledge" were among the "he said, she said" stories in the *New York Times.*[83]

If politicians have no choice but to watch what they say, they are not expected to engage in outright deception.[84] Yet that's exactly what many of them have done in recent years, using misleading messaging to mask their intentions.[85] The deceptions extend to the manufacture of issues. In *Beyond Ideology,* political scientist Frances Lee shows that congressional leaders have frequently introduced phony bills that are designed to create the kind of conflict that will catch journalists' attention and mobilize core constituents.[86] "Fight club politics" is how veteran Capitol Hill reporter Juliet Eilperin describes the tactic.[87]

The fog of war that has descended on America's politics includes efforts to confound the facts, a development that Jay Rosen calls "verification in reverse"—the taking of known facts and challenging them in order to create confusion and uncertainty.[88] In his 2008 book, *What Happened,* Scott McClellan, a real-life White House press secretary, tells of how he was instructed to mislead the press in the effort to win the public's support for the Iraq invasion. "He [Bush] and his advisers confused the propaganda campaign with the high level of candor and honesty so fundamentally needed to build and then sustain public support during a time of war," McClellan wrote. "In this regard, [Bush] was terribly ill-served by his top advisers, especially those involved directly in national security."[89]

7.

By airing deceptive claims and pairing them with opposing claims, the journalist leaves open the question of where the truth lies.[90] During the 2000 presidential election, a *Newsweek* writer dumped the question squarely in the audience's lap: "Who gains [from Bush's proposed tax cut]? Gore says that 42 percent of the benefits go to the richest one percent. Bush says the figure is only 21 percent. The truth lies in between; just where, no one knows."[91]

If the *Newsweek* reporter expected the public to sort out the figures, it wasn't going to happen.[92] Faced with contrasting claims, people tend to pick the more agreeable one, even when it's factually less plausible[93]—a condition that Lance Bennett calls "the democratization of truth."[94] Through a process that psychologists call "motivated reasoning," people are able to process information in a way that allows them in some situations to believe what they want to believe.[95] A study of news coverage of the long-term solvency of Social Security found, for instance, that exaggerated claims by GOP leaders resulted in an increase in the number of Republicans who falsely believed the program would soon "run out of money completely."[96] Similarly, a 2010 national survey found that a significant number of Democrats thought President Obama had cut the number of U.S. troops in Afghanistan, a view consistent with their personal desires but at odds with what Obama had done.[97]

In an experiment designed to show the power of motivated reasoning, Stanford psychologist Geoffrey Cohen exposed self-identified liberals to two hypothetical news stories, one containing a proposal for a generous new welfare program and the other containing a proposal for a less substantial new welfare program. Half of the subjects read stories that presented the proposals without reference to their sponsors. This group of liberals expressed a clear preference for the generous program—the more liberal alternative. The other half read stories that included an endorsement of the skimpy program by Democratic leaders. Reacting to the endorsement, these liberals expressed a preference for the less substantial program—the more conservative of the two options.[98]

Americans' partisan loyalties are not always so determinative of their thinking. In some instances, the facts are simply too obvious to ignore. Opposition to the Iraq War, for example, rose among Republicans and Democrats alike as the human and financial costs soared.[99] However, when the facts are less obvious and become the object of "he said, she said" partisan disputes, people often use party loyalty as a guide.[100]

Global warming is a case in point. During most of the 1990s, a substantial majority of Republicans and Democrats accepted global warming as fact and believed human activity was driving it.[101] However, after the Kyoto climate change agreement was negotiated in late 1997, global warming came under attack from the right, and Republicans' belief in climate change began to waver. They didn't have to look far to find challenges to the scientific evidence. A study found that conservative politicians, industry-funded think tanks, and other sources that claimed climate change was inconsequential or scientifically unsupported received the same level of news coverage in the mainstream press during the 1998 to 2002 period as did sources whose views were aligned more closely with those of the scientific community.[102]

Although scientific evidence of climate change continued to accumulate after 2002, so did attacks on the evidence, as a study by Duke University's Frederick Mayer revealed.[103] When the climate change film *An Inconvenient Truth* burst on the scene, garnering an Oscar and the Nobel Peace Prize for former vice president Al Gore in 2007, conservatives fired back, claiming that global warming was a hoax concocted by environmentalists and government-funded scientists. The claim gained momentum when the hacked e-mails of four climatologists at the University of East Anglia suggested (wrongly as it turned out) they had manipulated data to strengthen the case for climate change. By 2009 on Fox News, the "hoax narrative" was outpacing the global warming narrative by nearly two to one.[104] Overall, nearly 60 percent of Fox broadcasts included a message disputing the global warming thesis, whereas less than 20 percent of its broadcasts contained a message supporting the thesis.[105]

Fox's liberal foil, MSNBC, countered the hoax narrative with what Mayer calls the "denialist-conspiracy narrative"—the claim that the right-wing media were deliberately distorting the evidence in order to promote corporate interests. At its peak, this type of reporting accounted for half of MSNBC's global warming coverage.[106] For its part, CNN gave the hoax and denialist-conspiracy theories nearly equal time while granting more airtime to "he said, she said" disputes than either Fox or MSNBC. CNN anchor Wolf Blitzer began a segment of *The Situation Room* by saying, "So is global warming fact or fiction? Let's go to a debate. John Christy is professor of atmospheric science at the University of Alabama–Huntsville and Gavin Schmidt is a climate scientist at the NASA Goddard Institute for Space Studies."[107]

Other news outlets did not ignore these controversies but gave them much less time and space—indeed, the balance of their coverage had tipped in the direction of the scientific consensus.[108] In other respects, however, they were still playing the "he said, she said" card. On the basis of a study of climate change economics, journalist Eric Pooley concluded that the news media "failed to recognize the emerging consensus among economists that cap-and-trade would have a marginal effect on economic growth and gave doomsday forecasts coequal status with nonpartisan ones. In other words . . . the press allowed opponents of climate action to replicate the false debate over climate science in the realm of climate economics."[109]

Offered a range of scenarios, Republicans and Democrats embraced different versions of reality. Whereas 86 percent of Democrats in 2007 believed there was "solid evidence" of climate change, only 62 percent of Republicans thought so. By 2008, the number of Republicans with this opinion had slipped to 49 percent. By late 2009, only 35 percent of Republicans agreed that the earth was warming and a mere 18 percent thought it was warming "mostly because of human activity."[110]

News exposure once served as protection against faulty beliefs. Citizens who followed the news regularly were more likely than other citizens to hold realistic views.[111] It's still true, but less so. A 2010 University of Maryland survey that examined Americans' opinions on eleven issues—ranging from health care reform to climate change—found that "for some news sources on some issues, higher levels of exposure increased misinformation." Newspaper readers were better informed than TV viewers, but that was not saying much. On eight of the eleven issues, 40 percent or more of regular readers misjudged the facts. On six of the eleven issues, regular readers were nearly as misinformed as other citizens, and on one issue—the budgetary impact of the 2010 health care reform law—they were the more misinformed group.[112] In explaining the findings, the University of Maryland research team pointed to the inaccurate messages that now flow freely through the media system.[113]

8.

The objective model of American journalism offers a weak defense against factual distortions. Not only does the commitment to balance invite such distortions, it allows them to pass unchecked. The model's definition of accuracy is less a question of the truth of what is said than a question of whether someone actually said it,[114] a practice that Pooley calls "stenography."[115]

It was not always this way. Kovach and Rosenstiel note that objective journalism was originally conceived as a method of inquiry. Journalists were assumed to have a subjective view of the world and therefore were required to make every effort to separate fact from opinion.[116] Over time, objectivity took on nearly the opposite meaning. Rather than taking responsibility for ascertaining the facts, journalists aimed for "balance"—giving each side an opportunity to present its version of the facts.[117] In the words of author Joan Didion, journalistic balance is "a scrupulous passivity, an agreement to cover the story not as it is occurring but as it is presented."[118]

As Bennett notes, the balance model breaks down when newsmakers "begin to play loose with facts."[119] "Balanced" reporting then devolves into what James Fallows calls "false equivalencies"—the side-by-side placement of statements of differing factual integrity.[120] Journalist John McQuaid argues that "he said, she said" reporting "is unworkable because the public 'conversation' is too splintered, its practitioners too practiced and manipulative."[121]

McQuaid thinks the answer to the problem rests in exposing politicians' fabrications. He says "journalists should be ready to call BS when they see it."[122] Fair enough. The appropriate counter, if a false or misleading claim is flagrant enough, is to call it for what it is. In fact, some observers suggest that "he said, she said" journalism, although still prevalent, is diminishing—that journalists are increasingly inclined to challenge officials' claims.[123]

Yet if journalists were to apply a microscope to everything that politicians say, the public will only end up confused about what to believe and whom to trust. Some issues are so fluid or inexact that politicians have no choice but to fight over them.[124] A failure to do so would force them to debate the issue on their opponents' turf. Moreover, some disputes are normative in nature. When Democrats propose extending the scope of stem cell research and furnish their set of facts for why it's necessary, and Republicans oppose any such extension and furnish their set of facts for why it's a bad idea, the two sides are clashing over values. If their factual constructions are dishonest, journalists should call them out, but the underlying normative differences, as philosophers tell us, are factually unimpeachable.

It is also the case that political rhetoric is naturally overblown.[125] "Politicians are the same all over," Soviet leader Nikita Khrushchev said a half century ago. "They promise to build a bridge where there is no river."[126] Citizens routinely discount such claims, accepting them, as Doris Graber found in her study, "with the proverbial grain of salt."[127] If journalists were to jump on every such exaggeration, they would only muddy the waters, making it harder, not easier, for citizens to understand what's at stake in political conflict.

The 2012 presidential campaign offered a glimpse at the chaos that results when journalists magnify every factual inaccuracy, large or small. Barely a day passed during the campaign when some reporter somewhere didn't report an inaccuracy uncovered by FactCheck.org, PolitiFact.com, or some other political fact-checking entity.[128] The back-and-forth charges between journalists and candidates filled the air on so many subjects that voters could have been forgiven if they had covered their ears.* A 2012 election survey found that only

* Nonpartisan fact-checking organizations, such as FactCheck.org and Politi Fact.com, provide an invaluable service. These services can be devalued, however, when they trumpet small or inconsequential deviations from fact. Their work has also been devalued through the rise of ideologically oriented "fact-checking" organizations, which exist partly to challenge what their nonpartisan counter-

10 percent of respondents approved of the news media's performance,[129] leading one critic to say of election reporters: "You know, the ones who bring us daily, even hourly, tales of hypocrisy, corruption, jealousy, infidelity, gaffes, ambition, lies, double-crosses, distortions, unsubstantiated rumors, malicious unsourced quotes, self-serving opinions masked as analysis and downright stupidities."[130] The *Washington Post*'s David Broder put his finger squarely on the effect of unrestrained criticism when he said: "If the assumption is that nothing is on the level, nothing is what it seems, then citizenship becomes a game for fools, and there is no point in trying to stay informed."[131]

Journalists' credibility can be shredded as easily by overzealousness as by timidity.[132] There is no surer way for the press to take the bite out of its watchdog bark than to find fault with every claim, large and small. Research indicates that heightened public mistrust of both journalists and politicians is the only certain effect of reporting that attacks nearly everything politicians say.[133]

Holding leaders to account is not merely an issue of correcting their faulty claims. The purpose of such reporting should be to clarify the public's choices.[134] This can occur only if journalists pick their battles, focusing on critical issues where deceptive tactics run the risk of getting citizens to act in ways contrary to their core interests and values.[135] When confronting grave lies, wrote Lippmann, journalists have "no higher duty" than "to tell the truth and shame the devil."[136] The consequences of not doing so, as in the case of the preinvasion coverage of the Iraq conflict, are substantial. By picking their battles, reporters will have the public's attention and trust when it counts. What Alexander Hamilton said of judges—that

---

parts are saying, making it doubly important that nonpartisan fact-checking organizations concentrate on significant distortions.

their authority rests not on their power to decide but on their ability to exercise "judgment" when making decisions—applies also to journalists.[137]

9.

Whether closer scrutiny by journalists would lead politicians to refrain from deceptive claims is unclear.[138] "We're not going to let our campaign be dictated by fact checkers," said Romney campaign pollster Neil Newhouse during the 2012 Republican National Convention. Other public figures say they would welcome closer scrutiny, as long as it is applied evenhandedly. "If a major political figure says something that is entirely untrue and ridiculous," said a White House communications director, "the press [should] treat it as untrue and ridiculous."[139]

Yet politicians face enormous pressures—arm-twisting by powerful groups, persistent demands from constituents, intense pressure to raise campaign funds. Any worry they might have about media scrutiny could take a backseat to the strategic advantage of stretching the truth. For sure, politicians would try to turn press criticism to their advantage.[140] From the earliest days of partisan politics in America, politicians have taken press practices into account when devising their strategies.* Today, attacks on the press are a tactical ploy,

* As the rivalry heated up between Thomas Jefferson and Alexander Hamilton for influence within and outside the administration of George Washington, each of them convinced a backer to start a newspaper that would serve as the principal outlet for their political philosophies. Support was provided in the form of government patronage. As secretary of the treasury and of state, respectively, Hamilton and Jefferson controlled most of the government's lucrative printing contracts.

aimed at weakening the impact of the press's messages.[141] In a 2012 Republican presidential primary debate in South Carolina, CNN's John King opened the questioning by asking Newt Gingrich about his ex-wife's accusation of marital infidelity. Gingrich shot back: "I think the destructive, vicious, negative nature of much of the news media makes it harder to govern this country, harder to attract decent people to run for public office. I'm appalled you would begin a presidential debate on a topic like that."[142] The debate audience erupted with wild applause—for Gingrich, not King.

Where, in most cases, would the public side in a war of words between the journalist and the politician? At the time of Watergate, the public might have sided with the journalist. Today, the public—or at least its motivated partisans, like those at the South Carolina debate—would side with the politician. In an experiment designed to test the relative power of the media's corrective messages and partisan-based motivated reasoning, political scientists Brendan Nyhan and Jason Reifler exposed conservative Republicans to a mock *New York Times* story that included a portion of a George W. Bush speech in which he claimed his tax cuts had increased government revenue. In a subsequent paragraph, the story cited evidence that "both nominal tax revenues and revenues as a proportion of GDP declined sharply after Bush's first tax cuts were enacted in 2001 . . . and still had not rebounded to 2000 levels by either metric in 2004." Rather than accepting the corrective information, the Republican subjects became more convinced than ever that the Bush tax cuts had increased revenue. Nyhan and Reifler conclude: "Many citizens seem unable or unwilling to revise their beliefs in the face of corrective information, and attempts to correct those mistaken beliefs may only make matters worse."[143]

In an earlier study, Northwestern University's Dennis Chong and James Druckman found the same tendency, concluding that corrective information can have a "backfire effect." They found that motivated partisans "counterargue" when exposed to corrective messages on controversial issues, thereby convincing themselves that they were right in the first place.[144] The tendency is strongest among those who distrust the press.[145]

10.

Few developments in recent decades have done more to tarnish the reputations of both journalists and politicians than what former *Boston Globe* editor Michael Janeway calls their "parasitic" and yet "adversarial" relationship.[146] Each side has done its level best to malign the other, and each has succeeded to an unhealthy degree.[147] A recent study found, for example, that partisan criticism of the media is a prime factor (tabloidization being the other) in the public's growing distrust of the press.[148] Journalists and politicians now have reputations on par with those of trial lawyers and used-car salesmen.[149] Writing a few years before his death in 2011, David Broder observed: "The hardest question any Washington reporter faces these days, whenever talking with voters outside the capital, is simply: 'Can I believe anything I'm told by those politicians in Washington—or by the press?' "[150]

Some journalists are unfazed by the public's skepticism of their work. "We're not here to be loved," remarked a veteran broadcast journalist.[151] Perhaps so, but journalists' credibility suffers when they don't have the public's trust.[152] A Pew Research Center poll during the Iraq War found, for example, that Americans had more faith in what the military was telling them about the conflict than what journalists were saying.[153] A recent study by political scientists Brian Fogarty and

Jennifer Wolak showed that people find "media accounts less convincing than messages delivered directly by politicians."[154] In his 2012 book, *Why Americans Hate the Media and How It Matters*, Georgetown University's Jonathan Ladd presents evidence showing that those who trust the press are swayed by its messages, whereas those who distrust it are not.[155]

Somewhere in the evolving relationship between journalists and politicians, fidelity to truth has slipped away. The potential for destructive behavior on either side has always been there, as the McCarthy era revealed,[156] but it was kept largely in check by informal understandings. Journalists expected politicians to be reasonably honest and high-minded, and politicians expected journalists to act with a reasonable degree of trust and restraint.[157] Many politicians and journalists still operate by this unwritten code. Increasingly, however, the old norms have given way to strategic spin on the political side and the stirring up of controversy on the journalistic side.

These are powerful disruptions. They result in an undersupply of reliable information and contribute to public misunderstanding and confusion. They empower the bullies and the charlatans and allow deceptive notions to surface and thrive. If citizens want to believe that the temperature of the earth has not changed or that the defense industry starts America's wars, they have no trouble finding support for it in today's corrupted information environment.

The situation will be difficult to reverse. It is costly for politicians to work against those in their party who misrepresent issues. If they do so, they get attacked by special interests with a stake in the outcome and risk being challenged by die-hard activists within their own party. And it is costly for news organizations to ignore an unverified story that is spreading like wildfire from one news outlet to the next. If they do resist, they get accused of bias and of suppressing vital information, and risk losing audience members to outlets that are airing the story.

The way forward cannot be found in the practices of the past. Journalism has evolved to the point where it is almost defined by its contradictions. The press, as *Washington Post* columnist E. J. Dionne notes, is operating "under a whole set of contradictory rules and imperatives—to be neutral yet investigatory, to be fair-minded and yet have 'edge,' to be disengaged from politics and yet have 'impact.' "[158] Each of these contradictions can be traced to the unholy mix of disdain and dependency that marks journalists' relationships with officials. Journalists need a new paradigm, one that involves a different way of thinking about what constitutes a reliable source.

THREE

The Knowledge Problem

News and truth are not the same thing, and must be clearly distinguished.[1]

—Walter Lippmann

1.

In a 2012 article, Pulitzer Prize–winning journalist Linda Greenhouse challenged reporters who had given voice to David Rivkin's views on national security. Rivkin had served in the Reagan and first Bush administrations and invariably took "the other side" in stories that criticized the second Bush administration's handling of the war on terrorism. Said Greenhouse: "As a surrogate, a 'go-to proxy,' [Rivkin] is simply filling a role assigned to him by reporters and—let's assume—editors who accept unquestionably the notion that every story has another side that it is journalism's duty to present. But there is another side to *that* story, too—one that calls on journalists to do their best to provide not just the facts, but also—always—the truth."[2]

"Truth" is the holy grail of journalism. In the late 1990s, two dozen of the nation's top reporters, calling themselves the

Committee of Concerned Journalists, held a series of public forums to address what its members saw as declining news standards. Over a period of two years, the committee met with three thousand reporters and citizens to exchange ideas about the purpose of journalism.[3] The resulting "Statement of Shared Principles" identified "truth" as journalism's standard:

> "[J]ournalistic truth" is a process that begins with the professional discipline of assembling and verifying facts. Then journalists try to convey a fair and reliable account of their meaning, valid for now, subject to further investigation. Journalists should be as transparent as possible about sources and methods so audiences can make their own assessment of the information. Even in a world of expanding voices, accuracy is the foundation upon which everything else is built—context, interpretation, comment, criticism, analysis and debate. The truth, over time, emerges from this forum.[4]

The committee members were careful to say that "journalistic truth" is not truth in the ordinary sense of the word, much less in the way philosophers understand it. Journalistic truth is a "sorting out" process that occurs over time through interaction "among the public, newsmakers, and journalists."[5] Committee members Bill Kovach and Tom Rosenstiel explained that journalists get at "the truth in a complex world by first stripping information of any misinformation, disinformation, or self-promoting bias and then letting the community react. . . . The search for truth becomes a conversation."[6]

There is no reason to question reporters' determination to deliver what Carl Bernstein has called "the best obtainable version of truth."[7] And it's easy to find examples of good reporting. Yet reporters fall far short of delivering "truth." Studies show, for example, that economic coverage typically lags behind major shifts in the macroeconomic cycle. Existing story lines can linger in the news months after the economic conditions that gave rise to them have changed.[8] Nor is economic reporting the exception. Studies have found that social conditions are often misreported.[9] As for forecasting—predicting how events will unfold—journalists' judgments, as one study concluded, are "repeatedly, wildly wrong."[10]

If news is truth, there appear to be at least two versions of it, one for print journalists and one for television journalists.[11] A Washington State University study showed that local TV and newspaper reporters portray U.S. Senate campaigns differently—so differently, in fact, that voters could reasonably assume they are witnessing different contests. "The priorities of newspapers and local television news seldom overlapped," the research team concluded.[12]

When journalists speak of truth in news, they often have a narrow conception in mind, one that boils down to the accuracy of specific facts.[13] Did Senator Smith actually say the words attributed to her? Did last year's trade deficit actually top $400 billion? Some news organizations retain fact checkers to verify such claims. But fact checkers don't address the fundamental question: Is the story itself "true"? A story can be accurate in its particulars—what was said, when and where it happened, who witnessed it, and so on—and yet falter as a whole. Even if the facts check out, a story would not be true for that reason alone.[14] Early coverage of the war in Afghanistan, for example, was often accurate in its particulars but off the mark in its assessments of Afghan society and the probable course of the war.[15]

Even "the facts" can be elusive. A 2005 study of fourteen local newspapers funded by the Knight Foundation found that three-fifths of their stories contained an error. Some errors were minor, as in the misspelling of a name. Others were more significant, as in the case of a misleading headline or faulty claim. None of the newspapers had a low error rate. "Neither stature of the paper nor market size," the study concluded, "[was] closely associated with accuracy."[16]

Journalists gain little by claiming to be in the truth business and suffer more as a result when their reporting goes astray. David Broder came closer to describing the nature of news when he said: "My experience suggests that we often have a hard time finding our way through the maze of facts—visible and concealed—in any story. We often misjudge character, mistake plot lines. And even when the facts seem most evident to our senses, we go astray by our misunderstanding and misjudgment of the context in which they belong."[17]

2.

Of the many who have written on the subject of news, few have come closer to understanding its nature than Walter Lippmann, widely regarded as the leading journalist of the twentieth century. He knew firsthand the frailties of reporting and had no patience for the craft's myths. To Lippmann, the oft-heard claim that the news is a mirror of reality was nothing but self-serving nonsense.[18]

The claim that news is truth was also troubling to Lippmann. Although the news is presented as if it were fact, Lippmann saw it as filled with opinion.[19] Journalism, wrote Lippmann, "works marvelously well at times, particularly in the rapidity with which it can report the score of a game . . . or the result of an election. But where the issue is complex, as for example in the matter of the success of a policy, or the social conditions among a foreign people—that is to say, where the real answer is neither yes or no, but subtle, and a matter of balanced evidence . . . the report causes no end of derangement, misunderstanding, and even misrepresentation."[20] As Lippmann saw it, nearly all assertions about power politics are conjectural, as are those about personal motives. So too are claims about social movements, complex events, intricate policy problems, and the like. News about what is likely to happen is usually of this kind.

News reports on intricate subjects may include flashes of insight but typically contain questionable assertions. Perhaps journalists were correct in claiming that Hillary Clinton's 2002 Senate vote on the Iraq invasion was expedient, driven by her desire to become president.[21] But what is the measure of a politician's sincerity? And what level of expediency is disqualifying, given that all who step forward to run for the presidency exhibit it? Perhaps Clinton exceeded the level of ambition expected of a president. But what is the standard and who should define it?

The Clinton narrative focused on a single individual. What about developments that encompass an entire institution or thousands of people? Or those that cut across national boundaries? Can it be said in all honesty that in the years since September 11, 2001, journalists have provided Americans the "truth" about Muslim views of the United States? Coverage of the killing of Osama bin Laden, for example, rarely mentioned that his death intensified anti-American sentiment in parts of the Muslim world.[22]

If truth were the test, the machinery of news would grind to a halt. Whole areas of public life would be walled off to reporters because judgments about them are speculative. When Woodrow Wilson said he had spent much of his adult life in government and yet had never seen "a government," he was saying that government is a concept and not an object.[23] How can journalists claim to know "the truth" of something as complex and intangible as government? Political scientists spend their careers studying government without mastering the subject fully. How can journalists with much less time and specialized training somehow accomplish it?

Journalists are asked to make too many judgments under conditions of too little time and too much uncertainty for the news to be the last word. "When we expect [the press] to supply a body of truth," Lippmann wrote, "we employ a misleading standard of judgment. We misunderstand the limited nature of news [and] the illimitable complexity of society."[24]

3.

Almost alone among the professions, journalism is not rooted in a body of substantive knowledge.[25] The claim is not that journalists lack knowledge or skill, for that is far from true. Nor is the claim an entry into the perennial but ultimately fruitless debate over whether journalism is a craft rather than a profession.[26] The claim instead is a precise one: Journalism is not grounded in a systematic body of substantive knowledge that would protect its practitioners' autonomy and inform their judgment.*

Medicine, law, and the sciences, even economics and psychology, have disciplinary knowledge that guides practitioners' decisions, narrowing the choices and reducing the chances of

* As the term is used in this book, "knowledge" refers to established patterns and regularities organized around conceptual frameworks or theories. Knowledge is more than mere information or conventional understandings. It is systematic information. As the ensuing discussion will point out, journalism lacks such a knowledge base, both in an absolute sense and relative to other disciplines. A related point, which is central to an understanding of journalism's shortcomings, is that knowledge is a key to devising accurate interpretations of what is observed or factually recorded.

error. Journalists have no such advantage. Although there is a theoretical knowledge of journalism, it is not definitive, nor is its mastery a prerequisite for practice.[27] Although a majority of journalists have a college degree in journalism, many have a degree in a different field and some have no degree at all.[28]

Journalists are often in the thankless position of knowing less about the subject at hand than the newsmakers they are covering, a reversal of the typical situation, in which the professional practitioner is the more knowledgeable party. Only rarely do clients know more about the law than do their attorneys, whereas newsmakers normally know more about the issue at hand than the journalists covering them. During the Persian Gulf War, journalists who visited the Pentagon press office were greeted with a sign that read, "Welcome Temporary War Experts."[29]

The knowledge advantage that newsmakers have over journalists is not simply that they are privy to what's said in closed-door meetings or contained in briefing papers.[30] They are assisted by experts. The president would never rely on his own instincts across a host of issues without the advice of policy specialists; nor would any congressional committee chair, top bureaucrat, or lobbyist. To be sure, journalists acquire expertise as a result of being on the same news beat for lengthy periods, but this form of expertise does not compare with that of most professionals. Doctors, lawyers, and engineers are masters of their own house in a way that journalists are not.

Journalists' knowledge deficit does not appear to be a major concern within their profession. In 2008, the Knight Foundation created a blue-ribbon commission aimed at strengthening journalism so that it could better serve communities' "information needs." None of the panel's fourteen recommendations spoke to journalism's knowledge deficit.[31] Yet the public has a sense of it. In a Freedom Forum study, journalist Robert Haiman found that although the public "respects the professional and technical skills [of] journalists," it feels that journalists "don't have an authoritative understanding of the complicated world they have to explain to the public." In the five cities where he held public forums (Nashville; New London, Connecticut; Phoenix; San Francisco; and Portland, Oregon), Haiman heard repeated complaints from local civic and business leaders who questioned reporters' preparation. "We heard stories," he writes, "about reporters who did not know the difference between debt and equity, who did not know basic legal terminology used in a trial, and who had little idea of how manufacturing, wholesaling, distributing, and retailing actually work and relate to each other."[32]

If journalists are, as has been claimed, "the custodians of the facts,"[33] their armament is sometimes akin to that of a palace guard. It is difficult to protect the facts in those instances when someone else commands them.

4.

When it comes to a subject of more than average complexity, the truth in news typically comes from outside of journalism. The news media, Lippmann argued, "can normally record only what has been recorded for it by the working of institutions. Everything else is argument and opinion."[34]

Lippmann's point is best seen by looking back in time, comparing the accuracy of news before journalists had access to precise information with its accuracy after they acquired it. Consider the history of election forecasting. Through the first half of the twentieth century, reporters arrived at their election predictions by talking with party leaders, judging the size of crowds at election rallies, sharing notes with colleagues. Experienced journalists knew they could not rely solely on what they observed. A huge rally in Detroit was significant, but it did not necessarily reveal what small-town America was thinking. However, since other reporters were in the same boat, journalists could let fly with their forecasts, knowing they would not be called to account until the votes were in. The *Literary Digest* won fame by correctly predicting four presidential elections in a row. It acquired notoriety when it missed the fifth by a mile, calling the 1936 election for Alf Landon. Landon won only 37 percent of the popular vote and a meager 2 percent of the electoral vote—a shellacking almost unmatched in the history of presidential elections.[35]

Even polling in its early years did not protect journalists from faulty predictions. In a front-page story the day before the 1948 presidential election, the *New York Times* proclaimed that "the rosy prospect of victory from the Truman ticket finds no credence outside Mr. Truman's kitchen cabinet."[36] *Time* polled the forty-seven journalists traveling with Republican nominee Thomas Dewey; all of them predicted he would win.[37] *Newsweek* conducted a poll of fifty of "the nation's top political writers" shortly before the election; all of them forecast a Dewey victory. The *Newsweek* panel predicted that Dewey would win 54 percent of the two-party popular vote.[38] Even after early returns revealed stronger-than-expected support for Harry Truman, some journalists clung to their forecasts. "Dewey Defeats Truman" was the headline of the *Chicago Tribune*'s early edition.

Faced with the wrong winner on their hands, journalists devised a new version of truth. During the campaign, journalists had cast Truman in the image of a loser. *Newsweek* said he lacked the "stature" of a president: "a woefully weak little man, a nice enough fellow but wholly inept."[39] His whirlwind train tour was dismissed with the headline "Prayer for a Chain Reaction."[40] The Truman of legend—he of whistle-stopping fame—

did not become journalists' story line until after the election. The feisty style that had been labeled "intemperate" and "a sign of desperation" during the campaign became the "give-'em-hell, Harry" that we know today.[41]

Election reporting in 1948 was an awkward form of fiction that journalists would not be required to repeat. The science of polling was advancing rapidly, as was its practice. George Gallup would never again make the mistake of conducting his final poll two weeks out from an election. Since then, polling has enabled journalists to predict election outcomes accurately. Polling is not a flawless method. It is subject to confidence intervals and margins of error, creating the possibility of a faulty prediction in a close or fluid race. But forecasting based on polls is a quantum improvement over journalists' old way of predicting elections.

So it is in most areas of news: the more precise the system of record, the more precise the news coverage. Until the 1990s, for example, obesity was portrayed by journalists as a personal problem that was the result of family genetics, eating disorders, and the like. In 1996, the National Center for Health Statistics (NCHS) made public for the first time a large amount of systematic evidence on obesity, including the startling finding that half of Americans were overweight and a quarter were obese. Within a few years, according to Regina Lawrence's Shorenstein Center study, the framing of obesity stories had changed dramatically. Although the "personal" frame was still in use, most stories were now framed in "systemic" terms. NCHS had concluded that personal predispositions could not explain the rapid rise in obesity levels, particularly among children and adolescents. NCHS singled out systemic factors, including the aggressive marketing of sugar-laced cereals and cholesterol-laden fast foods. "We don't sell children guns, alcohol or drugs," Dr. Walter Willett of Harvard University told the *New York Times*, "but we do allow them to be exploited by food companies."[42]

There is, wrote Lippmann, "a very direct relation between the certainty of news and the system of record."[43] No one need quarrel, for example, with stories that recount statistics on the balance of trade. Journalists did not get better at reporting on trade because their discipline developed a formula for calculating it. They got better because government agencies instituted a systematic method for measuring it.

Knowledge does not always yield precise answers. It can complicate the reporters' task by alerting them to what's not known as well as to what's known. Sometimes, the effect of knowledge is to unearth new questions or uncertainties. Even the "facts" can be elusive. Once they are determined, facts serve as a point of agreement, but they are not always easy to pin down.[44] "Most people think science is about facts and are quite frustrated when they find that science is in large part about uncertainty," says Gilbert Omenn, former chair of the American Association for the Advancement of Science.[45] Nevertheless, the surest way to improve the accuracy of news is for journalists to make fuller use of knowledge. There's no lack of it, and it's expanding at a breathtaking pace. By one estimate, the storehouse of human knowledge is doubling every decade.[46] Enough of it touches on public affairs that few policy areas now fall outside its scope.

5.

When Lippmann spelled out his vision of journalism in *Liberty and the News* (1920) and *Public Opinion* (1922), the biggest detractors were his fellow journalists.[47] As they saw it, reporting was not an intellectual pursuit but instead a job for hard-nosed men of common sense.[48] Paul Radin, a leading anthropologist of the early twentieth century, characterized the journalist as "a man of action" rather than "a thinker."[49]

When the 1947 Hutchins Commission on Freedom of the Press echoed Lippmann's claim that journalism needed a deeper knowledge base,[50] the writers at *Editor & Publisher* fired back, dismissing the commission's report as the work of "eleven professors, a banker-merchant and a poet-librarian."[51] A *New York Herald Tribune* columnist belittled the report: "[A] good $150-a-week newspaperman would have been ashamed to do as little work for a three-week assignment."[52] *Los Angeles Times* managing editor L. D. Hotchkiss said, "Outside of Walter Lippmann, I can think of no working newspaperman who could stand confinement with [the commission] members for any length of time."[53]

Modern journalists are leagues apart from the crusty newsmen of yesteryear.[54] Most journalists today are college graduates and are receptive to expert judgments.[55] Roughly a fifth of the sources cited in their news stories are scholars, professionals, former officials, and the like.[56] Although some of these "experts" are more skilled at delivering sound bites than at analyzing policy,[57] the world of knowledge and the world of the newsroom are closer together today than ever before.[58]

There is also greater expertise within journalism. Although they are still a small fraction of the profession, the number of reporters with advanced degrees in fields such as science, health, economics, and law has steadily increased. A few journalists, like David Sanger and Andrew Revkin, have acquired substantial reputations inside and outside the profession for deeply informed reporting. American University's Matthew Nisbet calls them "knowledge journalists," noting that they regularly apply "deductive, specialized understanding to problems."[59]

Nevertheless, journalists have been slow to apply systematic knowledge to their everyday work. As Walter Pincus noted recently, there are major policy areas in which few journalists—anywhere—know the subject truly well.[60] American journalists are trained in gathering and presenting information,[61] which are substantial skills but not ones that require subject proficiency. In a comparative study, a German scholar and his American colleague examined the news-gathering methods used by journalists in the two countries. When it came to making use of systematic forms of information, such as studies and public records, American journalists were substantially less likely to do so than their German counterparts.[62]

Journalism education in the United States has mirrored journalism practice.[63] For the most part, students are instructed in the skills of the craft and taught how to construct a broadcast, print, or online story. Few journalism schools systematically train students how to access, gain command of, and apply subject matter knowledge. Three decades ago, a top-level commission of journalists and practitioners criticized journalism schools for being "little more than industry-oriented trade schools."[64] Changes have occurred since then, but journalism schools still lag far behind business and public policy schools in the application of knowledge. Economics, management science, and even social psychology are now an integral part of a business school or public policy school education. Although these schools still puzzle over how best to align practice and scholarship, they have achieved a fuller integration of the two than have journalism schools.[65]

6.

In their influential and widely adopted journalism text *The Elements of Journalism,* Kovach and Rosenstiel explain that journalists' "discipline of verification" is what allows them to home in on the truth. "The discipline of verification," they write, "is what separates journalism from entertainment, propaganda, fiction, or art. Entertainment—and its cousin 'infotainment'—focus on what is most diverting. Propaganda selects facts and invents them to serve the real purpose: persuasion and manipulation. Fiction invents scenarios to get at a more personal impression of what it calls truth. Journalism alone is focused on getting what happened down right."[66]

Kovach and Rosenstiel acknowledge that journalists' discipline of verification is largely "personal and idiosyncratic."[67] "The notion of an objective method of reporting," they say, "exists in pieces, handed down by word of mouth from reporter to reporter."[68] "While not following any standardized code," they write, "every journalist operates by relying on some often highly personal method of testing and providing information—his or her own individual discipline of verification."[69]

Whether a method that is "personal and idiosyncratic" qualifies as a discipline is open to question. If there is no "standardized code," wouldn't it be better to describe journalism as a practice guided by conventions? Recognizing the problem, Kovach and Rosenstiel propose five "intellectual principles" as the basis for "a science of reporting":

1. Never add anything that was not there.
2. Never deceive the audience.
3. Be as transparent as possible about your methods and motives.

4. Rely on your own original reporting.

5. Exercise humility.[70]

Each of these principles has its logic. Conspicuously absent from the list, however, is knowledge.

It's difficult to imagine that journalism can become a systematic discipline without knowledge at its core. Unless knowledge is a guide, the chances of miscalculation are high. In early 2011, reporters described the protest demonstrations taking place in Cairo's Tahrir Square as a "prodemocracy movement." "Protesters Press for Voice in Egyptian Democracy" is how the AP headlined the departure from power of President Hosni Mubarak on February 11.[71] Many of the protesters were indeed seeking to install a Western-style democratic system in Egypt. Other protesters, however, had a different political system in mind, one closer in kind to Egypt's governing traditions. As it turned out, their view prevailed in the aftermath of the Egyptian revolution.

It is not all that hard for journalists, or anyone else for that matter, to devise explanations. What's harder to do is to come up with valid explanations. Noting the dysfunctional behavior of political leaders in 2010, a leading journalist wrote: "Barring a transformation of the Democratic and Republican parties, there is going to be a serious third-party candidate in 2012 . . . one definitely big enough to impact the election's outcome."[72] Such commentary is harmless enough and enables the journalist to say "I told you so" when the prediction comes true. But a deeper understanding of the dynamics of America's party politics would have tempered the claim. Whatever the indicators in 2010 of a viable third-party effort, they could not possibly have been as persuasive as the counterindicators. Strong third-party candidacies are rare for a host of reasons. Political scientists Brendan Nyhan and John Sides identify some of them: "party loyalty, ballot access, fundraising difficulties, the lack of organizational infrastructure, voters' unwillingness to 'waste' their vote."[73] Even when institutional obstacles can be overcome, a more imposing one exists, as Americans Elect discovered in 2012. Formed by prominent Democrats and Republicans concerned about the rising level of party polarization, Americans Elect secured ballot access for a third-party candidate and obtained funding commitments from major donors. Yet it was forced to abandon its third-party effort upon failing to get a leading politician to head the ticket. It's been a century since the last truly prominent politician, Theodore Roosevelt, was willing to take on the challenge.*

Knowledge is the starting point as well as the end product of systematic inquiry, guiding the practitioner in what to look for as well as what to make of what is found. Without knowledge of the deeper forces at work in the situation, the choice among plausible alternatives is in large part guesswork, a point that Kovach and Rosenstiel readily acknowledge. "Although journalism may have developed various techniques and conventions for determining facts," they write, "it has done less to develop a system for testing the reliability of journalistic interpretation."[74]

Journalists' knowledge deficiency is a reason they are vulnerable to manipulation by their sources. Sometimes a source might be disinterested, but the safe bet is that newsmakers are slanting their arguments.[75] Knowing this, a good journalist will be on guard, but, says journalist Jack Fuller, it is not enough for the journalist "to smell this sort of thing."[76] Skepti-

* Roosevelt, a Republican and former president, ran in 1912 because he was angered by the policy direction of his handpicked successor, Republican incumbent William Howard Taft. Roosevelt narrowly outpolled Taft, but they split the Republican vote, enabling their Democratic opponent, Woodrow Wilson, to win the election with 42 percent of the popular vote.

cism is a weak defense against sources that fabricate facts or hide them. Unless reporters have a sense of where the truth resides, they find themselves in the position of "common carriers, transmitters of other people's ideas and thoughts, irrespective of import, relevance, and at times even accuracy."[77]

Without a working knowledge of the subject at hand, journalists are also vulnerable to the experts from whom they seek information, quotes, and story leads. Many experts are dispassionate in their pursuit of knowledge, but others have an agenda. Sometimes it stems from a core personal or political belief. In other instances, the agenda is that of a sponsor, as in the case of some medical researchers who accept funding from pharmaceutical firms. Reporters, says Fuller, "must be capable of dealing with experts from a position of strength."[78]

7.

In the 1970s, Philip Meyer, a Knight Ridder national correspondent who went on to become a journalism professor at the University of North Carolina, argued that reporters needed "new tools." Noting the rapid advance of the social sciences, Meyer said scholars were "doing what we journalists like to think of ourselves as best at: findings facts, inferring causes, pointing to ways to correct social problems, and evaluating the effects of such correction."[79] In *Precision Journalism,* Meyer argued that journalists should make "the new high-powered research techniques our own"[80] and proceeded chapter by chapter to show journalists how to apply social science methods such as polls and field experiments.

Meyer's pioneering ideas acquired a following in some journalism schools and influenced the work of some reporters, particularly those engaged in polling and data analysis.[81] The impact was limited, however, by the fact that the slow speed of primary research conflicts with the fast pace of daily journalism. The limits of time and observation make it difficult for journalists to apply the data gathering and analytic methods of the social scientist. Walter Lippmann suggested instead a pragmatic approach. Rather than becoming adept at conducting basic research, journalists would become adept at applying existing knowledge to reporting situations.[82]

Some in journalism question whether even that approach is realistic, arguing that the puzzles and routines of journalism have little in common with those of science. Even as late as the mid-1990s, a survey funded by the Freedom Forum found that most journalists and journalism educators were resistant to making journalism a more systematic discipline.[83]

In fact, there are some key differences between science and journalism. Deadlines, time and space limitations, the need to attract and hold the audience's attention—these factors are distinctly journalistic in nature.[84] Moreover, as Nyhan and Sides explain, reporters don't have the option of ignoring "events that are not well understood."[85]

If there is to be a "science" of journalism, it will have to take a form that reflects the type of work that journalists do. Given the range of subjects they cover, and the uncertainty surrounding many of them, journalists cannot be expected to become experts on the level of those who make a subject area their life's work. Moreover, "knowledge" for the journalist will not mimic the type of "knowledge" that typifies, say, an economist. Journalism is not a tidy discipline, nor are its subjects narrowly defined. It is one thing to explain the economy, which is difficult enough, and another thing to explain nearly the whole of public life.

Nevertheless, there are parallels between scientific inquiry and reporting. "Although the vocabularies differ," argues communication scholar Kevin Barnhurst, "the [journalistic and scientific] processes closely parallel each other. Both attend to occurrences out there, formulating guesses (which become events or hypotheses), both resolve issues to arrive at facts (or theories), and both seek to establish truth (or a paradigm)."[86] And just as good science writing is an artful blend of the simple and the complex, so also is good newswriting. "Great journalism," says the writer Jeffrey Scheuer, "simplifies complicated stories just enough to make them accessible and clear, without undue distortion."[87]

It is a mistake to assume that systematic analysis works well only for tightly defined disciplines. "It does not matter that the news is not susceptible of mathematical statement," wrote Lippmann. "In fact, just because news is complex and slippery, good reporting requires the exercise of the highest scientific virtues."[88]

8.

Change in the way a profession does its work doesn't happen just because there might be a better way. A receptive attitude within the profession is required, as are mechanisms for bringing about constructive change. Adjustments in management practices and business school education, for example, did not occur until advances in microeconomics and organizational theory made a new approach feasible.[89]

Journalism has reached a point where change is possible. Its culture is markedly different today from in times past. Skepticism about the value of knowledge has diminished as a result of undeniable scientific advances and the influx into the profession of college-educated practitioners. To be sure, tensions remain. Compared with faculties at other professional schools, for instance, scholars and practitioners on journalism school faculties are more deeply split over the issue of how to best train their students.[90] Still, journalism practice and education have increasingly embraced knowledge as a tool of reporting. "We can support research that strengthens and informs those who are making change and apply our scholarship to the practice ourselves," says former *Des Moines Register* editor Geneva Overholser, now on the faculty of the University of Southern California.[91]

The Internet has reduced the obstacles to knowledge-based reporting. At an earlier time, the difficulty of accessing systematic studies and public records made it impractical for journalists to consult these materials on a regular basis. Today, reliable information on a wide range of news subjects is readily accessible on the Web. "Never has it been so easy to expose an error, check a fact, crowdsource, and bring technology to bear in service of verification," says the Poynter Institute's Craig Silverman.[92] The process is not foolproof, however. The Internet is at once a gold mine of solid content and a hellhole of misinformation. Unless the reporter knows something about the subject at hand, the odds of making a mistake are uncomfortably high. Even peer-reviewed scholarly studies available online can be misleading—some are deeply flawed and most require interpretation to apply them accurately to reporting situations.

If all that knowledge-based journalism comes to mean is tapping the Internet for information, it will not reach its potential.[93] It will represent the injection of knowledge into news stories rather than the application of knowledge to reporting. There's a large difference between the two. As Cambridge University scientist W. I. B. Beveridge noted, knowledge enables the investigator to recognize things that would otherwise be misunderstood or go unnoticed.[94] Knowledge can enable reporters to recognize whether they are on the right track with their explanations; whether they are keeping things in proportion; whether they are weighing plausible alternatives; whether they are avoiding attribution errors; whether they are fending off source fabrications; whether they are on target with their trend analyses and comparisons; and whether they are challenging their taken-for-granted assumptions.

Knowledge could also keep journalists from becoming outmoded and from being outflanked. In a 2012 report for Columbia University's Tow Center for Digital Journalism, C. W. Anderson, Emily Bell, and Clay Shirky note that what journalists have traditionally done—identifying newsworthy events—is now being done also by citizens, while what media outlets have traditionally leveraged—analyzing recent developments—is now being done also by specialty sites and scholars. During the 2012 presidential campaign, for example, historian Jack Bohrer posted a ten-thousand-word article on Mitt Romney's family background that attracted more than 125,000 visitors and was passed along through social media to an additional 750,000 people.[95] Anderson, Bell, and Shirky argue that journalists, if they are to remain competitive, will have to change from "the production of initial observations to a role that emphasizes verification and interpretation."[96] If this claim is even somewhat correct, journalists and news outlets will have no choice but to base more of their work on knowledge.

FOUR

The Education Problem

We need be under no illusion that the stream of news can be purified by pointing out the value of purity. [It can] be made serviceable to democracy . . . by the training of the journalist.[1]

—Walter Lippmann

1.

Journalists like to say that the news is "the first rough draft of history."[2] Even when the claim is not used to excuse the small errors inherent in a fast-paced job, it is inadequate. The news is a story of how today differs from yesterday. Each day is a fresh start, a new reality. Journalism, says scholar Philip Schlesinger, is a "time machine."[3] The *New York Times*' James Reston called reporting "the exhilarating search after the 'Now.' "[4]

Much of what is truly historic is barely visible in the news. In the twentieth century, few developments had more impact on American politics than the northward trek of Southern blacks. As they streamed north to industrial cities in search of jobs, white families, pushed by racial fears and pulled by the lure of the suburbs, moved out. Within the span of a few decades, the political, social, and economic borders of urban America had been redrawn. Yet because it happened slowly over a long period of time, the black migration was seldom reported in the news and almost never emblazoned in headlines.[5] Columnist George Will remarked that a ribbon should have been stretched across the Mason-Dixon Line as the one millionth African American crossed it on the way north. Journalists would then have had a story to cover.[6]

Although the example reveals a gap between journalistic myth and reality, its purpose is to illustrate a defining feature of journalism. Unlike history, journalism is an intentionally shortsighted discipline.[7] Journalists are in the business of producing news, which is to say they are trained to see the world changing in important ways from one day to the next. There are always critical problems facing the nation and the world, but whether they will make headlines depends on whether they fit the time horizon imposed by the news cycle.

Efforts to strengthen journalism must account for its unique character. Journalism cannot be recast in a way that squeezes "the new" out of the news, as can be seen from journalist Christopher Beam's depiction of what a news story might look like if written through the long-range lens of political science:

> A powerful thunderstorm forced President Obama to cancel his Memorial Day speech near Chicago on Monday—an arbitrary event that had no effect on the trajectory of American politics. Obama now faces some of the most difficult challenges of his young presidency: the ongoing oil spill, the Gaza flotilla disaster, and revelations about possibly inappropriate conversations between the White House and candidates for public office. But while these narratives may affect fleeting public perceptions, Americans will ultimately

> judge Obama on the crude economic fundamentals of jobs numbers and GDP.[8]

News reports of this ilk would soon send people scurrying to find better ways to spend their time. Nevertheless, journalists need to figure out how to work the steady currents of public life more fully into their reporting. Journalists necessarily look to what is new about today. It's the window through which they find their stories. Yet, if they focus too tightly on today, they will tend, as Walter Lippmann said, "to make of moles mountains, and of mountains moles."[9] An ABC News report in 2012, for example, headlined a research study that found the risk of heart attack and stroke roughly doubled with the use of birth control pills. What was not headlined was that the risk associated with use of the pill is much lower than that associated with pregnancy.[10] A columnist wryly divided medical reporting into two types of stories: "new hope" and "no hope."[11]

Contextual information has never been journalism's strong suit.[12] In 1947, the Hutchins Commission on Freedom of the Press concluded that reporters routinely fail to provide a "comprehensive and intelligent account of the day's events in a context that gives them some meaning."[13] A University of Pennsylvania study found that competing bills in Congress are often reported by their sponsors' names without reference to what the bills contain or how they differ.[14] Communication scholar Doris Graber found that news stories typically provide the who, what, where, and when of developments but often omit the why.[15] When stories do offer a why, it is often too thin to be instructive. A study of economic news coverage, for example, concluded that journalists' explanations "tend to [be] episodic, shallow and formulaic, focusing on the most obvious short-term effects. . . . Linkages rarely go beyond the simplistic level of . . . [the] explanation that 'the dropping dollar got a lift today, and that pushed up stocks on Wall Street.' "[16]

The why of reporting helps people to understand the significance of events. "The who, when, what, and where," says writer Jeffrey Scheuer, "is about *collecting* the dots." The why is about "*connecting* the dots."[17] Context, says journalism professor Samuel Freedman, tells "how momentary events fit into the larger flow of politics or culture or history."[18] Contextual inadequacies help explain a research finding that initially puzzled scholars: the fact that people don't learn much from news stories unless they already know something about the topic. Scholars had assumed that poorly informed individuals would learn the most from exposure to a news story because they know the least. Yet they don't. The uninformed often don't know enough about the topic to make up for the scarcity of contextual information.[19]

Knowledge is a key to strengthening story context. For almost any development of even modest complexity, journalists cannot be counted upon to construct "a comprehensive and intelligent account" unless they are knowledgeable of the underlying factors.

2.

In his classic study *The Reflective Practitioner,* MIT's Donald Schön argues that the best practitioners are those who have learned to challenge their assumptions and correct the mistakes arising from them. Rather than deferring to routines and formulas, they apply them reflectively. "Through reflection," writes Schön, the practitioner "can surface and criticize the tacit understandings that have grown up around the repetitive experiences of a specialized practice."[20]

Every profession has its habitual ways of thinking and acting.[21] Newcomers get initiated into the profession's norms and conventions, which eventually become habitual.[22] When asked how they select their stories, journalists will often say, "I know news when I see it," as if the news were a naturally occurring phenomenon rather than something they have learned to see.[23] Following the 2012 presidential election, for instance, President Obama held a press conference to discuss the "fiscal cliff" that threatened to drag the nation's economy back into recession. However, the resulting headlines focused on Obama's heated response to a question about a different issue. Earlier in the day, several Republican senators had vowed to block Susan Rice's possible nomination as secretary of state over remarks she made after a deadly attack two months earlier on a U.S. consulate in Libya. When asked about it, Obama called their threat "outrageous," saying, "If Senator McCain and Senator Graham and others want to go after someone, they should go after me." With that, reporters had a controversy to report, one that by news standards trumped the president's predictable remarks about the fiscal cliff.

Journalistic routines teach reporters what to see, but also what not to see. During the two decades leading up to the Occupy Wall Street movement in 2011, the gap in income between America's wealthy and its poor steadily increased. Yet, as a study by *Fortune*'s Nina Easton found, the income gap rarely made news. Not until it took the form of a grassroots movement did it fully catch journalists' attention. "Before these protesters . . . set up camp in New York City's Zuccotti Park on September 17," wrote Easton, "few in the media took notice of a growing body of scholarly research showing that America's rich are getting richer, even in years when middle-class incomes stagnate."[24]

Every profession has such blinders. Yet they are larger in journalism than in most professions because it is closer to being a reflexive practice than a reflective one. Reporters operate under intense time constraints and depend on standardized routines to handle them. Journalism's reflexive character is also seen in what is called "pack" or "herd" journalism—the tendency of reporters to look to other reporters for their story lines.[25] "Ninety percent of the coverage," the *Baltimore Sun*'s Jack Germond remarked, "is derivative of what ten percent produce."[26]

Two types of knowledge would tip journalism in the direction of a reflective practice: "content knowledge," which is knowledge of a subject, and "process knowledge," which is knowledge of how reporting methods affect news content and impact. The first of these will require a division of labor in that no single journalist can master more than a fraction of what reporters are asked to cover. Even some subfields of journalism will require a degree of specialization. "As the pace of new developments in science and technology quickens," says former *Washington Post* science reporter Cristine Russell, "[science] journalists are increasingly confronted with covering complicated technical information as well as the potential social, legal, religious, and political consequences of scientific research. Avian flu, embryonic stem cell research, genetic engineering, global warming, teaching of evolution, and bioterrorism are just a few of the topics on [science] journalists' plates today."[27]

The second knowledge skill—an understanding of the communication process—has been nearly overlooked within the profession. Studies indicate that most journalists are largely unaware of how their reporting tools and story constructions affect story content and audience response.[28] It would be as if teachers had only a vague idea of the instructional techniques that help students learn. Admittedly, journalists don't have the face-to-face interactions with their readers and listeners that teachers have with their students. News audiences are out of sight and therefore harder to comprehend. Still, unless journalists develop a better understanding of their audience, they will miss opportunities to inform it. The next two sections will illustrate this by explaining two common process-related problems: attribution bias, which stems from how journalists gather their material, and framing bias, which stems from how journalists present it.

3.

Journalists' primary tools—observation and interviewing—have been mainstays of reporting for more than a century. Reporters are trained to look first to the scene of action and then to the statements of interested parties. Observation and interviewing are highly useful tools, which is why they have been employed for so long. They are also tools that require judgment and experience if they are to be used properly.[29] Nevertheless, like all tools, observation and interviewing have limits. They fail, says journalist Robert Niles, to provide "us instruction on *how* to test the accuracy of information we receive."[30] Even when they yield reliable information, observation and interviewing enable journalists to capture only those aspects of developments that are observable and that available parties are able and willing to talk about.[31]

Invented by American journalists in the nineteenth century,[32] the interview is likely the handiest reporting tool ever devised. Interviewing relieves the journalist of having to undertake more demanding forms of investigation, and the interviewee's words can be treated as "fact" insofar as the words were actually said.[33] Yet the interview is not foolproof. Who is interviewed, what is asked, and even the time and place of the interview can affect the answers. Responses are subject to mistakes of memory or even a source's determination to mislead a reporter, as was the case in front-page *New York Times* stories that stemmed from White House officials' hoodwinking of reporter Judith Miller during the lead-up to the 2003 Iraq invasion.

As for observation, its usefulness is limited by the fact that it occurs at a particular time and from a particular perspective. Aspects of public life that are not in the line of sight get less scrutiny than those that are. Lobbying activities, for example, are reported less often than election activities, not because they have far less influence on public policy, but because they are far less visible.

Of the distortions that stem from observation, few are more prevalent or more predictable than "fundamental attribution error"—the tendency of an observer to exaggerate the impact of a salient actor or event.[34] In the fall of 2002, for example, George W. Bush crisscrossed the country, campaigning on behalf of three dozen House and Senate Republican candidates. When the votes were counted, the press attributed much of the GOP's success to Bush's efforts. "The result was a huge lift for Mr. Bush," the *New York Times* reported. "[T]he president clearly appeared to have won last night."[35] The *Washington Post* was more lavish in its praise: "There was plenty of evidence that Bush's popularity was a crucial, if not decisive, factor Tuesday. Of the 23 House candidates for whom he campaigned, 21 were victorious or leading last night. Of the 16 Senate candidates he aided, 12 won or were leading."[36] Other news outlets showed even less restraint, saying Bush's influence was "historic," comparable to that of FDR's impact on the 1934 congressional elections.[37] Follow-up stories told of how Bush's "victory" had solidified congressional support for his threatened invasion of Iraq.[38]

For the most part, these claims were an artifact of journalists' perspective on the midterm campaign. A study by political scientists Luke Keele, Brian Fogarty, and James Stimson found that Republican congressional candidates in states and districts where Bush campaigned ran no more strongly than those in areas where he did not campaign. In a detailed constituency-by-constituency comparison of the 2000 and 2002 election returns, they found virtually identical Republican vote gains in both types of races. The study concluded: "Republicans that Bush campaigned for did no better than other Republicans."[39]

Reporters do not have the time to conduct the type of detailed analysis that would have allowed them to correctly assess Bush's influence. Yet, in line with fundamental attribution error, the outsized influence they attributed to Bush's campaign stops was predictable. With their gaze fixed on Bush, reporters naturally gave him the lion's share of the credit for Republican victories in places where he campaigned.*

Attribution errors are magnified by journalists' tendency to personalize developments. Personalization is a godsend for the reporter. It exploits the audience's tendency to credit or blame leaders for what has happened and allows reporters to dramatize and simplify events in a way that reference to struc-

* The news is filled with attribution errors of one type or another. Few are more common, however, than claims about leadership. Take, for instance, reporters' claim that President Obama during his first term failed to display the communication skills he had shown during the 2008 election campaign. "One of the persistent mysteries about the president," a prominent *Washington Post* reporter wrote, "is why . . . [he] has had so much difficulty making a connection with voters on economic issues." Perhaps Obama had lost his way with words. Yet reporters portray presidents as "connecting" with voters only when their public approval rating is high or on the rise. When the economy is performing poorly, the president invariably has a low or declining approval rating, which leads to negative portrayals of their public relations skills. A Syracuse University study found, for instance, that Ronald Reagan was not called the "Great Communicator" until the third year of his presidency. During the first two years, unemployment reached a postwar high and Reagan's public approval rating declined at the fastest pace of any president in the history of polling. Toward the end of Reagan's second year in office, however, the economy turned upward and, as it did, so did his public approval rating. Only then did the press begin to say that Reagan had a gift for "connecting" with voters and bestowed him with the now-famous nickname.

tural factors would not.[40] Yet personalization diverts attention from more salient aspects of developments.[41] A study found, for example, that candidates' personal strategies and styles account for more than three-fourths of reporters' explanations of presidential primary results. Differences in state electorates—such as the fact that South Carolina Republicans are more conservative than those of New Hampshire—account for a mere fifth of the explanations, even though they ordinarily have greater influence on primary election outcomes.[42] "Too often," says Pulitzer Prize–winning journalist Diana Sugg, "we tell the tale of a person because it's a great tale."[43]

Journalists' emphasis on events is also a source of attribution error. Journalists' assessments of trends are only slightly more accurate than would be expected on the basis of chance alone,[44] a situation that can be explained in part by how reporters interpret events. A study found, for instance, that unusual developments alert journalists to events of a similar nature, leading them to conclude that such events are increasing in frequency.[45] Stories about a deadly shark attack, for example, generate stories about other sightings, accompanied by exaggerated claims of the risks to swimmers.[46]

Given the many pressures they face, journalists have no choice but to find efficient and interesting ways to tell their stories. Philip Meyer is correct in saying that "a newspaper with a zero error level of factual errors is a newspaper that is missing deadlines, taking too few risks, or both."[47] Yet it is hard to justify errors that occur repeatedly and stem from the unreflective use of reporting tools.

4.

Citizens do not study the news. They "follow" it. This explains in large part what they learn and fail to learn from news exposure. Few news stories make a lasting impression on the audience. Studies indicate that most stories are forgotten within a few hours of exposure.[48]

Many of the larger lessons that people derive from news exposure are the result of the frames that journalists repeatedly employ.[49] Framing is the process by which reporters select certain aspects of a situation and build their stories around them, as opposed to other aspects of the situation.[50] The effect is to prime the audience to see the situation through the frame that the journalist has selected. For example, although every congressional debate includes cooperation and conflict, journalists tend to report such debates through a conflict frame, which highlights the conflictive aspects and subordinates the cooperative aspects, thereby leading people to view such debates as embodying conflict rather than also involving cooperation.[51]

Reporters rely on a limited number of frames. Stories on policy issues, for example, tend to be told either through a problem frame—which highlights the nature of the policy issue—or through a strategic frame—which highlights the political maneuvering surrounding the issue. The problem frame dominates when issues are addressed in broad terms, usually at an early stage in their development. When issues become politicized, however, the strategic frame takes over.[52] Journalists' tacit assumption—that politics is a strategic game—drives their story lines.

The political game prevails even in unlikely situations. When a U.S. special operations team in 2011 conducted a secret raid into Pakistan that killed Osama bin Laden, the killing dominated the news. During the week following his death, the major story line—accounting for a third of the bin Laden coverage—was the planning and execution of the military raid. But what was the second-biggest story line? The press could have focused on the reaction of the Arab world to the killing, or the operation's effect on U.S. relations with Pakistan, or the effect of bin Laden's death on terrorists' operational capacity. Instead, second billing—accounting for a sixth of the coverage—went to the impact of bin Laden's death on the political game: Would it help Barack Obama win a second term? "President Obama," said ABC's Ann Compton, "is getting a significant bump up in the polls."[53] Strategic framing, Kathleen Hall Jamieson and Paul Waldman observe, "can suppress the factual information citizens need to make sense of the political world."[54]

Factual information is also suppressed by journalists' reliance on "episodic frames"—which highlight only the facts of an event—instead of "thematic frames"—which address also the event's causes and consequences.[55] In a series of controlled experiments, Stanford's Shanto Iyengar showed that episodic framing leads people to respond narrowly to news stories. When exposed, for example, to an episodically framed story about an individual who is poor as a result of not having a job, people tend to attribute the problem to a personal failing, such as laziness. On the other hand, when the story is framed thematically, people also tend to take into account systemic factors, such as economic conditions.[56] Indiana University's Lesa Hatley Major found the same tendencies in people's responses to health coverage.[57]

Episodic framing has its place. Not every development has a discernible cause or is significant enough to warrant elaboration. If episodic framing was confined to such stories, its prevalence would not be an issue. The problem is that the episodic frame is used in covering even momentous events. In a study of terrorism coverage in the period before September 11, 2001, for example, former *Boston Globe* editor Matt Storin found that the press had largely ignored international terrorism except for the immediate coverage of terrorist attacks, such as the bombing of the USS *Cole* in a Yemen harbor in 2000, the same-day bombings of embassies in Kenya and Tanzania in 1998, and the first World Trade Center attack in 1993. Even the firing of cruise missiles at Osama bin Laden's training camp in Afghanistan in 1998 did not prompt journalists to raise their sights. Rarely did they explore the political, religious, and cultural forces that were contributing to the rise in transnational terrorism.[58] Looking back on the terrorism coverage in the aftermath of the attacks on the World Trade Center and the Pentagon in 2001, Richard Holbrooke said that "the media's role in the last decade was grossly irresponsible, because the stories mattered."[59]

If the news is to be a means of getting people to think and talk sensibly about public affairs, it must be more than "a passing parade of specific events, a 'context of no context.'"[60] It needs to include the contextual information that enables citizens to make sense of events. "We're supposed to make those connections," says Columbia University's Nicholas Lemann.[61]

5.

Knowledge by itself produces "brittle understandings."[62] Only in its application does the practitioner acquire a robust understanding of its meaning and uses. "Knowledge of how to use knowledge" is nearly as important to the practitioner as knowledge itself.

Lee Shulman, an education researcher, was among the first to document the importance of knowing how to use knowledge. Shulman found that good teaching is more than a question of whether teachers know their subjects and understand pedagogical techniques. To be effective in the classroom, they must also know how to blend content knowledge and pedagogical knowledge in ways that heighten student learning. This blended knowledge, which Shulman calls "pedagogical content knowledge," is acquired through reflective practice. Through trial and error, teachers learn "ways of representing and formulating the subject that make it comprehensible to others."[63]

Journalists face a similar challenge. They need to discover how to combine content knowledge and process knowledge in ways that strengthen their stories. As in learning a language, there are few shortcuts in the process.[64] Pulitzer Prize recipient Steve Coll relies heavily on knowledge in his work and says it's "the back and forth" between knowledge and practice that leads to proficiency.[65]

Coll's method is not the way most journalists work. "For all the accelerating pace of news and the growing demand for context and analysis, journalists remain largely communicators, not analysts," writes Tom Rosenstiel. "Our skills are in gathering information and transmitting it to people's homes. We are masters of motion, not thought."[66] The 2012 Tow Center report made nearly the same point: "Most journalists . . . do not spend most of their time conducting anything like empirically robust forms of evidence gathering."[67]

Knowledge-based journalism would require reporters to change their approach. Reflective practice, writes the University of Minnesota's Harry Boyte, requires a "willingness to suspend belief, to look at evidence and go where it leads, to hold ideas as provisional hypotheses, to enjoy new problems."[68] If journalists were to operate in this way, news stories would include a wider range of angles, more links between the immediate event and its antecedents, and more connections to other subjects. Knowledge-based journalism would also give new power to time-honored devices. In his research, Shulman found that successful teachers rely on "the most powerful analogies, illustrations, examples, explanations, and demonstrations" to convey their material.[69] Such devices have long been hallmarks of vigorous reporting. The reporter's challenge is to root them in knowledge.

6.

When he gave Columbia University the money to start one of the nation's first journalism schools, publisher Joseph Pulitzer said that he wished "to begin a movement that will raise journalism to the rank of a learned profession, growing in the respect of the community as other professions far less in the public interest have grown." Pulitzer went on to say: "My idea is to recognize that journalism is, or ought to be, one of the great intellectual professions; to encourage, elevate and educate in a practical way the . . . members of that profession, exactly as if it were the profession of law or medicine."[70]

Rather than embracing Pulitzer's aspiration, America's journalism programs set themselves up as trade schools, a development that failed to impress even those in the trade. A newspaper cartoon that hung in many newsrooms during the first half of the twentieth century showed a city editor asking a job applicant, "And what, may I ask, is a school of journalism?"[71] When Columbia University in 1935 cut its journalism program from two years to one year, the *New York Daily News* called it "a step in the right direction" while suggesting that the program was "still one year too long."[72] Equally damning was the response of those who shared Pulitzer's belief that journalism should strive to become an intellectual profession. The 1947 Hutchins Commission said of journalism programs: "The kind of training a journalist most needs today is not training in the tricks and machinery of the trade."[73]

An effect of journalism programs' trade orientation was to reduce their voice in setting the profession's ethical standards. Whereas law and medical schools largely set the professional standards in their fields, journalism schools' position as a feeder system for the news industry subjected them to "pressures more commercial than democratic in nature."[74] Four decades after the Hutchins Commission, the Project on the Future of Journalism and Mass Communication Education—a group composed of top journalism educators and practitioners—concluded that journalism schools were stuck in the past. "In the midst of what has been called a communication revolution," the group wrote, "the nation's journalism/mass communication schools seemed anything but revolutionary. Indeed, there was abundant evidence that they were nearly stagnant. In their fundamental structure and curricular offerings, they had not changed much in decades. . . . Although journalism schools had begun with lofty ideals and great expectations . . . many were little more than industry-oriented trade schools."[75]

Since then, journalism schools have made significant adjustments. Although training in industry-related skills is still the cornerstone of a journalism education, subject matter training is on the rise.[76] In Canada, for example, the University of Toronto has developed a new recruiting model, bringing in students who are subject matter experts—scholars, policy analysts, and the like. Says Robert Steiner, the program's director, "We recruit real specialists, instead of trying to teach a specialty to generalists."[77] Another example is Columbia University's new two-year graduate-level journalism program. Unlike Columbia's long-standing one-year master's program, the new program requires students to take subject-area courses in addition to practical skills courses. The program is "based on the supposition that a journalist can be educated in a subject matter more efficiently, and in a manner more specific to the practice of journalism, inside a journalism school than outside it."[78]

The most ambitious effort to bring knowledge more fully into journalism programs is the Carnegie-Knight Initiative on the Future of Journalism Education.[79] In announcing the initiative in 2005, Vartan Gregorian, the Carnegie Corporation's president, said that journalism should strive to be "the new knowledge profession." Arguing that the communication revolution has moved "journalists to the forefront of diffusing knowledge to the next generations," Gregorian said that democracy requires "journalists who are superbly trained, intellectually rigorous, steeped in knowledge about the subjects they report on, steadfast about their ethical standards and courageous in their pursuit of truth."[80] In its announcement of the initiative, the Knight Foundation said: "In today's changing world of news consumption, journalism schools should be exploring the technological, intellectual, artistic, and literary possibilities of journalism to the fullest extent, and should be leading a constant expansion and improvement in the ability of the press to inform the public as fully, deeply, and interestingly as it can about matters of the highest importance and complexity."[81]

The Carnegie-Knight Initiative included eleven top journalism programs: Arizona State University's Walter Cronkite School of Journalism and Mass Communication; the University of California's Berkeley Graduate School of Journalism; the Columbia University Graduate School of Journalism; the University of Maryland's Philip Merrill College of Journalism; the University of Missouri School of Journalism; the University of Nebraska's College of Journalism and Mass Communications; the University of North Carolina's School of

Journalism and Mass Communication; Northwestern University's Medill School of Journalism; the University of Southern California's Annenberg School for Communication and Journalism; Syracuse University's S. I. Newhouse School of Public Communications; and the University of Texas at Austin's College of Communication.* Each program was awarded a grant to develop course work aimed at deepening students' knowledge of their reporting subjects. "The goal," explained Gregorian, "is to offer students a deep and multilayered exploration of complex subjects . . . to undergird their journalistic skills."[82]

The participating schools were charged with discovering ways to bring disciplinary knowledge into the classroom. Some programs adopted a team-teaching approach, in which a journalism school faculty member supplied the journalism content for a course while an outside scholar provided the subject matter content. Other journalism schools took the concept a step further, creating journalism concentrations linked to subject-area programs elsewhere in the university. These concentrations created a set of journalism-centered courses rooted in an academic discipline, such as national security studies, religion, or science.

The Carnegie-Knight Initiative, which ended in 2011,† demonstrated that knowledge-based journalism could be taught successfully in journalism schools, and it offers lessons on how best to do it. However, the initiative was only a first step in redefining journalism education. None of the participating institutions extended knowledge-based training to all

---

* A twelfth university was Harvard. Its Joan Shorenstein Center on the Press, Politics and Public Policy at the John F. Kennedy School of Government (where I have a faculty appointment) had a coordinating and research role in the Carnegie-Knight Initiative.

† Some elements of the initiative continued after this date, but the large grants to each of the participating institutions were phased out in accord with the initial Carnegie-Knight plan.

students or applied it broadly across the curriculum. Moreover, the eleven participating schools constitute only a fraction of the nation's roughly five hundred journalism programs. If knowledge-based reporting is to become a cornerstone of journalism education, the pioneering work of the Carnegie-Knight Initiative will need to be expanded.

7.

For the first time in their history, journalism schools are positioned to play a major part in setting the standards for quality journalism. News outlets have traditionally set the standards, which journalism schools have then used as the benchmark for their training programs, enabling their students to step directly into the newsroom upon graduation. Today, the news industry is facing the challenge of declining audiences and shrinking revenues, which has centered its attention more on its financial health than on the quality of its journalism.[83] Plus, if knowledge-based reporting is to be a significant part of journalism's future, the university rather than the newsroom is the logical place to develop it. Knowledge competency is harder to acquire outside the university than within it. "It's hard to learn on the fly," as Nicholas Lemann put it.[84]

In a report for the Carnegie-Knight Initiative, Wolfgang Donsbach and Thomas Fiedler* identified five competencies that journalists need to acquire: (1) awareness of relevant his-

* Wolfgang Donsbach is chair of the communications program at the Technical University of Dresden in Germany and is past president of both the International Communication Association (ICA) and the World Association for Public Opinion Research (WAPOR). Thomas Fiedler was a reporter, columnist, and executive editor at the *Miami Herald* and is currently dean of the school of communication at Boston University.

tory, current affairs, and analytical thinking; (2) expertise in the specific subjects to be reported upon; (3) knowledge of the processes of journalism; (4) awareness of ethical standards; and (5) mastery of practical skills. Journalism programs have traditionally stressed the last of these competencies—practical reporting skills. "Learning by doing" has been the prevailing pedagogy. Students are taught the tools of the trade and the production requirements of the various media.

In the hierarchy of journalism education, subject matter knowledge is far down the list. Courses on how to shape and present materials rank at the top.[85] A 2012 survey asked journalism educators to identify what they thought should be "the seven core courses" of the journalism major. Except for media law and ethics, all seven of the top-ranked courses involved practical skills training, such as news reporting and feature writing.[86] A 2008 survey of newswriting course syllabi found that many of them focused almost entirely on technique. Some lacked even background reading assignments, save for *The Associated Press Stylebook* or a similar manual on grammar, punctuation, editing symbols, and the dos and don'ts of reporting.[87]

False choices can blind journalism schools to their options. Should they focus on skills training? Or on knowledge training? The answer is that their training would be strengthened by integrating the two. As Lee Shulman and Chris Argyris have demonstrated in the context of education schools and business schools, respectively, the optimal training program for the professional practitioner is one that combines knowledge and practice.[88] When taught by itself, knowledge does not get internalized because it is separated from the context in which practitioners work. Practice is likewise diminished when taught by itself. It trains students to work within the narrow confines of prescribed rules and routines.

Knowledge-based training would not crowd out the practical skills courses that students need, as the Carnegie-Knight Initiative revealed. Although the Knight Foundation was a full partner in the project from the start, it was concerned that knowledge-based training might compete with another of Knight's goals: helping journalism programs and students make the transition to digital reporting. As it happened, digital technology strengthened knowledge based reporting, while the latter in turn deepened digital-platform reporting. "The unity of these two [innovations] was a real strength," concluded Eric Newton, Knight's journalism program vice president.[89]

8.

Any large-scale effort to institute knowledge-based training in journalism programs would face resistance. Yet whatever the merits of the traditional approach, it is out of step with the complexity of contemporary society. Journalism schools need to aim higher, asking more of themselves and their students. Even numerical literacy, for example, is not required of all journalism students, despite the fact that solid reporting in many areas depends on it. Journalism students are more likely to understand the power of a picture than to recognize the power of data, even though aggregations of everything from voters to business firms cannot be interpreted properly without the ability to analyze data distributions. "We cannot accept," says Pulitzer Prize winner Jack Fuller, "the kind of ignorance of basic statistics that so often leads to preposterous reporting."[90]

Journalism schools might conclude that their faculties are poorly equipped to take on the task of knowledge-based instruction. That would be true if the goal was to make every student a subject matter expert. Only the largest journalism programs could take on that task, and even they would not be able to cover every reporting area or train every student in that way. All journalism programs, however, have the capacity to train their students in "knowledge of how to use knowledge"—the equivalent of teachers' pedagogical content knowledge. Like teachers, journalists are asked to address a wide range of subjects. Like teachers, journalists are required to learn how to communicate effectively with their audience. There is no logical reason why "knowledge of how to use knowledge" cannot be taught as readily in a school of journalism as in a school of education.*

Journalism schools have not made full use of their intellectual resources. Many of their instructors have subject-area expertise as a result of past experience or formal education and could work it into their course assignments. Some already do so, but it's not a uniform requirement. The mass communications scholars within journalism schools are also an underutilized resource.[91] They have knowledge, for example, of how the framing of news stories affects audience learning. Yet, in most journalism programs, they have little if any voice in practical skills courses and do not include practical reporting exercises in their own courses—a tendency that impoverishes them as well as their practitioner colleagues. Instructional resources elsewhere in the university are also available to journalism schools. A lesson of the Carnegie-Knight Initiative is the ease of persuading other faculties to get involved in journalism education.[92]

A "knowledge of how to use knowledge" approach would

* The "knowledge of how to use knowledge" approach especially makes sense from the perspective of undergraduate journalism students. Although some of them plan for a career in a specialized area such as science or foreign affairs, many of them are uncertain about their career interests or, upon graduation, have little choice but to take a job as a general assignment reporter.

move journalism education in an intellectual direction. If the primary goal of journalism training continues to be to instruct students in how to report and conduct interviews, they can learn these things almost as easily through supervised work on the college newspaper or in the college broadcast station as in the classroom. On the other hand, if "knowledge of how to use knowledge" is to be at the center of journalism training, the classroom is the proper venue.

9.

It would be premature here to offer a full-scale blueprint for a new form of journalism education. What NYU's Mitchell Stephens said of news—that it's "best understood in the places where it is made and where its impact is felt"—applies also to journalism education.[93]

Nevertheless, there are resources available that can help in the transition. The Carnegie-Knight Initiative, for example, includes a Web site dedicated to knowledge-based journalism. Based at Harvard's Shorenstein Center, Journalist's Resource (journalistsresource.org) curates studies on a wide range of news-related topics—everything from the economy to government to society.* The Internet is a vast source of information, but much of it is unreliable or out of date. Journalist's Resource provides an answer to information overload by vetting and posting the best available studies. "Tens of thousands of studies come out every single year," notes John Wihbey, editor of the Journalist's Resource Web site. "It becomes very difficult for journalists, journalism educators, and students to go

* Instructors at more than a hundred journalism schools are already making use of the content available through Journalist's Resource.

through and find the key items that would help them. We're trying to be a useful filter and curator."[94] A search for "carbon tax" on Journalist's Resource, for instance, produces three studies, each with a summary of the findings and a link to the original work. When "carbon tax" is entered on Google Scholar, a staggering twenty-five thousand results appear.

Journalist's Resource is more than a tool for reporters working on deadline. It is oriented toward journalism education. Each study on the Web site includes adaptable student assignments that build on the study, and each comes with teaching notes to help instructors apply it in the classroom. Journalist's Resource has also created semester-length syllabi for a number of practical skills courses. These differ from traditional syllabi in that the practical exercises have a knowledge component, and the readings include a substantial amount of material aimed at informing students on their chosen reporting subjects.

The goal of Journalist's Resource is to train students to treat knowledge as an everyday tool of journalism, just as they now treat interviewing and observation that way. Reporting cannot simply be a matter of "just calling a couple of people and getting a few quotes," says Alex Jones, the Shorenstein Center's director and a Pulitzer Prize recipient.[95] "There is a real need," Jones notes, "for deepening journalism with verified, high-quality knowledge that informs the kind of serious journalism that makes our democracy work."[96]

Knowledge-based training could improve the market position of journalism students. As things stand, they compete for reporting jobs not only with each other but with graduates in economics, political science, and other fields. This competition might be tipping toward these other graduates. The 2012 Tow Center report concluded that the marketplace is increasingly responsive to applicants with "in-depth knowledge about something other than journalism. The complexity of information and the speed with which people wish to have it explained and contextualized leaves little room for the average generalist."[97] Knowledge-based training would give journalism graduates a skill that other graduates do not have and could not easily acquire.*

10.

Whether journalism will meet the challenges posed by today's information environment is an open question. The press, like any institution, is conservative in its routines. Traditional ways of defining, structuring, and gathering the news are built into every facet of journalism practice. "What is of enduring importance," Wilbert Moore wrote in *The Professions*, "is the homely truth that new knowledge or innovations in technique

* This chapter has concentrated on undergraduate journalism education. The same general principles would apply to graduate-level journalism education, but the possibilities would be greater. One option would be to recruit students with subject-area expertise, as the University of Toronto has done. Another option would be a division of labor, such that some schools would offer graduate-level training in science journalism, others in legal reporting, and so on. This kind of specialization typifies graduate training in many other fields; in political science, for example, the University of Michigan is noted for its political behavior program, while the University of Chicago is noted for political theory. Yet a third option is a two-year program of the type that Columbia University now offers, in which the second year focuses on subject-area training to enhance the first year's practical skills training. Traditionally, graduate-level journalism has consisted of a one-year course of study in which students follow more or less the same curriculum as undergraduate majors; in other academic fields, however, a graduate education is a more advanced form of disciplinary training. If journalism programs were to develop more advanced graduate training, they would also be better positioned to offer midcareer and executive education programs similar to those offered by business and public policy schools.

and practice threaten the very basis upon which established professionals rest their claims to expert competence."[98]

Newer developments could also blunt a shift toward knowledge-based journalism. While the Internet provides access to a seemingly infinite storehouse of knowledge, it also pressures journalists to crank out stories and constantly update blogs, Twitter feeds, Facebook pages, and other social media. Although speed is an obstacle to reflective reporting, it would be a mistake to see knowledge as a component only of slower-paced, longer-form reporting. In any reporting situation, the journalist who knows more about the subject at hand has an advantage over the journalist who knows less. When reporters must file quickly, without the opportunity to observe or conduct interviews, they have no place to turn except to what they already know. Knowledge is the best remedy for hastily concocted, wrongheaded story lines.

FIVE

The Audience Problem

Now the problem of securing attention . . . is a problem of provoking feeling in the reader, of inducing him to feel a sense of identification with the stories he is reading. News which does not offer this opportunity to introduce oneself into the struggle which it depicts cannot appeal to a wide audience.[1]

—Walter Lippmann

1.

The code of ethics of the American Society of News Editors declares that journalism is "to serve the general welfare by informing the people." The Radio Television Digital News Association's ethics code says "professional electronic journalists should recognize that their first obligation is to the public." In its ethics code, the Society of Professional Journalists claims that "public enlightenment is the forerunner of justice and the foundation of democracy. The duty of the journalist is to further those ends."

Journalism's codes reflect the age-old idea that democracy requires a press free of government control and dedicated to informing the public. "Where the press is free and every man able to read," Thomas Jefferson said, "all is safe."[2] The notion that democracy and press freedom are inseparable has been the bedrock of First Amendment jurisprudence. "The Founding Fathers," the Supreme Court ruled in *New York Times Co. v. United States* (1971), "gave the free press the protection it must have to fulfill its essential role in our democracy. The press was to serve the governed, not the governors."[3]

Yet government is not the only threat to a free and responsible press. The press's civic obligation has always sat uneasily with its determination to make money. In the early decades of the republic, publishers were dependent on government printing contracts for revenue, which tied them to the political parties.[4] The partisan press was brought to its knees not by a fit of conscience, but by a better deal. The invention of the high-speed rotary press enabled publishers to print their papers more cheaply, driving up circulations and attracting a new set of sponsors that paid far more money than the political parties ever could—so much money, in fact, that newspapers avoided stories that would upset their advertisers.[5] "One set of masters," political scientist V. O. Key, Jr., wrote, "had been replaced by another."[6]

The press is unusual in that it is a private business with a public trust. It is obligated by its constitutionally protected position to serve the public interest but driven by its business needs to serve itself.[7] The twin imperatives have long been a source of conflict within and outside news organizations, but the business side cannot be ignored. It would be foolish to assume that knowledge-based journalism could gain a foothold in the newsroom if what it produces lacks audience appeal. News organizations are not—consciously at least—in the business of self-destruction.

Without implementing it on a broad scale, there is no way to prove that knowledge-based journalism would have substantial audience appeal. However, an examination of news consumption patterns suggests a considerable overlap between knowledge-based journalism's features and people's news preferences.

2.

Journalists speak of "the public's right to know" as if the public insists on knowing. Yet many journalists express doubts about the public's interest in knowing. One *New York Times* journalist has said that politics "is superficial because the voters let it be."[8] Or in the words of one *Washington Post* writer, the "public can't stand abstract politics."[9]

In fact, citizens are not of one mind about the news.[10] They say in surveys that they want more issue coverage but do not always pay attention to it. They grumble about sensationalism but succumb to lurid stories. Conflict is another aspect of news that reliably draws people's attention even as they complain about it in surveys.[11] Such contradictions stem in part from the simple fact that people have different news preferences. The contradictions also stem in part from "social desirability bias"—the tendency of survey respondents to overstate "good" behaviors and understate "bad" behaviors.[12] Just as some people inflate how often they vote, some people exaggerate their interest in serious news.[13]

In light of this tendency, political scientist Michael Robinson's study of Americans' news interests is among the most reliable assessments to date.[14] Instead of asking people about their preferences for particular types of news stories, Robinson looked at the stories they actually consumed, as measured by their responses to Pew surveys. Since 1986, the Pew Research Center has questioned more than two hundred thousand Americans about their news consumption. Robinson focused on the period from 1986 to 2007, during which time more than thirteen hundred different news stories—each of which was a headline story at the time—were included in the Pew surveys.* Robinson grouped these stories by type of content—natural disasters, elections, foreign policy, celebrity, and so on—and then examined how many adult Americans on average were following each type "very closely."† From this, he was able to determine a hierarchy of story types, arranged in order of most to least closely followed story type.

1.	War and terrorism	41%
2.	Bad weather	40%
3.	Natural and man-made disasters	39%
4.	Financial and economic problems and policy issues	35%
5.	Crime and social violence problems and policy issues	29%
6.	Health and safety problems and issues	28%
7.	Other domestic policy problems and issues	25%
8.	Campaigns and elections	22%
9.	"Inside Washington" politics	21%
10.	Political scandals	20%
11.	"Other" politics	20%
12.	Foreign policy/international affairs	18%
13.	Celebrity lives and deaths	17%
14.	Celebrity scandals	16%

News stories about wars, disasters, and major storms—events that disrupt everyday life and offer the drama of lives

* Robinson's method does not eliminate social desirability bias but greatly reduces it. As this chapter will show, Americans are not shy about expressing interest in "lowbrow" categories, such as disasters or weather stories. Nor are they shy about denying interest in socially desirable stories, such as foreign news.

† Robinson used "very closely" rather than "fairly closely" as his cutoff point for close attention to a news story. This approach provides the greatest amount of differentiation between story types.

lost and at risk—tend to attract the most attention. These types were followed very closely on average by roughly 40 percent of respondents and accounted for the four top stories during the period of the study: the *Challenger* disaster in 1986 (80 percent), the 9/11 terrorist attacks in 2001 (78 percent),* Hurricane Katrina in 2005 (73 percent), and the San Francisco earthquake in 1989 (73 percent). They also accounted for a number of other closely followed stories, including the terrorist bombing of the federal building in Oklahoma City in 1995 (58 percent).

Robinson's study indicates that stories involving celebrities tend to get much less attention. In fact, they rank dead last among Americans' news interests. On average, only 17 percent of those surveyed said they followed such stories very closely. That number would have been even lower, at 13 percent, without the deaths of Princess Diana in 1997 and John F. Kennedy, Jr., in 1999. Both tragedies were closely followed by nearly 55 percent of respondents. More typical in terms of attention level were the deaths of the Grateful Dead's Jerry Garcia in 1995 (9 percent) and the Beatles' George Harrison in 2001 (10 percent).

Even celebrity scandals, with an average of 16 percent, fail to attract much attention. Michael Jackson's arrest on sexual molestation charges was among the top stories in this category—29 percent gave it close attention. On the other hand, only 12 percent were attentive to Donald and Ivana Trump's messy 1992 divorce, and a meager 2 percent expressed keen interest in Nicole Kidman and Tom Cruise's 1998 marital separation.

Stories about public affairs rank in the middle of audience

* In terms of sustained attention, the 9/11 attacks topped the list. Americans were asked about the attacks in Pew surveys in September, October, November, and December of 2001. The *Challenger* disaster was at the top of the news for a much shorter period.

interest. However, attention to such stories depends on what's at issue. At the top are financial and economic stories—news about sharp changes in energy prices, large swings in the economy, abrupt shifts in the stock market, and so on. When people's pocketbooks are at issue, they take notice. On average, such stories were followed very closely by 35 percent of Americans. The 1987 stock market crash—when the Dow plummeted 500 points within hours, shedding 23 percent of its value—was of keen interest to 40 percent of Americans. Spikes in gas prices scored even higher, topping the 50 percent mark. Even the 2001 Enron bankruptcy scandal was closely followed by a third of Americans, twice the level of the typical celebrity scandal.

Next highest in the public affairs category are consequential stories about social problems—crime and social violence (29 percent) and health and safety (28 percent). The mass killing at Colorado's Columbine High in 1999 scored 68 percent, placing it in the top ten of the thirteen hundred stories examined. Also in the top ten was the rioting that followed the acquittal of Los Angeles police officers for the videotaped beating of Rodney King. The King story was closely followed by 70 percent of Americans, more than twice the number that expressed strong interest in O. J. Simpson's 1995 murder trial.

Domestic policy issues ranked next, drawing on average the close attention of a quarter of the respondents. They displayed particular interest in George W. Bush's 2005 attempt to privatize Social Security (35 percent), the 2004 flu vaccine shortage (44 percent), and the 1989 Supreme Court ruling upholding the right to burn the American flag (51 percent). In contrast, only 14 percent paid close attention to the 2002 campaign finance reform debate.

At the bottom of the public affairs category are political stories. However much these stories might fascinate those inside the Washington Beltway, they fail to engage most citizens. Stories about campaigns and elections (22 percent), Washington politics (21 percent), political scandals (20 percent), and "other politics"* (20 percent) ranked low on the interest scale. The closing weeks of a presidential campaign, when interest in election news tops the 50 percent mark, is an exception. Closer to the norm is the New Hampshire primary—an average of 17 percent of respondents over the course of the study reported paying close attention to the nation's kickoff presidential primary.

Political scandals fared no better. With a few exceptions, such as the 1998 Clinton-Lewinsky saga and the 2007 exposé of Walter Reed Army Medical Center's shabby treatment of wounded troops, political scandals have no more appeal than celebrity scandals. Less than 15 percent of the public closely followed House majority leader Tom DeLay's corruption-induced resignation in 2006, House Ways and Means chair Dan Rostenkowski's fraud indictment in 1994, or House Speaker Jim Wright's fall from grace for ethical violations in 1989.

International politics also ranks low on the scale. Although the breakup of the Soviet Union in 1991 was an exception (47 percent), foreign policy stories on average drew the close attention of only 18 percent of the public. Except for war, Americans' attention usually wanes when the focus shifts overseas, even when the United States is a direct participant. The American-led expansion of NATO into Eastern Europe in 1999, for example, was closely followed by only 6 percent of respondents.

Two tendencies in Robinson's study are particularly noteworthy, given that they contradict the conventional wisdom

* In the "other politics" category, Robinson included such things as interest group action, nonviolent rallies and demonstrations, and outside-of-Washington controversies, such as the "Stars and Bars" debate about the South Carolina state flag.

about Americans' news tastes. One is the low level of interest in celebrity-based stories—public affairs trump celebrity interest by a wide margin. The second is that news of domestic policy problems and issues outdraws news that is more emphatically "political," also by a decent margin. Policy trumps politics.* Robinson's findings coincide with those of an earlier Harvard study that used survey and experimental methods to assess Americans' news preferences. Unlike Robinson's study, which examined only top news stories, the Harvard study examined routine stories. As with Robinson's study, soft news stories—those focusing on celebrities and entertainers—ranked at the bottom of the list. Stories about policy problems and issues—jobs, school spending, and the like—ranked much higher. "Public affairs news," the Harvard study concluded, "is more appealing than soft news to most people."[15]

3.

Audience demand is only one half of the marketplace for news. The other half is the supply side—the stories that news outlets produce. Are the media's top stories also the ones of greatest interest to the public? As it happens, supply and demand do not coincide. News outlets overproduce some types of news relative to demand, while underproducing other types.

Washington-centered stories are overproduced. Of keen interest to the politically interested, they are of only passing

* Celebrity news and political news are consistently low performers. When Robinson divided his analysis into three "news eras" (1986–1990, 1991–2000, and 2001–2006), the ranking of these story types was similar in each period. Interest in celebrity stories during the three periods was, respectively, 19 percent, 18 percent, and 17 percent. Interest in political scandals was, respectively, 22 percent, 20 percent, and 19 percent.

interest to most citizens. Even the stories that address the fate of top leaders do not ordinarily attract close public attention. Although the press heavily covered Trent Lott's resignation as Senate majority leader in 2002 for praising Strom Thurmond's 1948 segregationist presidential bid, only 20 percent of Americans said they were following the story closely.[16] Run-of-the-mill Washington stories fare worse. Although such stories are often at or near the top of the day's news, they are far down the list of stories Americans follow closely. " 'Inside-the-Beltway stories,' " Robinson notes, are "heavily covered, but lightly watched."[17]

To be sure, citizens take some interest in political goings-on.[18] During the closing phase of a presidential campaign, people are attuned to their favorite candidate's chance of victory.[19] Relatively few citizens, however, intently follow the political wrangling that is the mainstay of national political coverage.[20] One reason is that their stake in the conflict is seldom made clear.[21] A Project for Excellence in Journalism election study, for example, found that reporters were seven times more likely to say how campaign developments might affect the candidates than to say how they might affect the voters.[22]

The oversupply of political stories reflects what the *Washington Post*'s Dan Balz calls "the gap" between the interests of "the media and ordinary folks."[23] Most journalists know a lot more about politics than they do about policy, and they like to cover what they know best—"talking mainly to each other," as Lance Bennett put it.[24] "Washington is weird that way," says *New York Times* media columnist David Carr. "Sometimes I hear what some of my friends are chasing and I'm like, really? That's it? Washington thrives on a kind of incrementalism that wouldn't reach the standard of news elsewhere."[25] In late 2010, for instance, the lame-duck Senate took up the issue of a nuclear arms control treaty that the Obama administration had negotiated with Russia. The news highlighted Obama's efforts to acquire the two-thirds vote to ratify the treaty, as well as the objections of some Senate Republicans and the fact that their numbers would increase when the new Congress convened in January. Seldom was there a substantial reference to what was at stake if the treaty was ratified or rejected. In the end, the Senate ratified the treaty, delivering what the headlines called "a victory for Obama,"[26] as if that was somehow the crux of the issue.

Political coverage, says NYU's Jay Rosen, allows journalists to "display their savviness, which is [their] unofficial religion."[27] Moreover, reporters spend much of their time tracking political leaders, which naturally leads them to find significance in what they do.[28] "Reporters like to concentrate on . . . tactics and devices," journalist Tom Wicker wrote. "In their usual footrace or game perspective on politics, they and their editors see these as being more critical than . . . most issues."[29] Twitter and other Web-based communication have heightened the tendency. CNN's Peter Hamby, who reported from the campaign trail in 2012, noted that journalists were tweeting from morning to night, making note of tiny shifts in what the campaigns were doing. "The 2012 media," Hamby writes, "was covering the campaign through a magnifying glass never-before seen in political journalism, treating every ordinary development—candidate travel plans, staffing decisions in Iowa, minuscule polling shifts, veepstakes voodoo—as if it were the invasion of Baghdad."[30] Said Reuter's Sam Youngman: "[Twitter] made me think smaller when I should have been thinking bigger."[31]

Political stories have the advantage of being relatively cheap to produce.[32] Alison Dagnes, a television producer turned scholar, notes that "it is infinitely easier to write about the process than it is [to write about] intricate public policy initiatives."[33] Such stories can be constructed in some cases simply by observing what political figures say and do in public forums—talking heads do it in real time during a presidential debate or press conference. "Much of the news Americans get each day," writes Walter Pincus, "was created to serve just that purpose—to be the news of the day."[34] The sheer ease of political reporting has made it—along with opinionated commentary—the staple of cable news outlets, which face the daily challenge of filling large blocks of time with relatively small reporting staffs.* CNN once touted the strength of its "reporting team." It now claims to have the "best political team on television." MSNBC's slogan was once "A Fuller Spectrum of News." It relabeled itself "The Political Channel." Fox News camouflages its political appetite by claiming to be what it is not: "Fair and Balanced."

4.

Although citizens express greater interest in news about policy problems than in news about politics, they aren't always thinking of policy in the way journalists do. Reporters typically focus on the policy initiatives of political leaders.[35] These initiatives draw the public's attention if they are clearly defined and if they clearly impinge on people's lives, as in the case of a tax increase. "They will note it, and form opinions about it," explained Doris Graber on the basis of her audience study.[36] On the other hand, if a policy proposal is remote in its consequences or overly complex, as in the case of monetary policy, the public usually tunes it out.[37]

---

* The ease of political reporting is matched only by the ease of interview segments, which are even less costly to produce. The Project for Excellence in Journalism reports that, between 2007 and 2012, interview segments increased by 31 percent across the three major cable news channels: CNN, MSNBC, and Fox.

The policy problems of greatest interest to citizens are those that directly affect their daily lives or the lives of those like them. It's a reason people give little thought to energy policy until gas prices rise. Such responses are a consequence of what scholars call the "surveillance function." People seek "reassurance that the world, both near and far, is safe [and] secure."[38] This outlook helps explain why turbulent weather, natural and human disasters, and the onset of war rank highly in the public's news preferences. It's also why people take more interest in Main Street economic issues, like high gas prices, than in Wall Street economic issues, like stock price manipulation.[39] It also helps explain why they are more attentive to crime reports than to celebrity stories. As Pete Hamill noted: "[People] have only marginal interest in the latest sensational sex scandal; they do care when death comes calling in their own neighborhood."[40]

News also serves what scholars call "the communal function."[41] Citizens are attracted to stories that arouse empathy for the fate of people with whom they can identify.[42] Consider the difference in Americans' attention to two top stories in 2007: the revelation of patient neglect at Walter Reed and the perjury trial of White House aide Scooter Libby. Although the Libby story received twice the amount of news coverage as the Walter Reed story, it drew only half as much public attention.[43] Americans were bothered by the slack medical treatment being given to service members who had been wounded fighting for their country in Iraq and Afghanistan. Libby's fate, in contrast, was at best a source of curiosity. He was a distant figure facing a self-inflicted problem.[44]

This is not necessarily to say that the Libby coverage was excessive. Watchdog reporting sends a signal to the powerful that corrupt practices will bring them unwanted headlines. The press would be remiss if it made small note of official wrongdoing. On the other hand, it's hard to justify stories that lack a public purpose and fail to attract wide interest, which is the case for many inside-the-Beltway stories. To be sure, the news would not be the news, nor would the public interest be served, if political wrangling was ignored by reporters. There's truth even in *Dallas Morning News* reporter Jacquielynn Floyd's claim that political coverage would be "a mighty dry and colorless affair" without it.[45] Yet if political infighting becomes the point of the coverage, the audience receives an incomplete picture, one that highlights the fireworks and buries the consequences.[46]

When health care reform was in the spotlight in 2009 and 2010, for example, the bulk of the coverage centered on political strategy and infighting, so much so that the public learned very little during the yearlong legislative battle.[47] It was a replay of the coverage of President Clinton's health care reform effort in the early 1990s. Kathleen Hall Jamieson and Joseph Cappella tracked the coverage of that earlier episode and found that stories on the substance of Clinton's health care proposal were hugely outnumbered by stories on who was getting the better of the fight. Their study also showed that the public, rather than becoming better informed as the debate progressed, became increasingly confused.[48]

To the journalist, each political story is different. To many citizens, such stories look and sound pretty much the same. A Syracuse University survey asked respondents to recall a news story they had seen within the past twenty-four hours and then asked them to describe their reaction to it. News stories about political infighting often elicited no reported reaction at all. Policy-related stories were 50 percent more likely to draw a response.[49] In the same vein, Doris Graber found that when news stories "discussed serious social problems," people were inclined to think about how the problems could be resolved.

But when stories focused on the political game, people reacted, if at all, with a feeling of resignation, believing that political gamesmanship is something they have no control over.[50]

To be sure, journalists occasionally dig into issues. The Newtown grade school massacre in 2012 that killed six adults and twenty children prompted numerous news stories about gun control laws.[51] During the Gulf oil spill in 2010, reporters made extensive use of technical and scientific knowledge to help Americans understand the spill and its consequences, even to the extent of teaching their audience a set of new terms—"dispersants," "relief wells," and the like.[52]

Such coverage is the exception, however, even though the story possibilities are many. Modern life is noteworthy not for its scarcity of policy questions, but for the abundance of them. News about a wide range of issues, from public education to homeland security, has the potential to attract the public's attention—if journalists had the knowledge and interest to explore them.[53] Climate change, for example, ranks high in terms of public interest, but gets only a moderate amount of news coverage.[54]

To be sure, citizens' policy interests are not the wonkish concerns of the policy analyst.[55] In a study of news consumers, Graber found that they complained about the "oversimplified treatment" of politics, but when presented with "more substantial exposure to issues," they usually failed to "seize" the opportunity.[56] Yet Americans' interest in issues is also more substantial than they may be given credit for, as is clear from the questions they ask in public gatherings or on call-in shows in which they have the chance to quiz politicians directly. Rarely do they ask about politicians' strategies and tactics, or inquire about the latest gaffe or scandal. They want to know what politicians intend to do about the problems they face.[57] It's a line of inquiry that journalists only occasionally pursue, in part because they are more interested in political strategy and in part because they are not deeply informed about most issues. And on many policy areas there is a near absence of journalistic expertise. "Education affects everyone," Walter Pincus wrote recently, "yet I cannot name an outstanding American journalist on this subject. Food is an important subject, yet regular newspaper coverage of agriculture and the products we eat is almost nonexistent unless cases of food poisoning turn up."[58]

Journalists' sense of their audience is wrong side up. What's happening at the top as it affects the fortunes of those at the top is not what interests most people.[59] As Bill Kovach and Tom Rosenstiel note, "Journalists need to focus on people and their problems, not on politicians and theirs."[60]

5.

Knowledge-based stories about people and their problems often cannot be told in a hurry or in a few words, which might be considered a problem in today's marketplace, where people expect to get their news in a flash.

In fact, the news audience does *not* routinely choose brevity over depth. The Project for Excellence in Journalism conducted an extensive study of 154 local TV stations, tracking for five years their audience ratings and news content to determine what people watched and why. Contrary to expectations, the project found that the longer the story—the more depth it possessed—the higher its audience rating. When the entire newscast was examined, a comparable finding emerged. Newscasts with a small number of well-produced longer stories had higher ratings than newscasts packed with shorter items. The study's authors concluded: "The consistent message that comes through all our research is that viewers reward stations that do a good job of gathering information and telling stories."[61]

Philip Meyer conducted a similar study of local papers. Using data from two dozen media markets, Meyer examined the relationship between newspapers' content and their circulation. He wanted to find out whether the quality of the reporting paid off with reader loyalty. Over the five-year span that Meyer studied, quality did matter: The newspapers that delivered the stronger content had the greatest success in holding on to their readers,[62] a finding supported by a subsequent Northwestern University study based on 35,000 consumers in 101 newspaper markets.[63]

National Public Radio's track record also illustrates the power of solid reporting. Compared with other broadcasters, NPR runs longer stories[64] and devotes less time to political infighting and more time to policy issues.[65] NPR also does more bottom-up stories—those that explore policy problems from the perspective of the citizen.[66] NPR now has one of the largest and most loyal audiences in the industry.[67] Since the 1980s, a period in which other broadcast news outlets have lost half or more of their audience, NPR's audience has increased by more than 500 percent.

If there was ever any doubt that quality matters, a 2013 survey by the Project for Excellence in Journalism should lay it to rest. Although a majority of those polled said they had heard little or nothing about the financial woes facing the news industry, or the resulting cutbacks in news staff and coverage, a third of the respondents said they had stopped paying attention to a particular news source because they had noticed a decline in the quality of its coverage. Moreover, those most likely to have stopped reading, watching, or listening to a news source because of a perceived decline were more highly educated and affluent than those who did not—in other words, they are the people who are generally more interested in news, and better able to pay for it. "The job of news organizations," the study's authors concluded, "is to come to terms with the fact that, as they search for economic stability, their financial future may well hinge on their ability to provide high quality reporting."[68]

6.

Conclusions based on traditional media might be thought irrelevant to Internet sites. They are "new media" with a different relationship to their users. Audiences for traditional media make an "appointment" with news, whether that's watching TV news at the dinner hour, looking at the paper over a morning cup of coffee, or tuning in to NPR while driving to work. Most people who rely on the Internet tap into news at irregular times.[69] Internet users are also more likely to "graze," consuming the news in bits and pieces over the course of the day.

Although grazing may suggest superficiality and often consists of quick hits, it turns out the practice is also a search strategy—a way to find worthwhile stories.[70] "Interest-driven search" is how Clay Shirky describes it.[71] Jim VandeHei, executive editor and cofounder of *Politico*, says the Web places a "premium on deeper-dive reporting," noting that *Politico*'s most heavily trafficked stories are "those that can't be done in a hurry," such as its probing stories in 2011 on the killing of Osama bin Laden and the congressional deadlock over the debt ceiling.[72] Adam Moss, editor of *New York*, notes that the in-depth stories on the magazine's Web site attract twenty to forty times more readers than do its brief postings.[73]

The "story" is emerging as the fundamental unit of Internet-based news. With traditional media, people typically hear of a particular story during the course of their exposure, as when reading a newspaper or watching TV news. With the Internet, people often access a story after first having heard of it through a tweet, Facebook post, e-mail, or other alert. Many such stories are in-depth pieces. "Long-form journalism is working [on the Web]," Moss said, noting that stories tend to get passed from one person to the next only when they're strong enough to stand on their own—"it's every piece for itself."[74] The same is true of "evergreen" stories—those that continue to draw traffic long after being posted.[75] As one team of researchers explained it, stories that draw a large audience on the Web are the ones "worth searching for."[76] The "worth searching for" principle aligns with the conclusion of the recent Tow Center report. Shallow reporting, its authors argue, increasingly fails to hold people's attention.[77] "A remarkable amount of what gets [accessed on the Internet]," they write, "is not singing cats but long, careful pieces of reporting or opinion."[78]

NYU's Mitchell Stephens argues that "instead of getting faster, [news outlets] could get wiser." He would have them "pull back from the race for breaking news and attempt to produce—at daily, not hourly, speed—the most insightful interpretations of that news."[79] The problem, says Stephens, is that most journalists are not trained for this type of reporting. "Quality journalism," he writes, "should be defined not by the ability to bear witness, to pursue facts, to array the five W's [who, what, where, when, why], but by the ability to write stories that are interpretive, informed, intelligent, interesting and insightful. . . . [This] will require more of journalists—more education in a subject, probably, more study, more thoughtfulness, fresher thinking. It will require the ambition not to recount, not only to uncover, but to explain, illuminate and enlighten."[80]

To be sure, the lure of solid reporting is easily exaggerated by those who care about journalism. Many of the most heavily trafficked public affairs stories on the Web are brief items that are as flimsy in their construction as they are light in their content. People have different tastes in news, and even those who prefer hard news like an occasional soft news story in the mix.[81] Furthermore, Internet sites that regularly refresh their content, typically in the form of short updates, have what Web analyst Jakob Nielsen calls "stickiness"—the willingness of users to return to the site regularly.[82]

Frequent updates, and light fare, clearly have a place in the news. Yet it is a mistake to assume that they are the key to attracting a loyal audience. It is a mistake, too, to conclude that knowledge is important for deeper pieces but not for brief updates. The hurried-up pace of today's reporting places a premium on reporters who know their subject well.

7.

News outlets face the harsh reality of a declining following. The news audience, as the next chapter will show, is not being replenished at a rate equal to the loss—today's young adults have much less interest in the news than their counterparts of a generation or two ago. Moreover, the redistribution of news consumers across an ever larger number of outlets—a trend that began in the 1980s—will continue, which means that most news outlets can expect their audience to shrink in the years ahead.[83]

In today's media system, a news organization's "brand" is increasingly important. The near monopoly on the audience that local papers and the broadcast networks once had, and which gave them readers and viewers almost by default, is gone. Cable and the Internet have reduced geography and spectrum allocation as decisive factors in determining where citizens will get their news. They have a wide range of choices and typically seek out brands they know and trust.

Although a loss of audience was inevitable, traditional news outlets accelerated the loss by being careless with their brands. Soft news in its early years helped news outlets to hold on to marginal news consumers—those with a weak interest in news who might otherwise have chosen to watch cable entertainment.[84] Holding on to them, however, required pumping out heavy doses of soft news, which hurt the reputation of news outlets, as well as the status of the news media generally.* "Pretty close to tabloid" was former FCC chair Newton Minow's description of 1990s television news.[85] The University of Illinois's Matt Ehrlich labeled it "the journalism of outrageousness."[86]

The hollowing out of hard news to make room for soft news alienated many of those who prefer hard news.† An irony of

* Although an analysis of soft news journalism is beyond the scope of this book, Harvard's Matthew Baum (*Soft News Goes to War*) conducted such a study in the context of war coverage. He found that citizens who otherwise would be less informed about public affairs do acquire "at least some information" from soft news exposure. Soft news could include more information if its stories were more thematic and less episodic (see chapter four). Many soft news stories have public policy implications, but the implications are seldom explored in any depth, a reason soft news consumers frequently reach erroneous conclusions from the information they receive.

† Soft news consumers are a misunderstood segment of the news audience. They consume less news on average than other news consumers and are less dependable in that their consumption varies with events. On the day when the story broke of Anna Nicole Smith's death of a drug overdose in a Florida hotel room, CNN's ratings jumped by a factor of three. "America's newest guilty pleasure" is how a CNN anchor described viewers' response. The number is deceiving, however. In tripling its audience with the Smith story, CNN temporarily gained a million extra viewers—a rousing success in terms of its business model, and yet a small gain in the context of the larger television news audience. According to Michael Robinson's study, CNN's extra viewers on the night of Smith's death were outnumbered twenty to one by those who chose instead to watch the ABC, CBS, and NBC evening

heightened audience competition is that what made sense in the short term turned out to be destructive in the long run. Initially, soft news enabled news outlets to hold on to marginal consumers—those who might have defected to entertainment programming. Yet heightened competition also meant that people with a substantial interest in news would be able to find outlets that did a good job of reporting. A NewsLab survey of former regular TV news viewers found that many of them had switched sources because they thought the newscasts had become too sensational, too contentious, too repetitive, and too flimsy—in other words, too much like showbiz and too little like news.[87] A 2011 study found the rise of infotainment to be one of the leading causes of the long-term decline in the size of the traditional news audience.[88]

A mistake that many traditional news outlets have made in response to declining circulations and ratings is to assume that people have a need for the newspaper or newscast when, in fact, what people have, and have always had, is a need to know. When the newspaper and the newscast were the only delivery vehicles for this information, it was convenient to assume that they, and not the information they contained, were the attraction. But now that people have a broad range of choices, they can satisfy their need to know in any number of ways. It is also the case that expanded choice has heightened audience members' expectations. In seeking to fulfill their need to know, they don't have to settle for marginally satisfying content.

Whatever the full explanation for the declining audience for traditional news, the time when a news outlet could success-

---

newscasts. In order to lure and hold soft news consumers, news outlets have to overproduce soft news relative to the overall demand for it. It gets more coverage from the press than it gets attention from the public. Smith's death, for example, was nearly in the top third among the most heavily covered news stories in 2007. In terms of audience attention, however, Smith's death was nearly in the bottom third.

fully be all things to all people is rapidly ending.* What works better in today's high-choice media system is news pitched to a targeted audience—"niche news."[89] Studies indicate that targeting increases an outlet's credibility with its users,[90] which results in increased loyalty.[91] The Project for Excellence in Journalism study that tracked local TV stations found, for example, that the worst-performing newscasts over a five-year span were those that aimed for a general audience by offering a full mix of traditional and soft news stories. The strongest performers were newscasts that concentrated on either traditional news or soft news, and did it better than their competitors.[92] Their performance reflects the outlook of digital innovator Clark Gilbert, who argues that the digital era requires news outlets to concentrate on areas where they can deliver distinctive content. "Invest where you can be the best," he says.[93]

8.

Journalists cannot be faulted for the fact that it's hard to inform the public. Convincing people that the news deserves their full attention is at once a noble thought and a fool's errand.[94] Nor can reporters be faulted when they lack the time to solidify their stories. Many of the shortcomings in news reporting owe, as political scientist Tim Cook explained, to the compro-

* With so many choices available, the news audience is realigning in a way similar to that of the radio audience. In radio's early decades, the leading stations offered a broad range of programming—everything from news to music to canned variety shows and sitcoms. But as the number of stations increased over time and as television siphoned off program listeners, the audience became more selective and most listeners drifted toward specialized outlets—talk stations, country music stations, oldies stations, Top 40 stations, news stations—that catered to their interests.

mises required "to crank out a daily product called news."[95] And there is no sin in the fact that news organizations are in the business of making money. It's a key to a strong newsroom. "You can't do [news] on the cheap and get away with it for long," notes Alex Jones.[96]

The news media's ongoing challenge is to strike a proper balance between "doing well" economically and "doing good" civically. Attention is one of democracy's scarcest resources,[97] and the press revels in it. What other institution can count upon a daily following in the tens of millions? No church or political party has anywhere near that kind of constituency. Journalists are the closest thing that the public has to an everyday teacher. Although journalists are not obliged to turn news stories into lesson plans, there is an educational opportunity in news that cannot be realized until journalists take citizens' interests and needs more fully into account in their reporting. "The point of having journalists around," says Jay Rosen, "is not to produce attention, but to make our attention more productive."[98]

SIX

The Democracy Problem

Reformers . . . assume . . . that somehow mysteriously there exists in the hearts of men a knowledge of the world beyond their reach.[1]

—Walter Lippmann

1.

Informed citizens do not spring forth from birth. The process of informing the public is an ongoing task, as well as a source of endless debate. Just how much information do citizens need in order to exercise proper judgment on the issues of the day? And just how important is information to the workings of democracy? Thomas Jefferson placed great value on it. Alexander Hamilton was less certain that information had to penetrate deeply into society.[2]

Agreement has long existed, however, on the basic ingredients of an informed public: good schools and good journalism, along with citizens who are willing to make use of them. Whatever might be the story of the schools, the story of journalism has recently taken a downward turn.

2.

For nearly two centuries, Americans' interest in news rose steadily, driven by breakthroughs in communication technology.[3] An early development was the invention of the hand-cranked rotary press, which enabled publishers to print newspapers more quickly and cheaply than was possible with the older, flat-plate press. In 1834, the *New York Sun* became the first newspaper to pass the savings along to readers, cutting the price of the paper from six cents to a penny. The *Sun*'s circulation rose to five thousand in four months and to ten thousand in less than a year.[4] By the early 1900s, propelled by the invention of newsprint and the steam-driven press, some metropolitan dailies were peddling more than one hundred thousand copies a day.[5]

Radio news came of age a few decades later. It served mainly as a headline service, airing brief accounts of the day's top stories.* Still, radio brought news to millions, many of whom did not read a daily paper. By the end of the 1930s, the number of homes with a radio set exceeded the number that subscribed to a newspaper.[6]

A bigger breakthrough came in the early 1960s, when the television networks launched their thirty-minute nightly newscasts. Television news soon gained a huge following, much of it "inadvertent"—viewers who watched less out of an interest in news than out of an addiction to television.[7] In most media markets, news was the only dinner-hour programming avail-

---

* Radio's headline tradition was established early in its history, in part because radio stations relied upon the wire services, which were pressured by newspapers to limit the amount of news that stations could air. Although the policy was later changed, the original arrangement restricted radio stations to two five-minute newscasts a day.

able, and habitual viewers stayed tuned. Some of them gradually developed a real liking for TV news, so much so that they seldom missed a newscast. By the 1970s, three out of every four adults were following the news on a regular basis[8]—nearly twice as many as when the newspaper was the sole source of daily news.[9]

3.

The era of broadcast television was short-lived. By 1990, more than half of American homes had been wired for cable, giving viewers a choice of programs at the dinner hour. Although some broadcast TV news viewers switched to cable entertainment, the bigger loss was in future years. The number of "inadvertent" viewers fell sharply, reducing the likelihood that those without a TV news habit would eventually acquire one.[10]

Cable also undercut young people's interest in news. The evening news in the 1960s and 1970s was a family ritual in many homes, and though the children might have preferred to watch something else, they sat through it. By the time they left high school, many had acquired a news habit.[11] Cable disrupted this pattern. Fewer parents were now watching the news, and even if they were, as a Kaiser Family Foundation study discovered, the children were often in another room watching something else.[12] Compared with their peers who grew up without cable, those from cable households were 40 percent less likely to follow the news regularly after leaving home.[13]

Adults under forty—the cable generation—consume much less news than their broadcast-era counterparts. In the 1970s, young adults watched nearly as much TV news as older adults.[14] They also were nearly as likely to read a daily paper.[15] This isn't true today.[16] Younger adults are now far less likely than older adults to follow the news closely, even when Internet-based news is taken into account.[17] Although the Web offers thousands of news sites, most young adults don't visit such sites regularly or hang around long when they do.[18] While eighteen- to thirty-four-year-olds account for more than two-fifths of Web traffic, they account for only a third of news site visits and a mere fifth of political site visits.[19]

Even so, young adults are only part of the story of Americans' flight from news. Within *every* age group, Americans devote less time each day to news than was the case even a decade or two ago.[20] Moreover, the individual variation in news consumption is higher than it was in the past. While cable and the Internet have made it easier for interested citizens to consume great quantities of news, they have also made the news easier for the less interested to avoid. At all hours of the day, there is an endless supply of movies, chat rooms, reality shows, sporting events, newscasts, electronic games, and the like. The choice is ours to make.[21]

Paeans to the wonders of the "information age" ignore the human element. The supply of news is greater than ever, but the determining factor is the demand for it. In the past two decades alone, the number of Americans who say "a lot" when asked whether they "enjoy keeping up with news" has fallen from 54 percent to 45 percent.[22] Among young adults, only 27 percent say they enjoy keeping up with news.[23] There are nearly as many people today who say they have little or no interest in news as those who express strong interest in it—a sharp change compared with the days before cable and the Internet. Americans are not walled off from news because of its high cost or inaccessibility. Many of them are simply not all that interested.[24]

4.

Television programming hollowed out the nation's street life by giving Americans a reason to stay home.[25] Cable and the Internet have turned us inward, to the point where we spend large chunks of our day alone, connected to others, if at all, through digital media.[26] As Marshall McLuhan noted, "We shape our tools and then our tools shape us."[27]

Watching television can be addictive, which is why in its early years it turned a generation of politically disengaged citizens into regular consumers of news. Digital media are no less addictive. A British study found that more than half of cell phone users suffer anxiety when they forget their phone at home or can't get a signal. The condition has even acquired a name—nomophobia.[28] Cognitive psychologist David Meyer calls digital media a modern-day "Skinner box," a reference to psychologist B. F. Skinner's famed stimulus-response studies from the 1930s.[29] Cell phones, TV remotes, and other devices offer instant gratification, conditioning us to want more of it. "We get an adrenalin jolt every time we receive a new stimulus—a reward for paying attention to the new," says Harvard Medical School professor Michael Rich.[30]

The flow of messages has accelerated, sometimes by the design of others, sometimes by our own hand. Tweets substitute for e-mail, text messages for phone calls, singles for albums, ten- and fifteen-second ads for thirty- or sixty-second ones. A 2012 Pew Internet and American Life Project survey found that American teenagers send and receive an average of sixty texts a day, up from fifty texts just two years earlier.[31] News bits also flow more quickly. In the 1960s, the typical TV news story presented eight images.[32] Five times that number now fly past our eyes during the typical story.[33] But even this pace is too slow for most viewers. In the past decade, the number of people who watch television news while clicking between it and other programming has more than doubled—such viewers now constitute a majority.[34]

Newspaper reading is one of the few remaining media activities that require close attention. Yet we now read less and do so for shorter periods,[35] particularly when we go online. Compared with those who read a printed version of the newspaper, Americans who read an online version devote significantly fewer minutes to it.[36]

As messages arrive at an ever faster pace, our ability to recall them diminishes. Most people have difficulty spontaneously recalling a news story a few minutes after exposure. When the story is accompanied by a scroll touting another story, the memory loss quickens.[37] It also quickens when people click between TV news shows.[38] Media multitasking further magnifies the "more is less" effect. MIT psychologist Sherry Turkle found that "when you multitask, there's a degradation of function . . . everything gets done a little worse."[39] A divided mind is a diminished mind.

A hard-to-admit truth about media abundance is that it impedes our ability to pay attention.[40] "What information consumes is rather obvious," Nobel laureate Herbert Simon noted. "It consumes the attention of its recipients. Hence a wealth of information creates a poverty of attention."[41] In a 2008 replication of a decade-old study, a British research team put a thousand people through a series of tests designed to assess their ability to concentrate. Attention spans were found to have declined by half from what they had been ten years earlier.[42]

5.

In a seminal 1947 article, "Some Reasons Why Information Campaigns Fail," sociologists Herbert Hyman and Paul Sheatsley concluded that even if "all the physical barriers" to informing the public were removed, there would remain imposing "psychological barriers." Such barriers include people's lack of interest and their knack for interpreting information in ways that reinforce their prior beliefs.[43]

The broadcast era lowered the barriers to political awareness, particularly for individuals with less education and less political interest.* "Television," Princeton's Markus Prior notes, "made it easier to learn about politics."[44] Broadcast news also created an "information commons." Each network tried to be all things to all people, with the result that all three networks featured nearly the same stories, told from more or less the same angle.[45] Although critics rightly noted that the nightly news was light on content and preoccupied with Washington

---

* Research indicates that broadcast news' influence on public information levels was largely confined to those who did not otherwise pay much attention to public affairs. The broadcast era resulted in a narrowing of the "information gap"—the difference between what the most attentive citizens know about public affairs and what the least attentive ones know. The information gap has widened since then as a result of the ease with which the politically less interested can avoid news exposure. The effect is clearest among young adults. According to political scientist Martin Wattenberg's *Is Voting for Young People?*, younger adults during the precable era consumed nearly as much news as older adults and were nearly as knowledgeable about public affairs. Today, they pay much less attention to news and they know much less. A 2011 Pew Research Center survey yielded a result that is by now all too familiar. Respondents were asked eight simple questions about people and issues in the news. Each question included four possible responses, one of which was correct. Guessing alone would have yielded the right answer 25 percent of the time. Among adults over fifty years of age, 65 percent picked the correct answer on average. Among adults under thirty, the figure was only 43 percent.

elites,[46] it was nonetheless the case that tens of millions of Americans, from all walks of life and every political leaning, were exposed each evening to a common version of the news.[47] They did not all respond in the same way, but they at least started from a shared rendition.[48]

The current media system has raised the barriers to news exposure and eroded the commons. It's not simply that citizens find it easier to avoid the news. They also have to contend with the onslaught of misinformation and infotainment that spews from today's media system. In the 1950s, cyberneticist Karl Deutsch noted that "noise" in the communication system was disrupting citizens' efforts to understand public affairs.[49] Today's media system is awash in noise, some of it designed to confuse or mislead us. Small wonder we regularly mix things up. If we were paying closer attention, we would know that climate change and weather conditions are not the same. Yet we insist on conflating them, which is why poll respondents are more likely to deny the existence of global warming during a cold winter.[50]

6.

Some observers believe that citizen-based Internet communication is an answer to the information problem.[51] They point to the many chat rooms and online discussion groups dedicated to public affairs, the informational Web sites devoted to public issues, the social networks through which information circulates.[52] They also note the emergence of "citizen journalists,"[53] pointing out the power of YouTube, Facebook, and Twitter. Handheld recording devices and Web technology enable citizens to create and disseminate stories through user-generated Web sites, social networks, and microblogging tools.[54] "In a networked world," one observer remarked, "there is no longer the 'journalist,' 'audience,' and 'source.' There is only 'us.'"[55] Another said: "We are all journalists now."[56]

Citizen journalism is an expanding field.* Gone is the day when, as journalist A. J. Liebling noted, freedom of the press belonged only to those with the money to buy a newspaper.[57] In many locations in the United States, online journalists are bringing to light developments that local newspapers have overlooked. "We are the traditional journalism model turned upside down," says Mary Lou Fulton, editor of a local online newspaper. "We [have] thousands of readers who serve as [our] eyes and ears, rather than having everything filtered through the views of a small group of reporters and editors."[58] Citizens

---

* The term "citizen journalist" is being used here to refer to a wide range of activities, which is the way the term is generally used. Proponents of citizen journalism have shied from a strict definition, seeing it as an evolving field. That's a sensible approach but can result in needless conceptual confusion. Some activities lumped under citizen journalism fall outside any reasonable conception of journalism. A photo taken on a cell phone by a casual observer can capture a powerful image that is then distributed widely. But is it journalism? Alex Jones sees it as "taking a picture." The camera holder is serving as a news source, a role as old as journalism but different from that of the journalist. Conceptual confusion also results when social networking per se is equated with journalism. Democracies have always had opinion leaders—informed citizens who help others interpret political developments. Community activists, civic volunteers, and campaign workers are among the other types of citizen mediators. To call them "citizen journalists" when they do their work through the Internet is to blur the unique contribution each of them makes to democratic life. Some of the public conversation that once took place in civic groups, churches, party organizations, the workplace, and among friends now takes place online. But this conversation was not called journalism in the past, and it is not journalism today—unless the basis for saying so is that it's occurring on the Web. To define journalism in that way robs the term of its meaning, just as nothing would be gained by calling parents "citizen doctors" when they administer a pain reliever to a sick child. On the other hand, a subset of these activities can reasonably be seen as journalism, such as the crowdsourcing that underpinned the reporting of the tsunami that devastated part of Japan in 2011.

have also uncovered major stories, as in the case of a waiter who used a cell phone to capture Republican nominee Mitt Romney's "47 percent"* remark at a private fund-raiser during the 2012 presidential campaign.[59]

It's impossible to look at what citizen journalists are doing and conclude that good reporting is the exclusive province of the professional journalist.[60] Nevertheless, citizen journalism's contribution to people's awareness of public affairs is less substantial than some of its proponents claim.[61] From an extensive study of Internet content and traffic, Matthew Hindman found scant evidence to support most "trickle-up theories." "In their enthusiasm," writes Hindman, "many have forgotten to do the math."[62] He found that most of the heavily trafficked news sites are hosted by traditional news outlets, which also produce the large majority of news items that circulate on the Web.[63] Although some types of Internet content—such as humorous videos—originate largely with users, news of public affairs is not among them. Moreover, the demand for citizen-generated public affairs content is small, accounting for less than 1 percent of Web traffic.[64] The quality of such user-generated information is also lower than that of traditional news outlets.[65] Most citizen journalists gloss over complicated topics and seldom conduct systematic research. "Many of their stories," explains Doris Graber, "are little more than responses to comments by randomly chosen members of the audience."[66]

For its part, the blogosphere is mainly a venue for punditry and advocacy rather than reporting.[67] Most blog sites are dedicated to the airing of opinion rather than the gathering of

* Romney said: "There are 47 percent of the people who will vote for the president no matter what . . . who are dependent upon government, who believe that they are victims. . . . These are people who pay no income tax . . . and so my job is not to worry about those people. I'll never convince them that they should take personal responsibility and care for their lives."

news. An Ohio State University study found that much of the information on blogs is closer in kind to what is transmitted on political talk shows than what is communicated by news outlets.[68] For their part, social networks have increasingly mimicked the content of personal conversation.[69] A 2011 Pew survey found that only a small fraction of the messages sent through social networks deal with public affairs.[70]

The emphasis on the information value of citizen journalism by some of its advocates has had the unintended effect of downplaying its most important contribution to democratic life. Responsible citizenship is as much an issue of participation in public affairs as it is an issue of being informed about public affairs, and, here, citizen journalism trumps traditional journalism by a wide margin. It enables ordinary citizens to participate directly in the communication process. "The Web is different," says the University of Michigan's W. Russell Neuman. "Each node on the Web can as easily speak as listen."[71] This is true also of blogs.* Although many blogs play fast and loose with the facts—a tendency that scholars Bruce Williams and Michael Delli Carpini describe as "politically relevant" but "politically debilitating"—they do enable people to voice their opinions.[72]

A commitment to participatory democracy led philosopher John Dewey to question Walter Lippmann's advocacy of professional journalism. In *The Public and Its Problems* (1927), Dewey concluded that professionalism would place a barrier between journalists and their audience. Dewey argued that journalists should instead try to engage citizens in the issues affecting

* Talk shows also engage the citizenry in more substantial ways than do the traditional media. This capacity became clear early in the talk show era, when Rush Limbaugh's prodding brought large numbers of conservative Republicans to the polls in the 1994 midterm elections, helping the GOP to win control of Congress for the first time in four decades and earning Limbaugh the label as the party's "electronic precinct captain."

their lives.[73] "Democracy must begin at home," wrote Dewey, "and its home is the neighborly community."[74] Dewey's idea fell by the wayside, in part because he did not clarify how citizen-centered journalism could be made to work in what was then an increasingly centralized news system. Today, as a result of the Internet's decentralizing effect, citizen-centered journalism is flourishing.[75] "A media system built on scarcity is being replaced by one based on abundance," notes CUNY's Jeff Jarvis.[76]

Although the news system as a whole is stronger because of it, citizen-based journalism is not—at least, not yet—a substitute for old-style journalism. When it comes to supplying trustworthy and relevant news on an ongoing basis, there is only one institution with the capacity to provide it: the traditional news media. They alone have the necessary infrastructure, personnel, and organizational routines, as well as norms that charge them with being "custodians of the facts."[77] "We can disagree about the respective merits of professional and nonprofessional reporting," writes Graber, "but if clear delineation of information about complex political issues is important in a democracy, citizen journalists, as a group, are a poor substitute for their professional counterparts."[78]

The problem with the traditional press is not its structure or its code, but its performance. Too often, it has placed profit and convenience ahead of its duty to inform the public. The fixation with celebrities, disasters, and crime; the reliance on the strategic frame at the expense of reporting on policy problems and issues; the habit of decontextualizing events—these and other journalistic tendencies have kept the news from being as informative as it could and should be.[79]

7.

Advocates of citizen journalism say reporters need to listen more closely to their audience.[80] It has always been good advice, and journalists have hurt their public standing by not always following it.[81] "It's hard to shake the feeling," wrote David Broder, "that we have isolated ourselves from the citizenry we serve, and are seen by many of them as just another big bureaucratic force, as unresponsive as all the rest."[82] Now that blogs, e-mails, and tweets make it easier for journalists to stay in touch with their audience, there's no good reason for them not to do so.[83]

Yet there is only so much that citizens can tell journalists. To claim otherwise is to grant citizens what they are lacking, and what they need journalists for. Journalists are in the business of making the unseen visible, of connecting citizens to the world beyond their direct experience. Citizens are expected to hold views on a wide range of issues, and yet have firsthand knowledge of only a few.[84] It's impossible to extract from citizens more information than they possess. "The truth about distant or complex matters," Lippmann said, "is not self-evident."[85]

The relationship between the public and the journalist is naturally one-sided. Citizens look to journalists to do what they do not have the time, inclination, or training to do for themselves. It's the reason that the path to a better-informed public, as it has for more than a century, runs through the nation's newsrooms.[86]

Some analysts say that the Internet age has made the press less relevant. Fewer people today worship at the altar of daily journalism. Yet from the perspective of a public bathed in a "stream of blather and misinformation," as Maureen Dowd puts it, the press is as indispensible as ever.[87] Never before has so much information been available to us, and yet never before have we had a greater need for information grounded in facts rather than spin and speculation. Reliable information on the issues of the day is an increasingly scarce commodity, and citizen journalism can't provide it on an everyday basis. "Serious reporting on national and international affairs isn't for amateurs," says Yale Law School's Bruce Ackerman.[88]

Ackerman's "isn't for amateurs" reproach holds for professional journalists as well as for citizens. Journalists' civic contribution will ultimately rest on whether through knowledge they are able to assert greater control over the facts. Journalists will falter, and ultimately fail, if their set of "facts" is seen by the public as little better than those offered up by talk show hosts, bloggers, and spin doctors. Knowledge offers journalists their best chance of delivering an authoritative version of the news, a point on which Dewey fully agreed with Lippmann. "The future of democracy is allied with the spread of the scientific attitude," wrote Dewey. "It is the sole guarantee against wholesale misleading by propaganda."[89]

APPENDIX

Knowledge-Based Journalism Resources

An array of knowledge-based material is available online for practicing journalists, journalism instructors and students, and interested citizens. Although much of the material is geared specifically to journalists, the following resources are useful for the general public and scholars as well.

JOURNALISM PRACTICE AND EDUCATION

Journalist's Resource: A free, open database that curates and synthesizes current studies on a variety of policy topics. The project identifies open-access studies whenever possible. Also available are a wide range of educational materials, from sample journalism syllabi to tip sheets on best practices for research. http://journalistsresource.org

Project for Excellence in Journalism, Pew Research Center: This nonpartisan "fact tank" analyzes and measures various aspects of the news business. www.journalism.org

Poynter Institute: A school and online project that fosters professional media development and training. The site features the latest news about the news industry and offers a wide variety of courses and training materials. www.poynter.org

Joan Shorenstein Center on the Press, Politics and Public Policy, Harvard Kennedy School: The center produces papers from leading journalists and scholars reflecting on the news media, and fosters dialogue on contemporary professional issues. http://shorensteincenter.org

Knight Foundation: With a focus on innovation in the news media, the organization supports new projects and community dialogue. www.knightfoundation.org/what-we-fund/innovating-media

Nieman Journalism Lab: A project that produces in-depth news articles on the latest developments in the news business. The Web site focuses on the intersection of media and technology. www.niemanlab.org

Journalist's Toolbox: A project supported by the Society of Professional Journalists (www.spj.org), the site curates useful links and information across topics and beats. www.journaliststoolbox.org

Investigative Reporters and Editors (IRE): An organization that supports and trains reporters, with an emphasis on developing and sharing techniques related to accountability journalism. Its NICAR project focuses on computer and data skills. www.ire.org

Tow Center for Digital Journalism, Columbia Journalism School: This project produces research-based reports that attempt to map the future of the news business. The university's *Columbia Journalism Review* (www.cjr.org) is a leading outlet for journalism-related articles and criticism. http://towcenter.org

FactCheck.org: A nonpartisan, nonprofit organization that monitors the factual accuracy of the public statements of major U.S. political players. It is a project of the Annenberg Public Policy Center of the University of Pennsylvania. http://factcheck.org

PolitiFact.com: A project of the *Tampa Bay Times* that monitors the factual accuracy of the public statements of major U.S. political figures. www.politifact.com

OTHER SITES

Google Scholar: Perhaps the most popular of the scholarly search engines, it maps the world of scholarship. This search engine is free, but access to the studies listed in the search results may be restricted. (For restricted items, click "All Versions" at the bottom of the search result to see whether an open version is available somewhere on the Web.) http://scholar.google.com

PubMed Central: This database, from the National Institutes of Health, has a great number of open-access full-text studies pertaining to public health and policy. The related PubMed database (www.ncbi.nlm.nih.gov/pubmed) has even more articles, but some have restricted access. www.ncbi.nlm.nih.gov/pmc

Microsoft Academic Search: This evolving database, similar to Google Scholar in some respects, also has tools for visualizing connections between researchers and their work. It provides "profiles" of many academics and charts how their findings have been cited. http://academic.research.microsoft.com

Social Science Research Network (SSRN): This open-access database has thousands of papers, many available for free download. www.ssrn.com

National Bureau of Economic Research (NBER): A nonprofit research organization that publishes top scholarship in economics. Many important articles first appear here as working papers, and much of the research has a public policy focus. http://nber.org

Pew Research Center: A leading survey and research organization that does polling and analysis of current issues. http://pewresearch.org

JSTOR: This nonprofit database covers more than a thousand academic journals. A university or library affiliation provides access to the full text of articles. By agreement, the database does not include the latest scholarly articles. www.jstor.org

Academic OneFile: This database, often available through public libraries, has access to thousands of journals. Not all articles are available in full text, but you can limit your search to full-text and peer-reviewed studies. www.gale.cengage.com/periodicalsolutions/academiconefile.htm

Directory of Open Access Repositories (Open DOAR): This site, run by the University of Nottingham (UK), aggregates databases from around the world. www.opendoar.org/find.php

Directory of Open Access Journals (DOAJ): A growing database that covers only open-access journals, which number more than a thousand. www.doaj.org

Mendeley: A database that crowdsources selected studies from participating scholars around the world. You can join this project and curate your own selection of studies. Some studies are restricted, but titles and abstracts are available for all of them. www.mendeley.com

Public Library of Science (PLOS): The flagship journal of this open-access academic project, *PLOS One*, features original peer-reviewed research on science and medical topics; many of the studies have policy implications. www.plosone.org/home.action

HighWire: A library and database project from Stanford University that provides full access to a large collection of science-related research. http://highwire.stanford.edu

Project MUSE: A project from Johns Hopkins University that includes more than two hundred open-access journals. http://muse.jhu.edu

Full Text Reports: A site that aggregates selected research studies and reports from across the universe of information. http://fulltextreports.com

Open CRS: The Congressional Research Service (CRS) is a reference service that provides reliable, unbiased background on policy issues. CRS reviews policy-related research and archives government reports that are in the public domain. https://opencrs.com

BIBLIOGRAPHY

Ackerman, Bruce, and James Fishkin. *Deliberation Day*. New Haven, CT: Yale University Press, 2004.

Adler, Richard. "News Cities: The Next Generation of Healthy Informed Communities." Aspen Institute Forum on Communications and Society, Aspen Institute, Washington, D.C., 2010.

Alterman, Eric. *What Liberal Media?* New York: Basic Books, 2003.

Altheide, David L. "Format and Symbol in Television Coverage of Terrorism in the United States and Great Britain." *International Studies Quarterly* 31 (1987): 161–76.

Altschull, J. Herbert. "The Journalist and Instant History." *Journalism Quarterly* 50 (1973): 545–51.

Alwood, Edward. *Dark Days in the Newsroom*. Philadelphia: Temple University Press, 2007.

Andersen, Kristi, and Stuart J. Thorson. "Public Discourse or Strategic Game? Changes in Our Conception of Elections." *Studies in American Political Development* 3 (1989): 271–73.

Anderson, C. W., Emily Bell, and Clay Shirky. "Post-Industrial Journalism: Adapting to the Present." Tow Center for Digital Journalism, Columbia University Graduate School of Journalism, New York, 2012.

Ansolabehere, Stephen, Roy Behr, and Shanto Iyengar. *The Media Game: American Politics in the Media Age*. New York: Macmillan, 1993.

Arnold, R. Douglas. *Congress, the Press, and Political Accountability*. Princeton, NJ: Princeton University Press, 2004.

Atwater, Tony, and Norma Green. "News Sources in Network Coverage of International Terrorism." *Journalism Quarterly* 65 (1988): 967–71.

Auletta, Ken. "Non-Stop News." *New Yorker*, January 25, 2010.

Barnhurst, Kevin G. "The Makers of Meaning." *Political Communication* 20 (2003): 1–22.

Barnhurst, Kevin G., and Catherine A. Steele. "Image Bite News: The Coverage of Elections on U.S. Television, 1968–1992." *Harvard International Journal of Press/Politics* 2 (1997): 40–58.

Bartels, Larry. *Presidential Primaries and the Dynamics of Public Choice.* Princeton, NJ: Princeton University Press, 1988.

Bates, Stephen. "Realigning Journalism with Democracy: The Hutchins Commission, Its Times, and Ours." Washington, D.C.: Annenberg Washington Program, Northwestern University, 1995.

Bauerlein, Mark. *The Dumbest Generation.* New York: Penguin, 2008.

Baum, Matthew A. "Partisan Media and Attitude Polarization: The Case of Healthcare Reform." In *Regulatory Breakdown: The Crisis of Confidence in U.S. Regulation*, ed. Cary Coglianese, 118–42. Philadelphia: University of Pennsylvania Press, 2012.

——. *Soft News Goes to War: Public Opinion and American Foreign Policy in the New Media Age.* Princeton, NJ: Princeton University Press, 2003.

Baum, Matthew A., and Tim Groeling. "New Media and the Polarization of American Political Discourse." *Political Communication* 25 (2008): 345–65.

——. "Shot by the Messenger." *Political Behavior* 31 (2009): 157–86.

Baumgartner, Jody C., and Jonathan S. Morris. *Laughing Matters: Humor and American Politics in the Media Age.* New York: Routledge, 2012.

Benkler, Yochai. *The Wealth of Networks.* New Haven, CT: Yale University Press, 2007.

Bennett, W. Lance. *News: The Politics of Illusion*. New York: Longman, 2002.

——. "Political Communication and Democratic Governance." In *Democracy in the Twenty-First Century*, ed. Peter Nardulli, forthcoming.

——. "Toward a Theory of Press-State Relations in the U.S." *Journal of Communication* 40 (1990): 103–25.

Bennett, W. Lance, Regina G. Lawrence, and Steven Livingston. *When the Press Fails: Political Power and the News Media from Iraq to Katrina.* Chicago: University of Chicago Press, 2007.

Bernt, Joseph P., Frank E. Fee, Jacqueline Gifford, and Guido H. Stempel III. "How Well Can Editors Predict Reader Interest in News?" *Newspaper Research Journal* 21 (2000): 2–10.

Bimber, Bruce. *Information and American Democracy: Technology in the Evolution of Political Power.* New York: Cambridge University Press, 2003.

Blendon, Robert. "Bridging the Gap between the Public's and the Economists' Views of the Economy." *Journal of Economic Perspectives* 11 (1997): 105–18.

Blom, Robin, and Lucinda D. Davenport. "Searching for the Core of Journalism Education." *Journalism and Mass Communication Educator* 67 (2012): 70–86.

Blumler, Jay G., and Michael Gurevitch. *The Crisis of Public Communication.* London: Routledge, 1995.

Boehlert, Eric. *Lapdogs: How the Press Rolled Over for Bush.* New York: Free Press, 2006.

Boykoff, Maxwell T. *Who Speaks for the Climate? Making Sense of Media Reporting on Climate Change.* New York: Cambridge University Press, 2011.

Boykoff, Maxwell T., and Jules M. Boykoff. "Balance as Bias: Global Warming and the U.S. Prestige Press." *Global Environmental Change* 14 (2004): 125–36.

Boyte, Harry C. "Civic Agency and the Politics of Knowledge." Kettering Foundation, 2009.

Bradlee, Ben. *A Good Life: Newspapering and Other Adventures.* New York: Simon & Schuster, 1995.

Brantner, Cornelia, Katharina Lobinger, and Irmgard Wetzstein. "Effects of Visual Framing on Emotional Responses and Evaluations of News Stories about the Gaza Conflict of 2009." *Journalism and Mass Communication Quarterly* 88 (2011): 523–40.

Broder, David. *Beyond the Front Page.* New York: Simon & Schuster, 1987.

Brownstein, Ronald. *The Second Civil War: How Extreme Partisanship Has Paralyzed Washington and Polarized America.* New York: Penguin, 2007.

Buchanan, Bruce. *Renewing Presidential Politics.* Lanham, MD: Rowman & Littlefield, 1996.

Buckingham, David. "News Media, Political Socialization and Popular Citizenship: Towards a New Agenda." *Critical Studies in Mass Communication* 14 (1997): 344–66.

Bucy, Erik P., and Maria Elizabeth Grabe. "Taking Television Seriously: A Sound and Image Bite Analysis of Presidential Campaign Coverage, 1992–2004." *Journal of Communication* 57 (2007): 652–75.

Cappella, Joseph, and Kathleen Hall Jamieson. *Spiral of Cynicism: The Press and the Public Good.* New York: Oxford University Press, 1997.

Carpenter, Serena. "How Online Citizen Journalism Publications and Online Newspapers Utilize the Objective Standard and Rely on External Sources." *Journalism and Mass Communication Quarterly* 85 (2008): 533–50.

Chong, Dennis, and James N. Druckman. "Framing Public Opinion in Competitive Democracies." *American Political Science Review* 101 (2007): 637–55.

Clyde, Robert W., and James K. Buckalew. "Inter-Media Standardization: A Q-Analysis of News Editors." *Journalism Quarterly* 46 (Summer 1969): 349–51.

Cobb, Roger W., and David M. Primo. *The Plane Truth: Airline Crashes, the Media, and Transportation Policy.* Washington, D.C.: Brookings Institution, 2003.

Cohen, Jeffrey E. *The Presidency in the Era of 24-Hour News.* Princeton, NJ: Princeton University Press, 2008.

Cook, Timothy E. *Governing with the News.* Chicago: University of Chicago Press, 1998.

Crouse, Timothy. *The Boys on the Bus.* New York: Ballantine, 1974.

Curran, James. *Media and Democracy.* London: Routledge, 2011.

Dagnes, Alison. *Politics on Demand: The Effects of 24-Hour News on American Politics.* Westport, CT: Praeger, 2010.

Dahlgren, Peter. *Media and Political Engagement.* New York: Cambridge University Press, 2009.

D'Alessio, David, and Mike Allen. "Media Bias in Presidential Elections: A Meta-Analysis." *Journal of Communication* 50 (2000): 133–56.

Davis, Richard. *Politics Online.* New York: Routledge, 2005.

De Vreese, Claes H., and Matthijs Elenbaas. "Media in the Game of Politics: Effects of Strategic Metacoverage on Political Cynicism." *International Journal of Press/Politics* 13 (2008): 285–309.

Delli Carpini, Michael X., and Scott Keeter. *What Americans Know about Politics and Why It Matters.* New Haven, CT: Yale University Press, 1997.

Dennis, Everett C., and John C. Merritt. *Media Debates: Great Issues for the Digital Age*, 5th ed. Belmont, CA: Wadsworth, 2006.

Dewey, John. *The Public and Its Problems.* New York: Holt, 1927.

Dionne, E. J. *They Only Look Dead.* New York: Simon & Schuster, 1996.

Doherty, Carol. "The Public Isn't Buying Press Credibility." *Nieman Reports*, Summer 2005.

Doig, Stephen K. "Reporting with the Tools of Social Science." *Nieman Reports*, Spring 2008.

Donsbach, Wolfgang. "Journalists and Their Professional Identities." In *The Routledge Companion to News and Journalism Studies*, ed. Stuart Allan. New York: Routledge, 2010.

Donsbach, Wolfgang, and Tom Fiedler. "Journalism School Curriculum Enrichment: A Mid-Term Report of the Carnegie-Knight Initiative on the Future of Journalism Education." Joan Shorenstein Center on the Press, Politics and Public Policy, John F. Kennedy School of Government, Harvard University, Cambridge, MA, 2008.

Downie, Leonard, Jr., and Robert G. Kaiser. *The News about the News: American Journalism in Peril.* New York: Vintage, 2003.

Druckman, James N. "Political Preference Formation." *American Political Science Review* 98 (2004): 671–86.

Easton, Nina. "Rebelling Against the Rich." Discussion Paper D-75, Joan Shorenstein Center on the Press, Politics and Public Policy, John F. Kennedy School of Government, Harvard University, Cambridge, MA, 2012.

Edelman, Murray. *Constructing the Political Spectacle.* Chicago: University of Chicago Press, 1988.

Edwardson, Mickie, Kurt Kent, and Maeve McConnell. "Television News Information Gain: Videotext versus a Talking Head." *Journal of Broadcasting and Electronic Media* 29 (1985): 367–85.

Efron, Edith. *The News Twisters.* Los Angeles: Nash, 1971.

Ehrlich, Matthew Carlton. "The Journalism of Outrageousness." *Journalism and Communication Monographs* 155 (February 1996).

Eilperin, Juliet. *Fight Club Politics.* Lanham, MD: Rowman & Littlefield, 2007.

Engelberg, Stephen. "Open Your Mind." *American Journalism Review*, March 1999.

Entman, Robert. *Democracy without Citizens: Media and the Decay of American Politics.* New York: Oxford University Press, 1989.

——. *Projections of Power: Framing News, Public Opinion, and U.S. Foreign Policy.* Chicago: University of Chicago Press, 2004.

Epstein, Edward Jay. *News from Nowhere.* New York: Vintage, 1974.

Fallows, James. *Breaking the News: How the Media Undermine American Democracy.* New York: Pantheon, 1996.

——. "Did You Have a Good Week?" *Atlantic Monthly,* December 1994.

Farnsworth, Stephen J., and S. Robert Lichter. *The Mediated Presidency: Television News and Presidential Governance.* Lanham, MD: Rowman & Littlefield, 2005.

——. "News Coverage of New Presidents in the *New York Times,* 1981–2008." *Politics and Policy* 40 (2012): 69–91.

Feldman, Lauren, Edward W. Maibach, Connie Roser-Renouf, and Anthony Leiserowitz. "Climate on Cable: The Nature and Impact of Global Warming Coverage on Fox News, CNN, and MSNBC." *International Journal of Press/Politics* 17 (2012): 3–31.

Fogarty, Brian J. "Determining Economic News Coverage." *International Journal of Public Opinion Research* 17 (2005): 149–72.

Fogarty, Brian J., and Jennifer Wolak. "The Effects of Media Interpretation for Citizen Evaluations of Politicians' Messages." *American Politics Research* 37 (2009): 129–54.

Fowles, Jib. *Why Viewers Watch.* Newbury Park, CA: Sage Publications, 1992.

Fried, Richard M. *Nightmare in Red: The McCarthy Era in Perspective.* New York: Oxford University Press, 1991.

Fröhlich, Remy, and Christina Holtz-Bacha. *Journalism Education in Europe and North America.* New York: Hampton Press, 2003.

Fuller, Jack. *News Values.* Chicago: University of Chicago Press, 1996.

——. *What Is Happening to News: The Information Explosion and the Crisis in Journalism.* Chicago: University of Chicago Press, 2010.

Gans, Herbert J. *Deciding What's News.* New York: Pantheon, 1979.

Gant, Scott. *We're All Journalists Now.* New York: Free Press, 2007.

Gardner, Howard, Mihaly Csikszentmihalyi, and William Damon. *Good Work: Where Excellence and Ethics Meet.* New York: Basic Books, 2001.

Geer, John G. *In Defense of Negativity.* Chicago: University of Chicago Press, 2006.

Gentzkow, Matthew, and Jesse M. Shapiro. "What Drives Media Slant? Evidence from U.S. Daily Newspapers." *Econometrica* 78 (2010): 35–71.

George, Cherian. "Beyond Professionalization." *Journalism and Mass Communication Educator* 66 (2011): 257–67.

Gilens, Martin, Lynn Vavreck, and Martin Cohen. "The Mass Media and the Public's Assessments of Presidential Candidates, 1952–2000." *Journal of Politics* 69 (2007): 1160–75.

Giles, Bob. "Universities Teach Journalists Valuable Lessons." *Nieman Reports,* Spring 2001.

Gillmor, Dan. *We the Media: Grassroots Journalism by the People, for the People.* Sebastopol, CA: O'Reilly Media, 2006.

Gitlin, Todd. *Media Unlimited.* New York: Henry Holt, 2002.

Glaser, Mark. "The New Voices: Hyperlocal Citizen Media Sites Want You (to Write)!" *Online Journalism Review,* USC Annenberg, November 2004.

Glasser, Theodore J. "Objectivity Precludes Responsibility." *Quill,* February 1984.

Godkin, Paul. "Rethinking Journalism as a Profession." *Canadian Journal of Media Studies* 4 (2008): 109–23.

Goldberg, Bernard. *Bias: A CBS Insider Exposes How the Media Distort the News.* Washington, D.C.: Regnery, 2002.

Graber, Doris A. *On Media: Making Sense of Politics.* Boulder, CO: Paradigm, 2012.

——. *Processing the News: How People Tame the Information Tide,* 2nd ed. New York: Longman, 1988.

——. *Processing Politics: Learning from Television in the Internet Age.* Chicago: University of Chicago Press, 2001.

Greenhouse, Linda. "Challenging 'He Said, She Said' Journalism." *Nieman Reports* 66 (Summer 2012).

Groeling, Tim. *When Politicians Attack.* New York: Cambridge University Press, 2010.

Groeling, Tim, and Matthew A. Baum. "Journalists' Incentives and Media Coverage of Elite Foreign Policy Evaluations." *Conflict Management and Peace Science* 26 (2009): 437–70.

Groeling, Tim, and Samuel Kernell. "Is Network News Coverage of the President Biased?" *Journal of Politics* 60 (1998): 1063–87.

Grubisich, Tom. "Grassroots Journalism: Actual Content vs. Shining Idea." *Online Journalism Review*, USC Annenberg, October 2005.

Gunther, Albert C., and Janice L. Liebhart. "Broad Reach or Biased Source? Decomposing the Hostile Media Effect." *Journal of Communication* 56 (2006): 449–66.

Hacker, Jacob S., and Paul Pierson. *Off Center: The Republican Revolution and the Erosion of American Democracy.* New Haven, CT: Yale University Press, 2005.

Haiman, Robert J. *Best Practices for Newspaper Journalists.* Arlington, VA: Freedom Forum, 2002.

Haller, H. Brandon, and Helmut Norpoth. "Reality Bites: News Exposures and Economic Opinion." *Public Opinion Quarterly* 61 (1997): 555–75.

Hamill, Pete. *News Is a Verb.* New York: Ballantine, 1998.

Hartley, John. *Understanding News.* London: Methuen, 1982.

Hartman, Todd K., and Christopher R. Weber. "Who Said What? The Effects of Source Cues in Issue Frames." *Political Behavior* 31 (2009): 537–58.

Hayes, Danny, and Matt Guardino. "Whose Views Made the News? Media Coverage and the March to War in Iraq." *Political Communication* 27 (2010): 59–87.

Herbst, Susan. *Reading Public Opinion: How Political Actors View the Democratic Process.* Chicago: University of Chicago Press, 1998.

Hindman, Matthew. *The Myth of Digital Democracy.* Princeton, NJ: Princeton University Press, 2009.

Hofstadter, Richard. "The Paranoid Style in American Politics." *Harper's Magazine*, November 1964.

Howard, Philip N. *New Media Campaigns and the Managed Citizen.* New York: Cambridge University Press, 2006.

Hyman, Herbert H., and Paul B. Sheatsley. "Some Reasons Why Information Campaigns Fail." *Public Opinion Quarterly* 11 (1947): 412–23.

Iyengar, Shanto. *Is Anyone Responsible? How Television Frames Political Issues.* Chicago: University of Chicago Press, 1991.

Iyengar, Shanto, Helmut Norpoth, and Kyu S. Hahn. "Consumer Demand for Election News: The Horserace Sells." *Journal of Politics* 66 (2004): 157–75.

Jacobs, Lawrence R., and Robert Y. Shapiro. *Politicians Don't Pander.* Chicago: University of Chicago Press, 2000.

Jamieson, Kathleen Hall. *Dirty Politics.* New York: Oxford University Press, 1992.

Jamieson, Kathleen Hall, and Karlyn Kohrs Campbell. *The Interplay of Influence,* 5th ed. Belmont, CA: Wadsworth, 2001.

Jamieson, Kathleen Hall, and Joseph N. Cappella. *Echo Chamber: Rush Limbaugh and the Conservative Media Establishment.* New York: Oxford University Press, 2008.

Jamieson, Kathleen Hall, and Paul Waldman. *The Press Effect: Politicians, Journalists, and the Stories That Shape the Political World.* New York: Oxford University Press, 2003.

Janeway, Michael. *Republic of Denial: Press, Politics, and Public Life.* New Haven, CT: Yale University Press, 1999.

Jarvis, Jeff. *What Would Google Do?* New York: HarperBusiness, 2009.

Jerit, Jennifer, and Jason Barabas. "Bankrupt Rhetoric: How Misleading Information Affects Knowledge about Social Security." *Public Opinion Quarterly* 70 (2006): 278–303.

Johnson, Thomas J., and Barbara K. Kaye. "Wag the Blog." *Journalism and Mass Communication Quarterly* 81 (2004): 622–42.

Johnston, Robert D. *The Politics of Healing.* New York: Routledge, 2004.

Jones, Alex S. *Losing the News.* New York: Oxford University Press, 2009.

Kalb, Marvin. "The Rise of the 'New News.'" Discussion Paper D-34, Joan Shorenstein Center on the Press, Politics and Public Policy, John F. Kennedy School of Government, Harvard University, Cambridge, MA, 1998.

Kang, HyunJin, Keunmin Bae, Shaoke Zhang, and S. Shyam Sundar. "Source Cues in Online News: Is the Proximate Source More Powerful Than Distal Sources?" *Journalism and Mass Communication Quarterly* 88 (2011): 719–36.

Keeter, Scott, and Cliff Zukin. *Uninformed Choice.* New York: Praeger, 1984.

Kepplinger, Hans Mattias, and J. Habermeier. "The Impact of Key Events on the Presentation of Reality." Unpublished paper, Institut für Publizistik, University of Mainz, Germany, 1995.

Kerbel, Matthew R. *If It Bleeds, It Leads.* New York: Basic Books, 2000.

——. *Remote and Controlled: Media Politics in a Cynical Age,* 2nd ed. Boulder, CO: Westview Press, 1999.

Keren, Michael. *Blogosphere: The New Political Arena.* Lanham, MD: Lexington Books, 2006.

Kiku, Adatto. "Sound Bite Democracy: Network Evening News Presidential Campaign Coverage, 1968 and 1988." Research Paper R-2, Joan Shorenstein Center on the Press, Politics and Public Policy, John F. Kennedy School of Government, Harvard University, Cambridge, MA, 1990.

King, Elliot. *Free for All: The Internet's Transformation of Journalism.* Evanston, IL: Northwestern University Press, 2010.

Klein, Ezra. "Unpopular Mandate." *New Yorker,* June 25, 2012.

Klein, Roger D. "Audience Reaction to Local TV News." *American Behavioral Scientist* 46 (2003): 1661–72.

Kline, David, and Dan Burstein. *Blog!: How the Newest Media Revolution Is Changing Politics, Business, and Culture.* New York: CDS Books, 2005.

Kovach, Bill, and Tom Rosenstiel. *The Elements of Journalism.* New York: Three Rivers, 2001.

——. *The Elements of Journalism,* revised ed. New York: Three Rivers, 2007.

Kuklinski, James H., Paul J. Quirk, Jennifer Jerit, David Schweider, and Robert F. Rich. "Misinformation and the Currency of Democratic Citizenship." *Journal of Politics* 62 (2000): 790–816.

Kuklinski, James H., Paul J. Quirk, David Schweider, and Robert F. Rich. "'Just the Facts, Ma'am': Political Facts and Public Opinion." *Annals of the American Academy of Political and Social Science* 560 (1998): 143–54.

Kurtz, Howard. *Spin Cycle: How the White House and the Media Manipulate the News.* New York: Touchstone, 1998.

Kuypers, Jim A. *Press Bias and Politics: How the Media Frame Controversial Issues.* Westport, CT: Praeger, 2002.

Ladd, Jonathan M. *Why Americans Hate the Media and How It Matters.* Princeton, NJ: Princeton University Press, 2012.

Lawrence, Regina. "Framing Obesity: The Evolution of News Discourse on a Public Health Issue." *International Journal of Press/Politics* 9, no. 3 (Summer 2004): 56–75.

Lawrence, Regina, and Melody Rose. *Hillary Clinton's Race for the White House: Gender Politics and the Media on the Campaign Trail.* Boulder, CO: Lynne Rienner, 2009.

Layton, Charles. "State of the American Newspaper. What Do People Really Want?" *American Journalism Review,* March 1999.

Lee, Francis E. *Beyond Ideology: Politics, Principles, and Partisanship in the U.S. Senate.* Chicago: University of Chicago Press, 2009.

Leigh, Robert D. *A Free and Responsible Press.* Chicago: University of Chicago Press, 1974.

Lemann, Nicholas. "The Limits of Language." In *What Orwell Didn't Know: Propaganda and the New Face of American Politics,* ed. András Szántó and Orville Schell. New York: Public Affairs, 2007.

Leubsdorf, Carl. "The Reporter and the Presidential Candidate." *Annals of the American Academy of Political and Social Science* 427, no. 1 (1976): 1–11.

Levy, Mark. "Disdaining the News." *Journal of Communication* 31 (1981): 24–31.

Leys, Colin. *Market-Driven Politics.* London: Verso, 2001.

Lichter, S. Robert, and Ted J. Smith. "Bad News Bears." *Forbes Media Critic* 1 (1994): 81–87.

Lippmann, Walter. *Liberty and the News.* Princeton, NJ: Princeton University Press, 2008 [1920].

——. *Public Opinion.* New York: Free Press, 1970 [1922].

Lowrey, Wilson, George L. Daniels, and Lee B. Becker. "Predictors of Convergence Curricula in Journalism and Mass Communication Programs." *Journalism and Mass Communication Educator* 60 (2005): 31–46.

Lupia, Arthur, and Mathew D. McCubbins. *The Democratic Dilemma: Can Citizens Learn What They Need to Know?* New York: Cambridge University Press, 1998.

MacKinnon, Rebecca. *Consent of the Networked: The Worldwide Struggle for Internet Freedom.* New York: Basic Books, 2012.

Maier, Scott R. "Accuracy Matters: A Cross-Market Assessment of Newspaper Error and Credibility." *Journalism and Mass Communication Quarterly* 82 (2005): 533–51.

Major, Lesa Hatley. "The Mediating Role of Emotions in the Relationship between Framing and Attribution of Responsibility for Health Problems." *Journalism and Mass Communication Quarterly* 88 (2011): 502–22.

Manheim, Jarol. *All of the People, All the Time: Strategic Communication and American Politics.* Armonk, NY: M.E. Sharpe, 1991.

Mann, Thomas E., and Norman J. Ornstein. *The Broken Branch: How Congress Is Failing America and How to Get It Back on Track.* New York: Oxford University Press, 2008.

——, eds. *Congress, the Press, and the Public.* Washington, D.C.: American Enterprise Institute and Brookings Institution, 1994.

——. *It's Even Worse Than It Looks.* New York: Basic Books, 2012.

Mayer, Frederick W. "Stories of Climate Change: Competing Narratives, the Media, and U.S. Public Opinion 2001–2010." Discussion Paper D-72, Joan Shorenstein Center on the Press, Politics and Public Policy, John F. Kennedy School of Government, Harvard University, Cambridge, MA, 2012.

McCauley, Michael P. *The Political Economy of Media: Enduring Issues, Emerging Dilemmas.* New York: Monthly Review Press, 2008.

——. *NPR: The Trials and Triumphs of National Public Radio.* New York: Columbia University Press, 2005.

McChesney, Robert, and Victor Pickard, eds. *Will the Last Reporter Please Turn Out the Lights.* New York: New Press, 2011.

McClellan, Scott. *What Happened: Inside the Bush White House and Washington's Culture of Deception.* New York: Public Affairs, 2008.

McCombs, Maxwell E., and Donald L. Shaw. "The Evolution of Agenda-Setting Research: Twenty-Five Years in the Marketplace of Ideas." *Journal of Communication* 43 (1993): 58–67.

McLeary, Paul. "Insightmag: A Must-Read." *Columbia Journalism Review,* January 29, 2007.

McLuhan, Marshall. *Understanding Media.* Cambridge, MA: MIT Press, 1964.

McManus, John H. *Market-Driven Journalism.* Thousand Oaks, CA: Sage, 1994.

Mele, Nicco. *The End of Big: How the Internet Makes David the New Goliath.* New York: St. Martin's Press, 2013.

Mencher, Melvin. "Will the Meaning of Journalism Survive?" *Nieman Reports,* June 2006.

Mensing, Donica. "Rethinking [Again] the Future of Journalism Education." *Journalism Studies* 11 (2010): 511–23.

Meyer, Philip. *Precision Journalism: A Reporter's Introduction to Social Science Methods.* Bloomington: Indiana University Press, 1973.

——. *The Vanishing Newspaper.* Columbia: University of Missouri Press, 2004.

Miller, Arthur H., Edie N. Goldenberg, and Lutz Erbring. "Type-Set Politics: Impact of Newspapers on Public Confidence." *American Political Science Review* 73 (1979): 67–84.

Mindich, David T. Z. *Just the Facts: How "Objectivity" Came to Define American Journalism.* New York: New York University Press, 2000.

Mooney, Chris, and Matthew C. Nisbet. "Undoing Darwin." *Columbia Journalism Review,* September/October 2005.

Morris, Jonathan S. "Slanted Objectivity? Perceived Media Bias, Cable News Exposure, and Political Attitudes." *Social Science Quarterly* 88 (2007): 707–28.

Morris, Jonathan S., and Rosalee A. Clawson. "Media Coverage of Congress in the 1990s: Scandal, Personalities, and the Prevalence of Policy and Process." *Political Communication* 22 (2005): 297–313.

Morris, Jonathan S., and Richard Forgette. "News Grazers, Television News, Political Knowledge, and Engagement." *Harvard International Journal of Press/Politics* 12 (2007): 91–107.

Mott, Frank Luther. *American Journalism: A History, 1690–1960.* New York: Macmillan, 1962.

Moy, Patricia, and Michael Pfau. *With Malice Toward All? The Media and Public Confidence in Democratic Institutions.* Westport, CT: Praeger, 2000.

Mutz, Diana. "Mass Media and the Depoliticization of Personal Experiences." *American Journal of Political Science* 36 (1992): 483–508.

Nadeau, Richard, Neil Neville, Elisabeth Gidengil, and André Blais. "Election Campaigns as Information Campaigns." *Political Communication* 25 (2008): 229–48.

Neuman, W. Russell, ed. *Media, Technology, and Society: Theories of Media Evolution.* Ann Arbor: University of Michigan Press, 2010.

Niles, Robert. "A Journalist's Guide to the Scientific Method, and Why It's Important." *Online Journalism Review,* USC Annenberg, August 2011.

Nisbet, Matthew. "Nature's Prophet." Discussion Paper D-78, Joan Shorenstein Center on the Press, Politics and Public Policy, John F. Kennedy School of Government, Harvard University, Cambridge, MA, 2013.

Nisbet, Matthew C., Dominique Brossard, and Adrianne Kroepsch. "Framing Science: The Stem Cell Controversy in the Age of Press/Politics." *Harvard International Journal of Press/Politics* 8 (2003): 36–70.

Nisbet, Matthew C., and Bruce V. Lewenstein. "Biotechnology and the American Media." *Science Communication* 23 (2002): 359–91.

Niven, David. *Tilt? The Search for Media Bias.* Westport, CT: Praeger, 2002.

Norris, Pippa, John Curtice, David Sanders, Margaret Scammell, and Holli A. Semetko. *On Message: Communicating the Campaign.* Thousand Oaks, CA: Sage, 1999.

Nyhan, Brendan. "Why the 'Death Panel' Myth Wouldn't Die: Misinformation in the Health Care Reform Debate." *Forum* 8, no. 1 (2010).

Nyhan, Brendan, and Jason Reifler. "When Corrections Fail: The Persistence of Political Misperception." *Political Behavior* 32 (2010): 303–30.

Nyhan, Brendan, and John Sides. "How Political Science Can Help Journalism (and Still Let Journalists Be Journalists)." *Forum* 9, no. 1 (2011).

Oppenheimer, Todd. "Reality Bytes." *Columbia Journalism Review,* September/October 1996.

Overholser, Geneva. "Keeping Journalism, and Journalism Education, Connected to the Public." *Nieman Journalism Lab,* September 2012.

Page, Benjamin I., and Robert Y. Shapiro. *The Rational Public.* Chicago: University of Chicago Press, 1992.

Patterson, Thomas E. "Bad News, Bad Governance." *Annals of the American Academy of Political and Social Science* 546, no. 1 (July 1996): 97–108.

———. "Time and News." *International Political Science Review* 19 (1998): 55–67.

———. "Doing Well and Doing Good." Working Paper RWP01-001, Joan Shorenstein Center on the Press, Politics and Public Policy, John F. Kennedy School of Government, Harvard University, Cambridge, MA, 2000.

——. *The Mass Media Election: How Americans Choose Their President.* Westport, CT: Praeger, 1980.

——. "More Style Than Substance: Television News in U.S. National Elections." *Political Communication and Persuasion* 8 (1991): 145–61.

——. *Out of Order.* New York: Knopf, 1993.

——. "Young People and News." Joan Shorenstein Center on the Press, Politics and Public Policy, John F. Kennedy School of Government, Harvard University, Cambridge, MA, 2007.

Patterson, Thomas E., and Robert D. McClure. *The Unseeing Eye.* New York: Putnam, 1976.

Perloff, Richard M. *Political Communication: Politics, Press, and Public in American Politics.* Mahwah, NJ: Lawrence Erlbaum, 1998.

Phelps, Andrew. "From White Paper to Newspaper." *Nieman Journalism Lab,* November 2011.

Pincus, Walter. "Newspaper Narcissism." *Columbia Journalism Review,* May/June 2009. www.cjr.org/essay/newspaper_narcissism_1.php.

Pinkleton, Bruce E., Erica Weintraub Austin, Yushu Zhou, Jessica Fitts Willoughby, and Megan Reiser. "Perceptions of News Media, External Efficacy, and Public Affairs Apathy in Political Decision Making and Disaffection." *Journalism and Mass Communication Quarterly* 89 (2012): 23–39.

Pooley, Eric. "How Much Would You Pay to Save the Planet?" Discussion Paper D-49, Joan Shorenstein Center on the Press, Politics and Public Policy, John F. Kennedy School of Government, Harvard University, Cambridge, MA, 2009.

Popkin, Samuel. *The Reasoning Voter: Communication and Persuasion in Presidential Campaigns.* Chicago: University of Chicago Press, 1991.

Postman, Neil. *Amusing Ourselves to Death.* New York: Penguin, 1985.

Powers, William. *Hamlet's BlackBerry.* New York: HarperCollins, 2010.

Prior, Markus. *Post-Broadcast Democracy.* Cambridge: Cambridge University Press, 2007.

Putnam, Robert. *Bowling Alone.* New York: Simon & Schuster, 2000.

Redlawsk, David. "Hot Cognition or Cool Consideration? Testing the Effects of Motivated Reasoning on Political Decision Making." *Journal of Politics* 64 (2002): 1021–44.

Reese, Stephen D. "The Progressive Potential of Journalism Education: Rethinking the Academic versus Professional Divide." *Harvard International Journal of Press/Politics* 4 (1999): 70–91.

Rideout, Christine F. "News Coverage and Talk Shows in the 1992 Presidential Campaign." *PS: Political Science and Politics* 26 (1993): 712–16.

Rideout, Victoria J., Ulla G. Foehr, Donald F. Roberts, and Mollyann Brodie. "Kids and Media at the New Millennium." Kaiser Family Foundation, Menlo Park, CA, 1999.

Ridout, Travis N., and Rob Mellon, Jr. "Does the Media Agenda Reflect the Candidates' Agenda?" *Harvard International Journal of Press/Politics* 12 (2007): 44–62.

Robinson, Michael J. "Public Affairs Television and the Growth of Political Malaise: The Case of 'The Selling of the Pentagon.'" *American Political Science Review* 70, no. 3 (1976): 409–32.

——. "Two Decades of American News Preferences." Pew Research Center for the People and the Press, 2007. http://pewresearch.org/pubs/574/ (accessed 2012).

Robinson, Michael, and Margaret Sheehan. *Over the Wire and on TV.* New York: Sage, 1983.

Romer, Daniel, Kathleen Hall Jamieson, and Sean Aday. "Television News and the Cultivation of Fear of Crime." *Journal of Communication* 53 (2003): 88–104.

Rosen, Jay. *What Are Journalists For?* New Haven, CT: Yale University Press, 2001.

Rosenstiel, Tom. *The Beat Goes On.* New York: Twentieth Century Fund, 1994.

Rosenstiel, Tom, Marion Just, Todd Belt, Atiba Pertilla, Walter Dean, and Dante Chinni. *We Interrupt This Newscast: How to Improve Local News and Win Ratings, Too.* New York: Cambridge University Press, 2007.

Rosenstiel, Tom, and Amy Mitchell. "The State of the News Media, 2011." Pew Research Center's Project for Excellence in Journalism, March 14, 2011. http://stateofthemedia.org/2011/overview-2/ (accessed 2013).

Russell, Cristine. "Covering Controversial Science: Improving Reporting on Science and Public Policy." Working Paper 2006-4, Joan Shorenstein Center on the Press, Politics and Public Policy, John F. Kennedy School of Government, Harvard University, Cambridge, MA, 2006.

Sabato, Larry J. *Feeding Frenzy: How Attack Journalism Has Transformed American Politics.* New York: Free Press, 1991.

Salerno, Steve. "Journalist-Bites-Reality." eSkeptic. February 12, 2008.

Scheuer, Jeffrey. *The Big Picture: Why Democracies Need Journalistic Excellence.* New York: Routledge, 2008.

Schlesinger, Philip. "Newsmen and Their Time Machine." *British Journal of Sociology* 28 (1977): 336–50.

Schön, Donald A. *The Reflective Practitioner: How Professionals Think in Action.* New York: Basic Books, 1983.

Schudson, Michael. *Discovering the News.* Cambridge, MA: Harvard University Press, 1978.

——. *The Power of News.* Cambridge, MA: Harvard University Press, 1995.

——. *Why Democracies Need an Unlovable Press.* Boston: Polity, 2008.

Scott, D. Travers. "Pundits in Muckrakers' Clothing." In *Blogging, Citizenship, and the Future of Media*, ed. Mark Tremayne. New York: Routledge, 2007.

Sellers, Patrick. *Cycles of Spin: Strategic Communication in the U.S. Congress.* New York: Cambridge University Press, 2010.

Seymour-Ure, Colin. *The Political Impact of Mass Media.* Beverly Hills, CA: Sage, 1974.

Shirky, Clay. *Cognitive Surplus: Creativity and Generosity in a Connected Age.* New York: Penguin Books, 2010.

Shoemaker, Pamela J., Timothy P. Vos, and Stephen D. Reese. "Journalists as Gatekeepers." In *The Handbook of Journalism Studies*, ed. K. Wahl-Jorgensen and T. Hanitzsch. New York: Routledge, 2009.

Shulman, Lee S. "Those Who Understand: Knowledge Growth in Teaching." *Educational Researcher* 15 (1986): 4–14.

Sigal, Leon. *Reporters and Officials: The Organization and Politics of Newsmaking.* Washington, D.C.: Heath, 1973.

Silverman, Craig. "A New Age for Truth." *Nieman Reports* 66 (Summer 2012).

Singer, Jane B. "The Journalist in the Network: A Shifting Rationale for the Gatekeeping Role and the Objectivity Norm." *Trípodos* 23 (2008): 61–76.

Sloan, W. David, and Lisa Mullikin Parcell. *American Journalism: History, Principles, Practices.* Jefferson, NC: McFarland, 2002.

Smolkin, Rachel. "Media Mood Swings." *American Journalism Review*, June 2003.

Sniderman, Paul M., Richard A. Brody, and Philip E. Tetlock. *Reasoning and Choice: Explorations in Political Psychology*. New York: Cambridge University Press, 1991.

Sparrow, Bartholomew H. *Uncertain Guardians: The News Media as a Political Institution*. Baltimore: Johns Hopkins University Press, 1999.

Starr, Paul. *The Creation of the Media*. New York: Basic Books, 2004.

Stein, Jay W. *Mass Media, Education, and a Better Society*. Chicago: Nelson-Hall, 1979.

Steiner, Robert. "In Toronto, We're Dumping the J-School Model to Produce a New Kind of Reporter." *Nieman Journalism Lab*, October 16, 2012.

Stempel, Guido H., III, and Hugh M. Cuthbertson. "The Prominence and Dominance of News Sources in Newspaper Medical Coverage." *Journalism Quarterly* 61 (1984): 671–76.

Stephens, Mitchell. "Beyond News: The Case for Wisdom Journalism." Discussion Paper D-53, Joan Shorenstein Center on the Press, Politics and Public Policy, John F. Kennedy School of Government, Harvard University, Cambridge, MA, 2009.

Stevens, John D. *Sensationalism and the New York Press*. New York: Columbia University Press, 1991.

Stimson, James A. *The Tides of Consent: How Public Opinion Shades American Politics*. New York: Cambridge University Press, 2004.

Storin, Matthew V. "While America Slept: Coverage of Terrorism from 1993 to September 11, 2001." Working Paper 2002-7, Joan Shorenstein Center on the Press, Politics and Public Policy, John F. Kennedy School of Government, Harvard University, Cambridge, MA, 2002.

Stroud, Natalie Jomini. *Niche News: The Politics of News Choice*. New York: Oxford University Press, 2011.

Sunstein, Cass R. *Going to Extremes: How Like Minds Unite and Divide*. New York: Oxford University Press, 2009.

——. *Republic.com 2.0*. Princeton, NJ: Princeton University Press, 2009.

Surowiecki, James. *The Wisdom of Crowds*. New York: Doubleday, 2004.

Taber, Charles S., and Milton Lodge. "Motivated Skepticism in the Evaluation of Political Beliefs." *Midwest Political Science Association* 50, no. 3 (July 2006): 755–69.

Taylor, Paul. *See How They Run.* New York: Knopf, 1990.

Tuchman, Gaye. "Objectivity as Strategic Ritual: An Examination of Newsmen's Notions of Objectivity." *American Journal of Sociology* 77 (1972): 660–79.

Valentino, Nicholas A., Thomas A. Buhr, and Matthew N. Beckmann. "When the Frame Is the Game." *Journalism and Mass Communication Quarterly* 78 (2001): 93–112.

Varga, Emily K., D. Jasun Carr, Jeffrey P. Nytes, and Dhavan V. Shah. "Precision vs. Realism on the Framing Continuum." *Political Communication* 27 (2010): 1–19.

Wattenberg, Martin J. *Is Voting for Young People?* New York: Pearson Longman, 2008.

Weaver, David H., Randal A. Beam, Bonnie J. Brownlee, Paul S. Voakes, and G. Cleveland Wilhoit. *The American Journalist in the 21st Century.* Mahwah, NJ: Lawrence Erlbaum, 2007.

Weaver, Paul H. "Is Television News Biased?" *Public Interest* 27 (Winter 1972): 57–74.

Weldon, Michele. *Everyman News: The Changing American Front Page.* Columbus: University of Missouri Press, 2007.

West, Darrell M. *The Rise and Fall of the Media Establishment.* Boston: Bedford/St. Martin's, 2001.

Williams, Bruce A., and Michael X. Delli Carpini. *After Broadcast News.* New York: Cambridge University Press, 2011.

Zaller, John. *The Nature and Origins of Mass Opinion.* New York: Cambridge University Press, 1992.

Zittrain, Jonathan. *The Future of the Internet—and How to Stop It.* New Haven, CT: Yale University Press, 2008.

Zuckerman, Ethan. *Rewire: Digital Cosmopolitans in the Age of Connection.* New York: W. W. Norton, 2013.

NOTES

INTRODUCTION

The Corruption of Information

1. Walter Lippmann, *Liberty and the News* (Princeton, NJ: Princeton University Press, 2008 [1920]), 6.
2. Gallup poll, February 2003.
3. Program on International Policy Attitudes (PIPA)/Knowledge Networks poll, February 2003.
4. "Misperceptions, the Media, and the Iraq War," report of the Program on International Policy Attitudes, University of Maryland, College Park, October 2, 2003, 9.
5. See, for example, Jeff Cohen, "Bush and Iraq: Mass Media, Mass Ignorance," *Common Dreams*, December 1, 2003, www.commondreams.org/views03/1201-13.htm.
6. PIPA/Knowledge Networks poll, February 2003.
7. Robert D. Johnston, *The Politics of Healing* (New York: Routledge, 2004), 136.
8. Richard Hofstadter, "The Paranoid Style in American Politics," *Harper's Magazine*, November 1964, 77.
9. See John Hudson, "How the U.S. Right Wing Convinced Egyptians Obama Is a Secret Muslim," *Atlantic Wire*, July 17, 2012, www.theatlanticwire.com/global/2012/07/how-us-right-wing-convinced-egyptians-obama-secret-muslim/54674/.
10. See Joshua Norman, "9/11 Conspiracy Theories Won't Stop," CBS News, September 11, 2011, www.cbsnews.com/8301-201_162-20104377.html.

11. *Wall Street Journal*/NBC News poll, August 2009.
12. Gallup poll, as reported in "In U.S., Global Warming Views Steady Despite Warm Weather," Gallup Politics, March 30, 2012, www.gallup.com/poll/153608/global-warming-views-steady-despite-warm-winter.aspx.
13. Jeffrey Scheuer, *The Big Picture: Why Democracies Need Journalistic Excellence* (New York: Routledge, 2008), 67–70.
14. Observation of Roderick Hart at the 2011 Breaux Symposium, Manship School of Mass Communication, Louisiana State University, Baton Rouge, March 29, 2011.
15. Walter Lippmann, *Public Opinion* (New York: Free Press, 1970 [1922]), 229.
16. Lippmann, *Liberty and the News*, 6.
17. Christopher Connell, *Journalism's Crisis of Confidence*, Carnegie Corporation of New York, 2006, 3.
18. Gallup poll, as reported in "U.S. Distrust in Media Hits New High," Gallup Politics, September, 21, 2012, www.gallup.com/poll/157589/distrust-media-hits-new-high.aspx.
19. Ibid.
20. Carol Doherty, "The Public Isn't Buying Press Credibility," *Nieman Reports*, Summer 2005, www.nieman.harvard.edu/reports/article/101115/The-Public-Isnt-Buying-Press-Credibility.aspx.
21. "Bottom-Line Pressures Now Hurting Coverage, Journalists Say," Pew Research Center's Project for Excellence in Journalism, May 23, 2004, www.people-press.org/2004/05/23/bottom-line-pressures-now-hurting-coverage-say-journalists/.
22. "The Web: Alarming, Appealing, and a Challenge to Journalistic Values," Pew Research Center for the People and the Press, March 17, 2008, www.stateofthemedia.org/files/2011/01/Journalist-report-2008.pdf; see also "News Leaders and the Future," Pew Research Center's Project for Excellence in Journalism, April 12, 2010, www.journalism.org/node/20072.
23. An example is the blogger Dave Winer. See his site at http://scripting.com/.
24. Alex S. Jones, *Losing the News* (New York: Oxford University Press, 2009), 100.
25. "Americans Spending More Time Following the News," Pew Research Center for the People and the Press, September 12, 2010, 56, http://

pewresearch.org/pubs/1725/where-people-get-news-print-online-readership-cable-news-viewers.

26. "The State of the News Media 2013: Overview," Pew Research Center's Project for Excellence in Journalism, March 18, 2013, http://stateofthemedia.org/2013/overview-5/.

27. Edwin Emery, *The Press and America: An Interpretive History of the Mass Media*, 4th ed. (Englewood Cliffs, NJ: Prentice-Hall, 1977), 350.

28. Michael Schudson, *Discovering the News* (Cambridge, MA: Harvard University Press, 1978).

29. See, for example, Yochai Benkler, *The Wealth of Networks* (New Haven, CT: Yale University Press, 2007); Dan Gillmor, *We the Media: Grassroots Journalism by the People, for the People* (Sebastopol, CA: O'Reilly Media, 2006); Elliot King, *Free for All: The Internet's Transformation of Journalism* (Evanston, IL: Northwestern University Press, 2010); Jay Rosen, *What Are Journalists For?* (New Haven, CT: Yale University Press, 2001).

ONE

The Information Problem

1. Lippmann, *Liberty and the News*, 6.
2. Lippmann, *Public Opinion*, 73.
3. Lippmann, *Liberty and the News*, 47.
4. Neil Postman, *Amusing Ourselves to Death* (New York: Penguin, 1985).
5. Gallup poll, "Americans' Concerns about Global Warming on the Rise," *Gallup Politics*, April 8, 2013, www.gallup.com/poll/161645/americans-concerns-global-warming-rise.aspx.
6. Political scientists disagree on the severity of the information problem. Some have interpreted the evidence as indicating widespread political ignorance. Others have argued that survey questions that test respondents on their factual information are a flawed indicator of the public's political awareness. It is safe to conclude, however, that policy awareness is not the public's strong suit. For opposing views on the question of how much the public knows, see Bruce Ackerman

and James Fishkin, *Deliberation Day* (New Haven, CT: Yale University Press, 2004), 5, and Doris Graber, *On Media: Making Sense of Politics* (Boulder, CO: Paradigm, 2012), 2.

7. Jane B. Singer, "The Journalist in the Network: A Shifting Rationale for the Gatekeeping Role and the Objectivity Norm," *Trípodos* 23 (2008): 63.
8. Ackerman and Fishkin, *Deliberation Day*, 5; see also Scott Keeter and Cliff Zukin, *Uninformed Choice* (New York: Praeger, 1984); Michael X. Delli Carpini and Scott Keeter, *What Americans Know about Politics and Why It Matters* (New Haven, CT: Yale University Press, 1997); Mark Bauerlein, *The Dumbest Generation* (New York: Penguin, 2008), 235.
9. See Stephen Engelberg, "Open Your Mind," *American Journalism Review*, March 1999.
10. Scott Althaus, "Free Falls, High Dives, and the Future of Democratic Accountability," in *The Politics of News/The News of Politics*, 2nd ed., ed. Doris Graber, Denis McQuail, and Pippa Norris (Washington, D.C.: Congressional Quarterly Press, 2007), 185.
11. Statement of guest on *On Being*, NPR, October 7, 2012, www.onbeing.org/program/pro-life-pro-choice-pro-dialogue/4863.
12. Todd K. Hartman and Christopher R. Weber, "Who Said What? The Effects of Source Cues in Issue Frames," *Political Behavior* 31 (2009): 537–58.
13. For reasons not fully understood, conservatives have a stronger preference for like-minded communication. According to Pew Research data, the most popular liberal talk show, *The Ed Schultz Show*, has only a sixth as many listeners as does conservative Rush Limbaugh's show.
14. Kathleen Hall Jamieson and Joseph N. Cappella, *Echo Chamber: Rush Limbaugh and the Conservative Media Establishment* (New York: Oxford University Press, 2008), 93–96.
15. Estimated from Arbitron and Nielson data.
16. Many of the more thoughtful talk shows use humor rather than bombast as the vehicle for advancing their agenda. See Jody C. Baumgartner and Jonathan S. Morris, eds., *Laughing Matters: Humor and American Politics in the Media Age* (New York: Routledge, 2012).
17. Nicholas Lemann, "The Limits of Language," in *What Orwell Didn't Know: Propaganda and the New Face of American Politics*, ed. András Szántó and Orville Schell (New York: Public Affairs, 2007), 15.

18. See Jamieson and Cappella, *Echo Chamber*, 244–47.
19. Glenn Beck, on his Internet-based GBTV show, October 9, 2011.
20. Quoted in Alison Dagnes, *Politics on Demand: The Effects of 24-Hour News on American Politics* (Westport, CT: Praeger, 2010), 111.
21. Brendan Nyhan, "The Politics of Health Care Reform," *Forum* 8 (2010): 9.
22. *Glenn Beck Show*, February 11, 2009.
23. *Countdown with Keith Olbermann*, February 15, 2010.
24. "Partisanship and Cable News Audiences," Pew Research Center for the People and the Press, October 30, 2009, http://pewresearch.org/pubs/1395/partisanship-fox-news-and-other-cable-news-audiences; Jonathan S. Morris, "Slanted Objectivity? Perceived Media Bias, Cable News Exposure, and Political Attitudes," *Social Science Quarterly* 88 (2007): 725.
25. "Americans Spending More Time Following the News," 56.
26. Ibid.
27. Cass R. Sunstein, *Going to Extremes: How Like Minds Unite and Divide* (New York: Oxford University Press, 2009); see also Matthew A. Baum, "Partisan Media and Attitude Polarization: The Case of Healthcare Reform," in *Regulatory Breakdown: The Crisis of Confidence in U.S. Regulation*, ed. Cary Coglianese (Philadelphia: University of Pennsylvania Press, 2012), 118–42; Cass R. Sunstein, *Republic.com 2.0* (Princeton, NJ: Princeton University Press, 2009).
28. Jamieson and Cappella, *Echo Chamber*, 195–98.
29. David Kline and Dan Burstein, *Blog!: How the Newest Media Revolution Is Changing Politics, Business, and Culture* (New York: CDS Books, 2005), 11.
30. Richard Davis, *Politics Online* (New York: Routledge, 2005), 43.
31. Matthew A. Baum and Tim Groeling, "New Media and the Polarization of American Political Discourse," *Political Communication* 25 (2008): 360; Natalie J. Stroud, "Media Use and Political Predispositions," *Political Behavior* 30 (2008): 341–66.
32. Matthew Hindman, *The Myth of Digital Democracy* (Princeton, NJ: Princeton University Press, 2009), 138.
33. Cited in Ken Auletta, "Non-Stop News," *New Yorker*, January 25, 2010, 38.
34. Peter Dahlgren, *Media and Political Engagement* (New York: Cambridge University Press, 2009), 165.
35. Ezra Klein, "Unpopular Mandate," *New Yorker*, June 25, 2012, 33; see

also Dean A. Ziemke, "Selective Exposure in a Presidential Campaign," in *Communication Yearbook*, ed. Dan Nimmo (New Brunswick, NJ: Transaction, 1980), 500.

36. Nyhan, "Why the 'Death Panel' Myth Wouldn't Die: Misinformation in the Health Care Reform Debate," *Forum* 8, no. 1 (2010); Charles S. Taber and Milton Lodge, "Motivated Skepticism in the Evaluation of Political Beliefs," *Midwest Political Science Association* 50, no. 3 (July 2006): 755–69; Kari Edwards and Edward E. Smith, "A Disconfirmation Bias in the Evaluation of Arguments," *Journal of Personality and Social Psychology* 71 (July 1996): 5–24.

37. Leon Festinger, Henry W. Rieckman, and Stanley Shachter, *When Prophecy Fails* (New York: Harper Torchbooks, 1964), 31.

38. Brendan Nyhan and Jason Reifler, "When Corrections Fail: The Persistence of Political Misperception," *Political Behavior* 32 (2010): 303–30.

39. Ibid., 315.

40. Statement of John Carroll while a fellow at the Joan Shorenstein Center on the Press, Politics and Public Policy, John F. Kennedy School of Government, Harvard University, 2006.

41. Edith Efron, *The News Twisters* (Los Angeles: Nash, 1971), 50.

42. See, for example, Jim A. Kuypers, *Press Bias and Politics: How the Media Frame Controversial Issues* (Westport, CT: Praeger, 2002).

43. David D'Alessio and Mike Allen, "Media Bias in Presidential Elections: A Meta-Analysis," *Journal of Communication* 50 (2000): 133–56.

44. *Media Monitor*, Center for Media and Public Affairs, various dates.

45. Thomas E. Patterson, "Bad News, Bad Governance," *Annals of the American Academy of Political and Social Science* 546, no. 1 (July 1996): 97–108.

46. Statement made by Keller during his appearance on NPR's *On Point*, September 22, 2010.

47. Jeffrey E. Cohen, *The Presidency in the Era of 24-Hour News* (Princeton, NJ: Princeton University Press, 2008), 90.

48. See, for example, Stephen J. Farnsworth and S. Robert Lichter, *The Mediated Presidency: Television News and Presidential Governance* (Lanham, MD: Rowman & Littlefield, 2005); Stephen J. Farnsworth and S. Robert Lichter, "News Coverage of New Presidents in *The New York Times*, 1981–2008," *Politics and Policy* 40 (2012): 69–91.

49. Mark Rozell, "Press Coverage of Congress," in *Congress, the Press, and the Public*, ed. Thomas E. Mann and Norman J. Ornstein (Washington, D.C.: Brookings Institution, 1994), 59–129.
50. Farnsworth and Lichter, *The Mediated Presidency*, 175–76.
51. Quoted in Peter Hamby, "Did Twitter Kill the Boys on the Bus?," draft paper, Shorenstein Center, May 2013, 67.
52. Quoted in David Shaw, "Beyond Skepticism: Have the Media Crossed the Line into Cynicism?," *Los Angeles Times*, April 17, 1996, A1.
53. See, for example, Ida Tarbell, *The History of the Standard Oil Company* (New York: Cosimo Classics, 2010 [1905]).
54. Tim Groeling and Samuel Kernell, "Is Network News Coverage of the President Biased?," *Journal of Politics* 60 (1998): 1063–87.
55. See Ruth Markus, "A Campaign Isn't Just for Gaffes," *Minneapolis Star Tribune*, August 1, 2012, A11.
56. Quoted in Thomas E. Patterson, "More Style Than Substance: Television News in U.S. National Elections," *Political Communication and Persuasion* 8 (1991): 157.
57. Quoted in Doreen Carvajal, "For News Media, Some Introspection," *New York Times*, April 5, 1998, 28.
58. Shaw, "Beyond Skepticism."
59. Lippmann, *Public Opinion*, 214.
60. Patricia Moy and Michael Pfau, *With Malice Toward All? The Media and Public Confidence in Democratic Institutions* (Westport, CT: Praeger, 2000); see also Claes H. de Vreese and Matthijs Elenbaas, "Media in the Game of Politics: Effects of Strategic Metacoverage on Political Cynicism," *International Journal of Press/Politics* 13 (2008): 286.
61. See John G. Geer, *In Defense of Negativity* (Chicago: University of Chicago Press, 2006).
62. William J. Cromie, "American Public Is Misinformed, Distrustful, New Study Finds," *Harvard Gazette*, December 5, 1996, www.news.harvard.edu/gazette/1996/12.05/AmericanPublici.html; see also Robert Blendon, "Bridging the Gap between the Public's and the Economists' Views of the Economy," *Journal of Economic Perspectives* 11 (1997): 105–18.
63. The degree to which references to policy trends was accurate, however, varied with time and issue. The "if it bleeds, it leads" phenomenon distorted what journalists said about crime, and journalists were behind the curve in the economic upswing that began in 1992.

64. *Congressional Quarterly Weekly Report*, December 31, 1994, 3620.
65. Cited in Thomas E. Patterson, *Out of Order* (New York: Knopf, 1993), 244.
66. Brian J. Fogarty, "Determining Economic News Coverage," *International Journal of Public Opinion Research* 17 (2005): 149–72.
67. See, for example, H. Brandon Haller and Helmut Norpoth, "Reality Bites: News Exposure and Economic Opinion," *Public Opinion Quarterly* 61 (1997): 555–75.
68. See, for example, Blendon, "Bridging the Gap"; Diana Mutz, "Mass Media and the Depoliticization of Personal Experiences," *American Journal of Political Science* 36 (1992): 483–508.
69. "Pessimistic Public Doubts Effectiveness of Stimulus, TARP," Pew Research Center, April 28, 2010, www.people-press.org/2010/04/28/pessimistic-public-doubts-effectiveness-of-stimulus-tarp/.
70. Clay Ramsay, Steven Kull, Evan Lewis, and Stefan Subias, "Misinformation and the 2010 Election: A Study of the U.S. Electorate," Program on International Policy Attitudes, University of Maryland, College Park, December 10, 2010, 5, http://drum.lib.umd.edu/bitstream/1903/11375/4/Misinformation_Dec10_rpt.pdf.
71. CNN poll, January 25, 2010.
72. Ramsay et al., "Misinformation and the 2010 Election," 2.
73. Tom Rosenstiel and Amy Mitchell, "The State of the News Media, 2011," Pew Research Center's Project for Excellence in Journalism, March 14, 2011, http://stateofthemedia.org/2011/overview-2/.
74. Thomas E. Patterson, "Doing Well and Doing Good," Working Paper RWP01-001, Joan Shorenstein Center on the Press, Politics and Public Policy, John F. Kennedy School of Government, Harvard University (hereafter cited as Shorenstein Center), December 2000, 3, http://shorensteincenter.org/wp-content/uploads/2012/03/soft_news_and_critical_journalism_2000.pdf.
75. Quoted in James McCartney, "News Lite," *American Journalism Review*, June 1997, 21.
76. Tom Brokaw, statement made at a Kennedy School forum, Harvard University, May 9, 1997.
77. Patterson, "Doing Well and Doing Good," 3–5. Also see Michele Weldon, *Everyman News: The Changing American Front Page* (Columbus: University of Missouri Press, 2007), 37; Weldon found in a study of twenty daily newspapers that soft news increased by a third during the 2001–2004 period.

78. Jones, *Losing the News*, 2–3.

79. Walter C. Dean and Atiba Pertilla, "I-Teams and 'Eye Candy': The Reality of Local TV News," in Tom Rosenstiel, Marion Just, Todd Belt, Atiba Pertilla, Walter Dean, and Dante Chinni, *We Interrupt This Newscast* (New York: Cambridge University Press, 2007), 31–35; see also Matthew R. Kerbel, *If It Bleeds, It Leads* (New York: Basic Books, 2000).

80. "AJR's 2009 Count of Statehouse Reporters," *American Journalism Review*, April/May 2009, http://ajr.org/article.asp?id=4722.

81. "Midwest Local TV Newscasts Devote 2.5 Times as Much Air Time to Political Ads as Election Coverage, Study Finds," press release announcing results from University of Wisconsin News-Lab study, Midwest Democracy Network, November 21, 2006, www.midwestdemocracynetwork.org/files/pdf/MNI_Nov06_Release.pdf. On the other hand, local newspapers continue to provide election coverage—see, for example, R. Douglas Arnold, *Congress, the Press, and Political Accountability* (Princeton, NJ: Princeton University Press, 2004).

82. Center for Media and Public Affairs data, 1998.

83. Edwin Emery, *The Press and America*, 2nd ed. (Englewood Cliffs, NJ: Prentice-Hall, 1962), 215.

84. Michael J. Robinson, "Two Decades of American News Preferences, Part 2: News Interest across Decades and 'News Eras,'" Pew Research Center for the People and the Press, August 22, 2007, 11, www.pewresearch.org/files/old-assets/pdf/NewsInterest1986-2007Part2.pdf; "Anna Nicole Smith, Anatomy of a Feeding Frenzy," Pew Research Center's Project for Excellence in Journalism, April 4, 2007, 8, www.journalism.org/node/4872.

85. E-Poll, 2010, http://blog.epollresearch.com/tag/lindsay-lohan/.

86. Douglas Mataconis, "Casey Anthony Trial Got More News Coverage Than GOP Candidates," *Outside the Beltway*, July 6, 2011, www.outsidethebeltway.com/casey-anthony-trial-got-more-news-coverage-than-gop-candidates/.

87. "Casey Anthony Murder Trial Garners Extensive Media Coverage," *Los Angeles Times*, July 6, 2011, http://articles.latimes.com/2011/jul/06/entertainment/la-et-casey-anthony-trial-sidebar-20110706.

88. "1993—The Year in Review," *Media Monitor* 8, no. 11 (January/February 1994).

89. Studies have shown that crime news has a particularly dramatic effect

on people's perceptions. See, for example, Daniel Romer, Kathleen Hall Jamieson, and Sean Aday, "Television News and the Cultivation of Fear of Crime," *Journal of Communication* 53 (2003): 88–104; Roger D. Klein, "Audience Reaction to Local TV News," *American Behavioral Scientist* 46 (2003): 1661–72.

90. Sentencing Project data, 2001, and UK Home Office data, 2001.
91. Justice Department statistics, 1992–1994.
92. According to Justice Department statistics, the rate of violent crime was 747 per 100,000 inhabitants in 1993 and 714 per 100,000 inhabitants in 1994.
93. Sentence modeled after a sentence by Lippmann, *Public Opinion*, 7.
94. George Zipf, *Human Behavior and the Principle of Least Effort* (Boston: Addison-Wesley, 1949).
95. Samuel Popkin, *The Reasoning Voter: Communication and Persuasion in Presidential Campaigns* (Chicago: University of Chicago Press, 1991). See also Paul M. Sniderman, Richard A. Brody, and Philip E. Tetlock, *Reasoning and Choice: Explorations in Political Psychology* (New York: Cambridge University Press, 1991); Arthur Lupia, "Shortcuts versus Encyclopedias: Information and Voting Behavior in California Insurance Reform Elections," *American Political Science Review* 88 (1994): 63–76.
96. James H. Kuklinski, Paul J. Quirk, Jennifer Jerit, David Schweider, and Robert F. Rich, "Misinformation and the Currency of Democratic Citizenship," *Journal of Politics* 62 (2000): 790–816; Richard R. Lau and David Redlawsk, "Advantages and Disadvantages of Cognitive Heuristics in Political Decision Making," *American Journal of Political Science* 45 (2001): 951–71; David Redlawsk, "Hot Cognition or Cool Consideration? Testing the Effects of Motivated Reasoning on Political Decision Making," *Journal of Politics* 64 (2002): 1021–44.
97. Quoted in Kathleen Hall Jamieson and Paul Waldman, *The Press Effect: Politicians, Journalists, and the Stories That Shape the Political World* (New York: Oxford University Press, 2003), 167.
98. See John D. Stevens, *Sensationalism and the New York Press* (New York: Columbia University Press, 1991).
99. Quoted in Stephen Bates, "Realigning Journalism with Democracy: The Hutchins Commission, Its Times, and Ours," Annenberg Washington Program, Northwestern University, Washington, D.C., 1995, 30.

100. Walter Pincus, "Newspaper Narcissism," *Columbia Journalism Review*, May/June 2009, www.cjr.org/essay/newspaper_narcissism_1.php.

101. Michael Schudson, "What Time Means in a News Story," Occasional Paper No. 4, Gannett Center for Media Studies, Columbia University, New York, 1986, 1.

102. *Good Morning America* broadcast, July 20, 2012.

103. Example from Steve Salerno, "Journalist-Bites-Reality!," eSkeptic, February 12, 2008, www.skeptic.com/eskeptic/08-02-13/.

104. See headlines at ibid.

105. "BSE Cases in North America, by Year and Country of Death, 1993–2008," Centers for Disease Control and Prevention, 2008, www.cdc.gov/ncidod/dvrd/bse/images/bse_cases_namerica_2008.gif. No cases have been reported since the 2008 study. All three of the BSE victims had spent considerable time abroad, and the CDC believes they contracted the disease outside the United States.

106. Salerno, "Journalist-Bites-Reality!"

107. Based on author's conservation with former CNN News president Rick Kaplan, July 19, 2001.

108. Thomas Patterson, *The Vanishing Voter* (New York: Knopf, 2002), 92.

109. Cited in Frank Rich, "The End of the Beginning," *New York Times*, September 29, 2001, A23. The reference to Tenet's testimony appeared first in a *Washington Post* column by Geneva Overholser.

110. James Risen, "C.I.A. Chief Sees Russia Reviving Its Challenge to U.S.," *New York Times*, February 8, 2011, A11.

111. Patterson, *The Vanishing Voter*, 92.

112. Rich, "The End of the Beginning."

113. Quoted in Bates, "Realigning Journalism with Democracy," 11.

114. Salerno, "Journalist-Bites-Reality!"; John H. McManus, *Market-Driven Journalism* (Thousand Oaks, CA: Sage, 1994), 162–63; Eric Jensen, "Scientific Sensationalism in American and British Press Coverage of Therapeutic Cloning," *Journalism and Mass Communication Quarterly* 89 (2012): 40–51; Richard Davis, *The Press and American Politics* (Upper Saddle River, NJ: Prentice-Hall, 2000), 24–27.

115. Doris Graber, *Mass Media and American Politics* (Washington, D.C.: CQ Press, 1980), 68. The study Graber was referring to is Robert W. Clyde and James K. Buckalew, "Inter-Media Standardization: A

Q-Analysis of News Editors," *Journalism Quarterly* 46 (Summer 1969): 349–51.

116. Richard M. Perloff, *Political Communication: Politics, Press, and Public in American Politics* (Mahwah, NJ: Lawrence Erlbaum, 1998), 80.

117. "Campaign 2000 Final: How TV News Covered the General Election Campaign," *Media Monitor* 14, no. 6 (November/December 2000): 2.

118. Murray Edelman, *Constructing the Political Spectacle* (Chicago: University of Chicago Press, 1988), 32.

119. Meg Greenfield, "Chronic Political Amnesia," *Newsweek*, September 22, 1980, 96.

120. This sentence plays off analyst Paul Virilio's observation that "there is no politics possible at the speed of light." Cited in Thomas Keenen, "Live Feed: War, Humanitarianism, and Real-Time Television," unpublished fellowship proposal, Department of English, Princeton University, Princeton, NJ, 1997. A classic study of news attention is G. Ray Funkhouser, "The Issues of the Sixties: An Exploratory Study of the Dynamics of Public Opinion," *Public Opinion Quarterly* 37 (1973): 62–75.

121. Quoted in Jones, *Losing the News*, 196.

122. James Fallows, "Did You Have a Good Week?," *Atlantic Monthly*, December 1994, 32–33.

123. Quoted in Auletta, "Non-Stop News," 42.

124. Quoted in Charles Sam Courtney, *Ignorant Armies* (Bloomington, IN: Trafford, 2007), 86; see also Dylan Byers, "The News Cycle Is Dead," *Politico*, September 3, 2012, www.politico.com/blogs/media/2012/09/the-news-cycle-is-dead-134216.html.

125. Adam Moss, remark made at the twenty-fifth anniversary seminar of the Shorenstein Center, October 14, 2011.

126. Philip Meyer, *The Vanishing Newspaper* (Columbia: University of Missouri Press, 2004), 84–86.

127. A 2011 *Washington Post* survey, for example, found that more than a fourth of Americans continued to believe, two years after the disinformation entered the news stream, that the health care reform act contained a "death panels" provision.

128. See, for example, Colleen Seifert, "The Continued Influence of Misinformation on Memory: What Makes a Correction Effective?," *Psychology of Learning and Motivation* 41 (2002): 265–92; Ullrich K. H. Ecker, Stephan Lewandowsky, and Joe Apai, "Terrorists Brought Down the

Plane!—No, Actually It Was a Technical Fault: Processing Corrections of Emotive Information," *Quarterly Journal of Experimental Psychology* 64 (2011): 283–310.

129. See, for example, Carl Hulse and Kate Zernike, "Bloodshed Puts New Focus on Vitriol Politics," *New York Times*, January 8, 2011; Jeff Zeleny and Jim Rutenberg, "In the Shock of the Moment, the Politicking Stops . . . Until It Doesn't," *New York Times*, January 9, 2011.

130. CNN survey, January 17, 2011.

131. Nick Baumann, "Exclusive: Loughner Friend Explains Alleged Gunman's Grudge Against Giffords," *Mother Jones*, January 10, 2011; see also Public Policy Polling, January 18, 2011.

132. Quoted in "Communication as a Fermenting Agent: A Keynote View," *SDC Magazine*, May 1967, 4, cited in Jay W. Stein, *Mass Media, Education, and a Better Society* (Chicago: Nelson-Hall, 1979), 40.

133. Albert Camus, "Rules of Engagement," *Harper's Magazine*, July 2011, 16. Originally written in 1939, the article was censored by French authorities and went unpublished until discovered in an archive.

134. Public statement of Stanley Baldwin, March 17, 1931, quoted in Colin Seymour-Ure, *The Political Impact of Mass Media* (Beverly Hills, CA: Sage, 1974), 156.

135. Jamieson and Waldman, *The Press Effect*, 12.

136. "A Statement of Shared Principles," Committee of Concerned Journalists, Washington, D.C., www.concernedjournalists.org/node/380.

137. Quoted in Jackie Ogburn, "Good Persons, Good Workers, Good Citizens," *Insights*, Sanford School of Public Policy, Duke University, Durham, NC, April 2011, 20.

138. Howard Gardner, Mihaly Csikszentmihalyi, and William Damon, *Good Work: Where Excellence and Ethics Meet* (New York: Basic Books, 2001), 33.

139. "News Leaders and the Future," Pew Research Center's Project for Excellence in Journalism, April 12, 2010, www.journalism.org/node/20072.

140. "Statement of Concern," Committee of Concerned Journalists, 1999.

TWO

The Source Problem

1. Lippmann, *Liberty and the News*, 58.
2. This sentence's construction follows that of a sentence by Lippmann, *Public Opinion*, 228: "If the press is not so universally wicked, nor so deeply conspiring, as Mr. Sinclair would have us believe, it is very much more frail than the democratic theory has as yet admitted."
3. Leon Sigal, *Reporters and Officials: The Organization and Politics of News-making* (Washington, D.C.: Heath, 1973), 69.
4. Michael Schudson, *Why Democracies Need an Unlovable Press* (Boston: Polity, 2008), 52.
5. See, for example, Herbert J. Gans, *Deciding What's News* (New York: Pantheon, 1979); Dominic L. Lasorsa and Stephen D. Reese, "News Source Use in the Crash of 1987: A Study of Four National Media," *Journalism Quarterly* 67 (1990): 60–71.
6. See Edward Alwood, *Dark Days in the Newsroom* (Philadelphia: Temple University Press, 2007); Richard M. Fried, *Nightmare in Red: The McCarthy Era in Perspective* (New York: Oxford University Press, 1991).
7. Ben Bradlee, *A Good Life: Newspapering and Other Adventures* (New York: Simon & Schuster, 1995), 352.
8. Schudson, "What Time Means in a News Story."
9. Quoted in Shaw, "Beyond Skepticism."
10. Marvin Kalb, "The Rise of the 'New News,'" Discussion Paper D-34, Shorenstein Center, October 1998, 13, www.hks.harvard.edu/presspol/publications/papers/discussion_papers/d34_kalb.pdf.
11. See, for example, Max Kampelman, "The Power of the Press," *Policy Review*, Fall 1978, 7–41; Irving Kristol, "Crisis Over Journalism," in *Press, Politics, and Popular Government*, ed. George Will (Washington, D.C.: American Enterprise Institute, 1972), 50; Michael Robinson and Margaret Sheehan, *Over the Wire and on TV* (New York: Sage, 1983), 2.
12. Gaye Tuchman, "Objectivity as Strategic Ritual: An Examination of Newsmen's Notions of Objectivity," *American Journal of Sociology* 77 (1972): 665.
13. Timothy Crouse, *The Boys on the Bus* (New York: Ballantine, 1974), 323.

14. Quoted in Barbara Gamarekian, "In Pursuit of the Clever Quotemaster," *New York Times*, May 12, 1989, Y10.
15. "He said, she said" journalism was not a totally new technique. It had been devised in the early 1900s but was used sparingly until attack journalism came into vogue in the 1970s. See Kristi Andersen and Stuart J. Thorson, "Public Discourse or Strategic Game? Changes in Our Conception of Elections," *Studies in American Political Development* 3 (1989): 271–73.
16. Paul H. Weaver, "Is Television News Biased?," *Public Interest* 27 (Winter 1972): 69.
17. Quoted in Robinson and Sheehan, *Over the Wire and on TV*, 226.
18. Patterson, *Out of Order*, 82.
19. Carl Leubsdorf, "The Reporter and the Presidential Candidate," *Annals of the American Academy of Political and Social Science* 427, no. 1 (1976): 6.
20. Weaver, "Is Television News Biased?," 69.
21. "They're No Friends of Bill," *Media Monitor*, July/August 1994, 2; see also Daniel R. Hallin, "Sound Bite News," *Journal of Communication* 42 (1992): 10; Kiku Adatto, "Sound Bite Democracy: Network Evening News Presidential Campaign Coverage, 1968 and 1988," Research Paper R-2, Shorenstein Center, 1990, 4.
22. Patterson, *Out of Order*, 75.
23. Kathleen Hall Jamieson, *Dirty Politics* (New York: Oxford University Press, 1992), 184–85; see also Jane Blankenship and Jong Guen Kang, "The 1984 Presidential and Vice-Presidential Debates: The Printed Press and 'Construction' by Metaphor," *Presidential Studies Quarterly* 23 (1991): 307–18.
24. Larry J. Sabato, *Feeding Frenzy: How Attack Journalism Has Transformed American Politics* (New York: Free Press, 1991), 1.
25. Joseph Cappella and Kathleen Hall Jamieson, "News Frames, Political Cynicism, and Media Cynicism," *Annals of the American Academy of Political and Social Science* 546 (1996): 79.
26. Jonathan S. Morris and Rosalee A. Clawson, "Media Coverage of Congress in the 1990s: Scandal, Personalities, and the Prevalence of Policy and Process," *Political Communication* 22 (2005): 297–313
27. Kathleen Hall Jamieson and Karlyn Kohrs Campbell, *The Interplay of Influence*, 5th ed. (Belmont, CA: Wadsworth, 2001), 42.
28. "The Campaign and the Press at Halftime," report of the Times Mir-

ror Center for the People and the Press, supplement to *Columbia Journalism Review*, July/August 1992, 4.

29. Thomas E. Mann and Norman J. Ornstein, eds., *Congress, the Press, and the Public* (Washington, D.C.: American Enterprise Institute and Brookings Institution, 1994): 59–129.

30. David Broder, "War on Cynicism," *Washington Post*, July 6, 1994, A19.

31. Maureen Dowd, "Raffish and Rowdy," *New York Times*, March 31, 1996, E15.

32. Quoted in Andrew Noyes, "FBI Director Lightens Up at Press Club," *National Journal*, May 16, 2008.

33. Comment of John Zaller to the author, December 4, 2004.

34. Jorgen Westerstahl and Folke Johansson, "News Ideologies as Moulders of Domestic News," *European Journal of Communication* 1 (1986): 126–43.

35. Tim Groeling and Matthew A. Baum, "Journalists' Incentives and Media Coverage of Elite Foreign Policy Evaluations," *Conflict Management and Peace Science* 26 (2009): 437–70.

36. "Campaign '96: The Media and the Candidates," final report to the Markle Foundation, Center for Media and Public Affairs, 1998. See also Erik P. Bucy and Maria Elizabeth Grabe, "Taking Television Seriously: A Sound and Image Bite Analysis of Presidential Campaign Coverage, 1992–2004," *Journal of Communication* 57 (2007): 652–75; Bruce Buchanan, *Renewing Presidential Politics* (Lanham, MD: Rowman & Littlefield, 1996), 149; Larry Bartels, *Presidential Primaries and the Dynamics of Public Choice* (Princeton, NJ: Princeton University Press, 1988), 32.

37. Matthew A. Baum and Tim Groeling, "Shot by the Messenger," *Political Behavior* 31 (2009): 157–86.

38. Tim Groeling, *When Politicians Attack* (New York: Cambridge University Press, 2010), 9.

39. Auletta, "Non-Stop News," 46.

40. Chris Mooney and Matthew C. Nisbet, "Undoing Darwin," *Columbia Journalism Review*, September/October 2005, 2.

41. Matthew C. Nisbet, Dominique Brossard, and Adrianne Kroepsch, "Framing Science: The Stem Cell Controversy in the Age of Press/Politics," *Harvard International Journal of Press/Politics* 8 (2003): 36–70.

42. See Jonathan Morris, "Car Crashes and Soap Operas: Melodramatic

Narrative on Cable News," in *Americana: Readings in American Popular Culture*, ed. Leslie Wilson (Hollywood, CA: Press Americana, 2006), 102.

43. Example from Natalie Jomini Stroud, *Niche News: The Politics of News Choice* (New York: Oxford University Press, 2011), 3–5.
44. Ibid.
45. "Campaign 2004: The Summer," *Media Monitor* 18, no. 5 (September/October 2004): 3.
46. W. Lance Bennett, "Toward a Theory of Press-State Relations in the U.S.," *Journal of Communication* 40 (1990): 103–25.
47. W. Lance Bennett, "Press-Government Relations in a Changing Media Environment," in *Oxford Handbook of Political Communication*, ed. Kathleen Hall Jamieson and Kate Kenski (New York: Oxford University Press, forthcoming).
48. Jamieson and Waldman, *The Press Effect*, chapter 7.
49. Quoted in Dagnes, *Politics on Demand*, 15.
50. Example from Brendan Nyhan blog, "Bush vs. His Economists, IV," October 10, 2006, www.brendannyhan.com/blog/2006/10/bush_vs_his_eco.html.
51. Kovach and Rosenstiel, *The Elements of Journalism* (2001), 94.
52. See William A. Gamson and Andre Modigliani, "Media Discourse and Public Opinion on Nuclear Power," *American Journal of Sociology* 95 (1989): 1–37.
53. Jack Fuller, *What Is Happening to News: The Information Explosion and the Crisis in Journalism* (Chicago: University of Chicago Press, 2010), 139.
54. Theodore J. Glasser, "Objectivity Precludes Responsibility," *Quill*, February 1984, www.columbia.edu/itc/journalism/j6075/edit/readings/glasser.html.
55. Tuchman, "Objectivity as a Strategic Ritual," 676; Bartholomew H. Sparrow, *Uncertain Guardians: The News Media as a Political Institution* (Baltimore: Johns Hopkins University Press, 1999), 26.
56. Jay Rosen, PressThink blog, April 19, 2009. See also W. Lance Bennett, Regina G. Lawrence, and Steven Livingston, *When the Press Fails: Political Power and the News Media from Iraq to Katrina* (Chicago: University of Chicago Press, 2007), 54–55.
57. Dana Milbank, "For Bush, Facts Are Malleable," *Washington Post*, October 22, 2002, A1.

58. John Zaller, *The Nature and Origins of Mass Opinion* (New York: Cambridge University Press, 1992), 315.
59. Danny Hayes and Matt Guardino, "Whose Views Made the News? Media Coverage and the March to War in Iraq," *Political Communication* 27 (2010): 59–87, cited in James Curran, *Media and Democracy* (London: Routledge, 2011), 25.
60. "The *Times* and Iraq," editors' note, *New York Times*, May 26, 2004.
61. Quoted in Howard Kurtz, "The *Post* on WMDs: An Inside Story," *Washington Post*, August 12, 2004, A1.
62. Quoted by Carol Matlack, "Crossing the Line," *National Journal* 21 (March 25, 1989): 727.
63. Quoted in Shaw, "Beyond Skepticism."
64. Campaign adviser Joseph Napolitan, quoted in Robert McNeil, *The People Machine* (New York: Harper and Row, 1968), 139.
65. Quoted in Steven E. Schier, *By Invitation Only: The Rise of Exclusive Politics in the United States* (Pittsburgh: University of Pittsburgh Press, 2000), 5.
66. See, for example, Philip N. Howard, *New Media Campaigns and the Managed Citizen* (New York: Cambridge University Press, 2006); Pippa Norris, John Curtice, David Sanders, Margaret Scammell, and Holli A. Semetko, *On Message: Communicating the Campaign* (Thousand Oaks, CA: Sage, 1999); Hugh Heclo, "Campaigning and Governing: A Conspectus," in *The Permanent Campaign and Its Future*, ed. Norman J. Ornstein and Thomas E. Mann (Washington, D.C.: American Enterprise Institute and Brookings Institution, 2000), 3; Michael Janeway, *Republic of Denial: Press, Politics, and Public Life* (New Haven, CT: Yale University Press, 1999), 163; Jarol Manheim, *All of the People, All the Time: Strategic Communication and American Politics* (Armonk, NY: M.E. Sharpe, 1991).
67. Edward L. Bernays, *Propaganda* (New York: Horace Liveright, 1928), 27.
68. See Lawrence R. Jacobs and Robert Y. Shapiro, *Politicians Don't Pander* (Chicago: University of Chicago Press, 2000).
69. Joshua Green, "Meet Mr. Death," *American Prospect*, December 19, 2001, http://prospect.org/article/meet-mr-death.
70. Jamieson, *Dirty Politics*, 215.
71. Thomas E. Mann and Norman J. Ornstein, *The Broken Branch: How Congress Is Failing America and How to Get It Back on Track* (New York: Oxford University Press, 2008), vii; see also Thomas E. Mann and

Norman J. Ornstein, *It's Even Worse Than It Looks: How the American Constitutional System Collided with the New Politics of Extremism* (New York: Basic Books, 2012).

72. See, for example, Patrick Sellers, *Cycles of Spin: Strategic Communication in the U.S. Congress* (New York: Cambridge University Press, 2010).

73. Baum, "Partisan Media and Attitude Polarization." Baum also found that compared with other Republicans, those who relied upon Fox for their news were much more likely to oppose the bill on grounds that it exemplified big government.

74. Neal Desai, Andre Pineda, Majken Runquist, and Mark Fusunyan, "Torture at Time: Waterboarding in the Media," student paper, Shorenstein Center, April 2010, http://dash.harvard.edu/bitstream/handle/1/4420886/torture_at_times_hks_students.pdf?sequence=1.

75. Rob Dietz, "Timeline of a Smear," Media Matters, January 30, 2007, http://mediamatters.org/research/2007/01/30/timeline-of-a-smear/137882.

76. Paul McLeary, "Insightmag: A Must-Read," *Columbia Journalism Review*, January 29, 2007, quoted in Dagnes, *Politics on Demand*, 110.

77. See, for example, Harvey Molotch and Marilyn Lester, "Accidental News: The Great Oil Spill as Local Occurrence and National Event," *American Journal of Sociology* 81, no. 2 (1975): 235–58.

78. Lippmann, *Public Opinion*, 158.

79. Aristotle, *The Rhetoric* (Princeton, NJ: Princeton University Press, 1984), 32–33.

80. Quoted in Klein, "Unpopular Mandate," 31.

81. Patterson, *Out of Order*, 9–10, 158.

82. Francis X. Clines, "Reagan Ridicules Mondale 'Realism,'" *New York Times*, July 26, 1984, www.nytimes.com/1984/07/26/us/reagan-ridicules-mondale-realism.html.

83. Steven R. Weisman, "Presidential Aide Scoffs at Mondale Tax Pledge," *New York Times*, July 31, 1984, www.nytimes.com/1984/07/31/us/presidential-aide-scoffs-at-mondale-tax-pledge.html.

84. See Mann and Ornstein, *It's Even Worse Than It Looks*; Ronald Brownstein, *The Second Civil War: How Extreme Partisanship Has Paralyzed Washington and Polarized America* (New York: Penguin, 2008).

85. W. Lance Bennett, "Press-Government Relations in a Changing Media Environment," in *Oxford Handbook of Political Communication*.

86. Frances E. Lee, *Beyond Ideology: Politics, Principles, and Partisanship in the U.S. Senate* (Chicago: University of Chicago Press, 2009).
87. Juliet Eilperin, *Fight Club Politics* (Lanham, MD: Rowman & Littlefield, 2007).
88. Jay Rosen, "Why Political Coverage Is Broken," PressThink blog, August 26, 2011, http://pressthink.org/2011/08/why-political-coverage-is-broken/.
89. Scott McClellan, *What Happened: Inside the Bush White House and Washington's Culture of Deception* (New York: Public Affairs, 2008), 312.
90. Chris Wells, Justin Reedy, John Gastil, and Carolyn Lee, "Information Distortion and Voting Choices: The Origins and Effects of Factual Beliefs in Initiative Elections," *Political Psychology* 30 (2009): 953–69.
91. Quoted in Jamieson and Waldman, *The Press Effect*, 189.
92. Stephen Ansolabehere, Roy Behr, and Shanto Iyengar, *The Media Game: American Politics in the Television Age* (New York: Macmillan, 1993), 236.
93. Taber and Lodge, "Motivated Skepticism in the Evaluation of Political Beliefs"; Edwards and Smith, "A Disconfirmation Bias in the Evaluation of Arguments."
94. W. Lance Bennett, "Press-Government Relations in a Changing Media Environment," in *Oxford Handbook of Political Communication*.
95. Murray Edelman, *Politics as Symbolic Action* (Chicago: Markham, 1971), 69.
96. Jennifer Jerit and Jason Barabas, "Bankrupt Rhetoric: How Misleading Information Affects Knowledge about Social Security," *Public Opinion Quarterly* 70 (2006): 278–303.
97. Ramsay et al., "Misinformation and the 2010 Election," 14.
98. Example from Klein, "Unpopular Mandate," 31.
99. See "Public Attitudes Toward the War in Iraq: 2003–2008," Pew Research Center for the People and the Press, March 19, 2008, http://pewresearch.org/pubs/770/iraq-war-five-year-anniversary.
100. Wells et al., "Information Distortion and Voting Choices."
101. Eric Pooley, "How Much Would You Pay to Save the Planet?," Discussion Paper D-49, Shorenstein Center, January 2009, www.hks.harvard.edu/presspol/publications/papers/discussion_papers/d49_pooley.pdf.
102. Maxwell T. Boykoff and Jules M. Boykoff, "Balance as Bias: Global

Warming and the U.S. Prestige Press," *Global Environmental Change* 14 (2004): 126.

103. Frederick W. Mayer, "Stories of Climate Change: Competing Narratives, the Media, and U.S. Public Opinion 2001–2010," Discussion Paper D-72, Shorenstein Center, February 2012, 8, www.hks.harvard.edu/presspol/publications/papers/discussion_papers/d72_mayer.pdf.

104. Ibid., 11.

105. Lauren Feldman, Edward W. Maibach, Connie Roser-Renouf, and Anthony Leiserowitz, "Climate on Cable: The Nature and Impact of Global Warming Coverage on Fox News, CNN, and MSNBC," *International Journal of Press/Politics* 20 (2011): 9.

106. Mayer, "Stories of Climate Change," 12; see also Feldman et al., "Climate on Cable," 9.

107. Mayer, "Stories of Climate Change," 33.

108. Maxwell T. Boykoff, *Who Speaks for the Climate? Making Sense of Media Reporting on Climate Change* (New York: Cambridge University Press, 2011), 133.

109. Pooley, "How Much Would You Pay to Save the Planet?," 4–5.

110. Ibid., 2.

111. Thomas E. Patterson, *The Mass Media Election: How Americans Choose Their President* (New York: Praeger, 1980), 156–59.

112. Ramsay et al., "Misinformation and the 2010 Election," 20–23.

113. Ibid., 13.

114. Fuller, *What Is Happening to News*, 139–41.

115. Pooley, "How Much Would You Pay to Save the Planet?," 5.

116. Bill Kovach and Tom Rosenstiel, *The Elements of Journalism*, rev. ed. (New York: Three Rivers Press, 2007), 83–84.

117. Sidney Blumenthal, "Afterword," in Lippmann, *Liberty and the News*, 80–81.

118. Quoted in Linda Greenhouse, "Challenging 'He Said, She Said' Journalism," *Nieman Reports* 66 (Summer 2012): 22.

119. W. Lance Bennett, "Press-Government Relations in a Changing Media Environment," in *Oxford Handbook of Political Communication*.

120. Fallows uses the term to headline his blog in the *Atlantic*.

121. Quoted in Jay Rosen, PressThink blog, April 12, 2009, http://archive.pressthink.org/2009/04/12/hesaid_shesaid.html.

122. Ibid.

123. Ibid.

124. James H. Kuklinski, Paul J. Quirk, David Schweider, and Robert F. Rich, "'Just the Facts, Ma'am': Political Facts and Public Opinion," *Annals of the American Academy of Political and Social Science* 560 (1998): 148.
125. Patterson, *Out of Order*, 8.
126. "Biography of Nikita Khrushchev," National Cold War Exhibition, www.nationalcoldwarexhibition.org/explore/biography.cfm?name =Khrushchev,%20Nikita.
127. Doris Graber, *Processing the News: How People Tame the Information Tide*, 2nd ed. (New York: Longman, 1988), 141.
128. Scott Lehigh, "Fact Checks for the Fall Campaign," *Boston Globe*, August 15, 2012, A13.
129. Public Policy Polling survey, conducted for Daily Kos/SEIU, July 26–29, 2012.
130. Andrew Malcolm, "Poll Finds Americans Are Disgusted with Political Media," Investors.com (*Investors' Business Daily*), August 9, 2012, http://news.investors.com/politics-andrew-malcolm/080912 -621566-daily-kos-poll-finds-americans-think-very-little-of -media-covering-politics.htm?p=full.
131. Broder, "War on Cynicism."
132. Mark Levy, "Disdaining the News," *Journal of Communication* 3 (1981): 24–31; see also Jay G. Blumler and Michael Gurevitch, *The Crisis of Public Communication* (London: Routledge, 1995), 203.
133. See, for example, Michael J. Robinson, "Public Affairs Television and the Growth of Political Malaise: The Case of 'The Selling of the Pentagon,'" *American Political Science Review* 70, no. 3 (1976): 409–32; Joseph N. Cappella and Kathleen Hall Jamieson, *Spiral of Cynicism: The Press and the Public Good* (New York: Oxford University Press, 1997); Arthur H. Miller, Edie N. Goldenberg, and Lutz Erbring, "Type-Set Politics: Impact of Newspapers on Public Confidence," *American Political Science Review* 73 (1979): 67–84; Matthew R. Kerbel, *Remote and Controlled: Media Politics in a Cynical Age*, 2nd ed. (Boulder, CO: Westview, 1999), 85; Adatto, "Sound Bite Democracy," 74; de Vreese and Elenbaas, "Media in the Game of Politics," 286.
134. Jamieson and Waldman, *The Press Effect*, 197.
135. John Zaller, "A New Standard of News Quality: Burglar Alarms for the Monitorial Citizen," *Political Communication* 20 (2003): 128.
136. Lippmann, *Liberty and the News*, 59.

137. *Federalist* No. 78.

138. Kathleen Hall Jamieson and Bruce W. Hardy, "Unmasking Deception: The Function and Failures of the Press," in *The Politics of News*, 2nd ed., ed. Doris A. Graber, Denis McQuail, and Pippa Norris (Washington, D.C.: CQ Press, 2008), 117–38.

139. Dan Pfieffer, quoted in Auletta, "Non-Stop News," 46.

140. John H. McManus, "Objectivity: It's Time to Say Goodbye," *Nieman Reports*, Summer 2009, 79, www.nieman.harvard.edu/reports/article/101564/Objectivity-Its-Time-to-Say-Goodbye.aspx.

141. Jonathan M. Ladd, *Why Americans Hate the Media and How It Matters* (Princeton, NJ: Princeton University Press, 2012), 199.

142. Dylan Byers, "The John King–Newt Gingrich Debate," *Politico*, January 20, 2012, www.politico.com/blogs/media/2012/01/the-john-king newt-gingrich-exchange-111596.html.

143. Nyhan and Reifler, "When Corrections Fail," 319, 324.

144. Dennis Chong and James N. Druckman, "Framing Public Opinion in Competitive Democracies," *American Political Science Review* 101 (2007): 641.

145. See, for example, Albert C. Gunther and Janice L. Liebhart, "Broad Reach or Biased Source? Decomposing the Hostile Media Effect," *Journal of Communication* 56 (2006): 449–66.

146. Janeway, *Republic of Denial*, 166.

147. Jamieson and Waldman, *The Press Effect*, 30.

148. Ladd, *Why Americans Hate the Media and How It Matters*, 126.

149. Ibid., 1.

150. David Broder, "A Lonely Warning on Debt," *Washington Post*, May 4, 2006, B7.

151. Quoted in Jeffrey Katz, "Tilt?," *Washington Journalism Review*, January/February 1993, 25.

152. See, for example, Hyunjin Kang, Keunmin Bae, Shaoke Zhang, and S. Shyam Sundar, "Source Cues in Online News: Is the Proximate Source More Powerful than Distal Sources?," *Journalism and Mass Communication Quarterly* [illegible] ([illegible]): [illegible]; Bruce E. Pinkleton, Erica Weintraub Austin, Yushu Zhou, Jessica Fitts Willoughby, and Megan Reiser, "Perceptions of News Media, External Efficacy, and Public Affairs Apathy in Political Decision Making and Disaffection," *Journalism and Mass Communication Quarterly* 89 (2012): 23–39.

153. "Who Do You Trust for War News?," Pew Research Center for the People and the Press, April 5, 2007, http://pewresearch.org/pubs/445/who-do-you-trust-for-war-news.
154. Brian J. Fogarty and Jennifer Wolak, "The Effects of Media Interpretation for Citizen Evaluations of Politicians' Messages," *American Politics Research* 37 (2009): 141.
155. Ladd, *Why Americans Hate the Media and How It Matters*, 159.
156. See Edwin R. Bailey, *Joe McCarthy and the Press* (New York: Pantheon, 1981).
157. W. Lance Bennett, "Press-Government Relations in a Changing Media Environment," in *Oxford Handbook of Political Communication*.
158. E. J. Dionne, *They Only Look Dead* (New York: Simon & Schuster, 1996), 246.

THREE

The Knowledge Problem

1. Lippmann, *Public Opinion*, 226.
2. Greenhouse, "Challenging 'He Said, She Said' Journalism," 24.
3. Kovach and Rosenstiel, *The Elements of Journalism* (2001), 2–4.
4. "A Statement of Shared Principles," Committee of Concerned Journalists.
5. Kovach and Rosenstiel, *The Elements of Journalism* (2007), 41.
6. Ibid., 44–45.
7. Quoted in ibid., 43.
8. S. Robert Lichter and Ted J. Smith, "Bad News Bears," *Forbes Media Critic* 1 (1994): 81–87.
9. Westerstahl and Johansson, "News Ideologies as Moulders of Domestic News."
10. Curran, *Media and Democracy*, 97–110; see also Patterson, *Out of Order*, 176–79.
11. See, for example, Thomas E. Patterson and Robert D. McClure, *The Unseeing Eye* (New York: Putnam, 1976).
12. Travis N. Ridout and Rob Mellon, Jr., "Does the Media Agenda Reflect the Candidates' Agenda?," *Harvard International Journal of Press/Politics* 12 (2007): 58.

13. Kovach and Rosenstiel, *The Elements of Journalism* (2001), 5.
14. Fuller, *What Is Happening to News*, 139.
15. Rachel Smolkin, "Media Mood Swings," *American Journalism Review*, June 2003, www.ajr.org/Article.asp?id=3040.
16. Scott R. Maier, "Accuracy Matters: A Cross-Market Assessment of Newspaper Error and Credibility," *Journalism and Mass Communication Quarterly* 82 (2005): 546.
17. David Broder, *Beyond the Front Page* (New York: Simon & Schuster, 1987), 19, quoted in Jamieson and Waldman, *The Press Effect*, 195.
18. Lippmann, *Public Opinion*, 216.
19. This paragraph is modeled upon a paragraph by Lippmann, *Public Opinion*, 217.
20. Lippmann, *Liberty and the News*, 24–25.
21. "Election Study Finds Media Hit Hillary Hardest," Center for Media and Public Affairs, Washington, D.C., December 21, 2007. Journalists' impugning of Clinton's ambition can be seen in this example from the study, a quote from Andrea Mitchell on *NBC Nightly News*: "Critics say her best-known Senate vote, on Iraq, was driven by politics, not by principle."
22. See, for example, "Pakistanis Disapprove of Bin Laden's Killing," Pew Global Attitudes Project, http://pewresearch.org/databank/dailynumber/?NumberID=1277.
23. Quoted in Thomas E. Patterson, *The American Democracy*, 5th ed. (New York: McGraw-Hill, 2001), 161.
24. Lippmann, *Public Opinion*, 228.
25. See J. Goldstein, "Foucault Among the Sociologists: The 'Disciplines' and the History of the Professions," *History and Theory* 18 (1984): 175.
26. Everett C. Dennis and John C. Merritt, *Media Debates: Great Issues for the Digital Age*, 5th ed. (Belmont, CA: Wadsworth, 2006), 190–99.
27. See Paul Godkin, "Rethinking Journalism as a Profession," *Canadian Journal of Media Studies* 4 (2008): 111.
28. For a detailed profile of the education and training backgrounds of journalists, see David H. Weaver, Randal A. Beam, Bonnie J. Brownlee, Paul S. Voakes, and G. Cleveland Wilhoit, *The American Journalist in the 21st Century* (Mahwah, NJ: Lawrence Erlbaum, 2007), 31–53.
29. Cited in Sparrow, *Uncertain Guardians*, 58.
30. Andrew Rich, *Think Tanks, Public Policy, and the Politics of Expertise* (New York: Cambridge University Press, 2004).

31. "Informing Communities: Sustaining Democracy in the Digital Age," Report of the Knight Commission on the Information Needs of Communities in a Democracy, April 7, 2010.
32. Robert J. Haiman, *Best Practices for Newspaper Journalists*, a handbook prepared for the Free Press/Fair Press Project, Freedom Forum, Arlington, Virginia, September 3, 2002, 23.
33. Jamieson and Waldman, *The Press Effect*, 12.
34. Lippmann, *Public Opinion*, 228.
35. James Monroe won by a wider margin in 1820, but the party system at the time consisted of a single party (the "Era of Good Feelings"). In 1964, Lyndon Johnson topped FDR's popular vote margin though not his electoral vote margin.
36. Anthony Leviero, "Truman Confident of a Groundswell," *New York Times*, November 1, 1948, 1, 19.
37. Patterson, *Out of Order*, 95.
38. "Experts See Dewey Victory but Tight Race for Senate," *Newsweek*, November 1, 1948, 12.
39. "Seldom an Encouraging Word," *Newsweek*, November 1, 1948, 17.
40. "Prayer for a Chain Reaction," *Newsweek*, October 25, 1948, 24.
41. "Democrats," *Time*, October 18, 1948, 24.
42. Regina Lawrence, "Framing Obesity: The Evolution of News Discourse on a Public Health Issue," *International Journal of Press/Politics* 9, no. 3 (Summer 2004): 56–75.
43. Lippmann, *Public Opinion*, 217.
44. Scheuer, *The Big Picture*, 46–47.
45. Quoted in Cristine Russell, "Covering Controversial Science: Improving Reporting on Science and Public Policy," Working Paper 2006-4, Shorenstein Center, Spring 2006, 36.
46. Todd Oppenheimer, "Reality Bytes," *Columbia Journalism Review* 35 (September/October 1996): 40–42.
47. Emery, *The Press and America* (1962), 735.
48. Kevin Barnhurst, unpublished book manuscript, chapters 2 and 7.
49. Paul Radin, *Primitive Man as Philosopher* (New York: Dover, 1927).
50. Robert D. Leigh, *A Free and Responsible Press* (Chicago: University of Chicago Press, 1947), 23.
51. Quoted in Bates, "Realigning Journalism with Democracy," 23.
52. Lewis Gannett, "A Free and Responsible Press," *New York Herald Tribune*, March 28, 1947, 24.

53. Quoted in Bates, "Realigning Journalism with Democracy," 10.
54. Guido H. Stempel III and Hugh M. Cuthbertson, "The Prominence and Dominance of News Sources in Newspaper Medical Coverage," *Journalism Quarterly* 61 (1984): 671–76; Tony Atwater and Norma Green, "News Sources in Network Coverage of International Terrorism," *Journalism Quarterly* 65 (1988): 967–71; D. Charles Whitney, Marilyn Fritzler, Steven Jones, Sharon Mazzarella, and Lana Rakow, "Geographic and Source Biases in Network Television News, 1982–1984," *Journal of Broadcasting and Electronic Media* 33 (1989): 159–74.
55. Kevin G. Barnhurst, "The Makers of Meaning," *Political Communication* 20 (2003): 1–22.
56. Whitney et al., "Geographic and Source Biases in Network Television News."
57. Lawrence Soley, *The News Shapers: The Sources Who Explain the News* (New York: Praeger, 1992).
58. Barnhurst, unpublished book manuscript.
59. Matthew Nisbet, "Nature's Prophet," Discussion Paper D-78, Shorenstein Center, March 2013, http://shorensteincenter.org/wp-content/uploads/2013/03/D-78-Nisbet1.pdf.
60. Pincus, "Newspaper Narcissism."
61. Dennis and Merritt, *Media Debates*, 196.
62. The survey was conducted by Wolfgang Donsbach and Thomas Patterson. The statement is based on the author's examination in 2012 of the survey's data.
63. See Remy Fröhlich and Christina Holtz-Bacha, *Journalism Education in Europe and North America* (New York: Hampton Press, 2003).
64. "Planning for Curricular Change in Journalism Education," Project on the Future of Journalism and Mass Communication Education, School of Journalism, University of Oregon, Eugene, 1984, 5.
65. See Rakesh Khurana and J. C. Spender, "Herbert A. Simon on What Ails Business Schools: More Than 'A Problem in Organizational Design,'" *Journal of Management Science* 49 (2012): 619–39.
66. Kovach and Rosenstiel, *Elements of Journalism* (2001), 79–80.
67. Ibid., 79.
68. Ibid., 83.
69. Ibid.
70. Ibid., 89.
71. Lee Keath and Hadeel Al-Shalchi, "Protesters Press for Voice in Egyptian Democracy," Associated Press, March 12, 2011.

72. Thomas Friedman of the *New York Times*, cited in Brendan Nyhan and John Sides, "How Political Science Can Help Journalism (and Still Let Journalists Be Journalists)," *Forum* 9 (2011): 8.
73. Ibid.
74. Kovach and Rosenstiel, *Elements of Journalism* (2001), 85.
75. Lippmann, *Public Opinion*, 217–18; Heclo, "Campaigning and Governing," 3.
76. Fuller, *What Is Happening to News*, 139.
77. Pincus, "Newspaper Narcissism."
78. Quoted in Bob Giles, "Universities Teach Journalists Valuable Lessons," *Nieman Reports*, Spring 2001, www.nieman.harvard.edu/reports/article/101711/Universities-Teach-Journalists-Valuable-Lessons.aspx.
79. Meyer, *Precision Journalism*, 4, 14.
80. Ibid., 13.
81. Stephen K. Doig, "Reporting with the Tools of Social Science," *Nieman Reports*, Spring 2008, 48–49.
82. Lippmann, *Public Opinion*, 227.
83. B. Medsger, "Winds of Change: Challenges Confronting Journalism Education," Freedom Forum, Arlington, Virginia, 1996.
84. Michelle K. McGinn and Wolff-Michael Roth, "Preparing Students for Competent Scientific Practice: Implications of Recent Research in Science and Technology Studies," *Educational Researcher* 28, no. 3 (April 1999): 14–24. See also N. Roll-Hansen, "Science, Politics, and the Mass Media: On Biased Communication of Environmental Issues," *Science, Technology, and Human Values* 19 (1994): 324–41; Matthew Yglesias, "Political Science and Political Journalism," ThinkProgress blog, March 12, 2009.
85. Nyhan and Sides, "How Political Science Can Help Journalism," 1.
86. Barnhurst, unpublished book manuscript, chapter 3 and page 11.
87. Scheuer, *The Big Picture*, 104.
88. Lippmann, *Liberty and the News*, 74.
89. See Khurana and Spender, "Herbert A. Simon on What Ails Business Schools."
90. See Stephen D. Reese, "The Progressive Potential of Journalism Education: Rethinking the Academic versus Professional Divide," *Harvard International Journal of Press/Politics* 4 (1999): 70–91.
91. Geneva Overholser, "Keeping Journalism, and Journalism Education, Connected to the Public," *Nieman Journalism Lab*, Sep-

tember 11, 2012, www.niemanlab.org/2012/09/geneva-overholser-keeping-journalism-and-journalism-school-connected-to-the-public/?utm_source=Daily+Lab+email+list&utm_medium=email&utm_campaign=8454ca109d-DAILY_EMass.IL.

92. Craig Silverman, "A New Age for Truth," *Nieman Reports* 66 (Summer 2012): 4.
93. For a comparable example from another profession, see Christopher Johns, "Framing Learning through Reflection within Carper's Fundamental Ways of Knowing Nursing," *Journal of Advanced Nursing* 22 (1995): 226.
94. Quoted in Melvin Mencher, "Will the Meaning of Journalism Survive?," *Nieman Reports*, June 2006, www.nieman.harvard.edu/reports/article/100501/Will-the-Meaning-of-Journalism-Survive.aspx.
95. Hamby, "Did Twitter Kill the Boys on the Bus?," 64.
96. C. W. Anderson, Emily Bell, and Clay Shirky, "Post-Industrial Journalism: Adapting to the Present," Tow Center for Digital Journalism, Columbia University Graduate School of Journalism, New York, 2012, http://towcenter.org/research/post-industrial-journalism/.

FOUR

The Education Problem

1. Lippmann, *Liberty and the News*, 59.
2. Jack Slater, "Who Said It First? Journalism Is the First Rough Draft of History," *Slate*, August 30, 2010.
3. Philip Schlesinger, "Newsmen and Their Time Machine," *British Journal of Sociology* 28 (1977): 336.
4. Quoted in Paul Taylor, *See How They Run* (New York: Knopf, 1990), 25.
5. See James N. Gregory, *The Southern Diaspora: How The Great Migrations of Black and White Southerners Transformed America* (Chapel Hill: University of North Carolina Press, 2005).
6. Comment made by George Will at the annual meeting of the American Association of Political Consultants, Washington, D.C., 1977. Another example of the disjunction between journalism and history is airline safety; see Roger W. Cobb and David M. Primo, *The Plane Truth: Air-*

line Crashes, the Media, and Transportation Policy (Washington, D.C.: Brookings Institution, 2003), 46.

7. Melvin L. DeFleur and Everett E. Dennis, *Understanding Mass Communication*, 7th ed. (Boston: Houghton Mifflin, 2002), 73–74.
8. Cited in Nyhan and Sides, "How Political Science Can Help Journalism," 1.
9. Lippmann, *Public Opinion*, 219.
10. Jennifer Mahand, "Birth Control Linked to Heart Attack, Stroke," ABC News, June 13, 2012, http://abcnews.go.com/Health/birth-control-linked-heart-attack-stroke/story?id=16559498.
11. Victor Cohn, quoted in Russell, "Covering Controversial Science," 32.
12. Robert Entman, *Democracy Without Citizens: Media and the Decay of American Politics* (New York: Oxford University Press, 1989); Shanto Iyengar, *Is Anyone Responsible?: How Television Frames Political Issues* (Chicago: University of Chicago Press, 1991).
13. Quoted in Mencher, "Will the Meaning of Journalism Survive?"
14. Cappella and Jamieson, *Spiral of Cynicism*, cited in Doris A. Graber, *Processing Politics: Learning from Television in the Internet Age* (Chicago: University of Chicago Press, 2001), 140.
15. Graber, *Processing Politics*, 145.
16. Lichter and Smith, "Bad News Bears," 82.
17. Scheuer, *The Big Picture*, 46–47.
18. Quoted in ibid., 94.
19. See, for example, Richard Nadeau, Neil Neville, Elisabeth Gidengil, and André Blais, "Election Campaigns as Information Campaigns," *Political Communication* 25 (2008): 229–48.
20. Donald A. Schön, *The Reflective Practitioner: How Professionals Think in Action* (New York: Basic Books, 1983), 61.
21. Ibid.
22. J. John Loughran, "Effective Reflective Practice," *Journal of Teacher Education* 53 (2002): 33.
23. See Michael Schudson, *Discovering the News* (Cambridge, MA: Harvard University Press, 1978).
24. Nina Easton, "Rebelling Against the Rich," Discussion Paper D-75, Shorenstein Center, September 2012, 2, http://shorensteincenter.org/wp-content/uploads/2012/09/D-75_easton1.pdf.
25. For an early study of this tendency, see J. Herbert Altschull, "The

Journalist and Instant History," *Journalism Quarterly*, 50 (1973): 545–51.

26. Quoted in Sparrow, *Uncertain Guardians*, 119.
27. Russell, "Covering Controversial Science," 2.
28. Joseph P. Bernt, Frank E. Fee, Jacqueline Gifford, and Guido H. Stempel III, "How Well Can Editors Predict Reader Interest in News?," *Newspaper Research Journal* 21 (2000): 2–10.
29. Anderson et al., "Post-Industrial Journalism."
30. Robert Niles, "A Journalist's Guide to the Scientific Method, and Why It's Important," *Online Journalism Review*, USC Annenberg, August 23, 2011, www.ojr.org/ojr/people/robert/201108/2004/.
31. Barnhurst, unpublished book manuscript, chapters 2 and 10; C. Tavris, "How to Publicize Science," in *Reporting Science: The Case of Aggression*, ed. J. H. Goldstein (Hillsdale, NJ: Lawrence Erlbaum, 1986), 21–32.
32. Before journalists developed the interview as a reporting tool, reporting was based largely on documents and personal observation. By the early 1900s, the interview was a mainstay of American journalism. It gradually became a reporting tool in other countries, though more limited in its use.
33. Kathleen Hall Jamieson and Karlyn Kohrs Campbell, *The Interplay of Influence*, 5th ed. (Belmont, CA: Wadsworth, 2001), 72.
34. Edward E. Jones and Victor A. Harris, "The Attribution of Attitudes," *Journal of Experimental Social Psychology* 3 (1967): 1–24.
35. Adam Nagourney, "G.O.P. Retakes Control of the Senate in a Show of Presidential Influence; Pataki, Jeb Bush, and Lautenberg Win," *New York Times*, November 6, 2002, A6.
36. Dana Milbank and Mike Allen, "White House Claims Election Is Broad Mandate," *Washington Post*, November 7, 2002, A27.
37. Luke J. Keele, Brian J. Fogarty, and James A. Stimson, "Presidential Campaigning in the 2002 Congressional Election," *PS: Political Science and Politics* 37 (2004): 827.
38. Ibid.
39. Ibid., 831.
40. Jack Fuller, *News Values* (Chicago: University of Chicago Press, 1996), 212; Hugh Heclo, "The Presidential Illusion," in *The Illusion of Presidential Government*, ed. Hugh Heclo and Lester M. Salamon (Boulder, CO: Westview, 1981), 8.

41. John Hartley, *Understanding News* (London: Methuen, 1982), 78.
42. Patterson, *The Mass Media Election*, 51.
43. Quoted in Kovach and Rosenstiel, *The Elements of Journalism* (2001), 187.
44. Westerstahl and Johansson, "News Ideologies as Moulders of Domestic News."
45. Hans Mattias Kepplinger and J. Habermeier, "The Impact of Key Events on the Presentation of Reality," unpublished paper, Insitut für Publizistik, University of Mainz, Germany, 1995.
46. Boykoff, *Who Speaks for the Climate?*, 118–19.
47. Meyer, *The Vanishing Newspaper*, 89.
48. Patterson, *The Mass Media Election*, 77–80.
49. Matthew C. Nisbet and Bruce V. Lewenstein, "Biotechnology and the American Media," *Science Communication* 23 (2002): 364.
50. Robert Entman, "Framing: Towards Clarification of a Fractured Paradigm," in *McQuail's Reader in Mass Communication Theory*, ed. Denis McQuail (London: Sage, 2002), 391–92.
51. See, for example, Emily K. Varga, D. Jasun Carr, Jeffrey P. Nytes, and Dhavan V. Shah, "Precision vs. Realism on the Framing Continuum," *Political Communication* 27 (2010): 1–19; Iyengar, *Is Anyone Responsible?*; James N. Druckman, "Political Preference Formation," *American Political Science Review* 98 (2004): 671–86; de Vreese and Elenbaas, "Media in the Game of Politics," 290; Nicholas A. Valentino, Thomas A. Buhr, and Matthew N. Beckmann, "When the Frame Is the Game," *Journalism and Mass Communication Quarterly* 78 (2001): 93–112.
52. Jacobs and Shapiro, *Politicians Don't Pander*, 181.
53. "Osama Bin Laden's Death Continues to Dominate the News," Pew Research Center's Project for Excellence in Journalism, May 9, 2011, 2, www.journalism.org/index_report/pej_news_coverage_index_may_2_8_2011.
54. Jamieson and Waldman, *The Press Effect*, 93–94; in the book, the last sentence in the quoted material appeared before the rest. See also Martin Gilens, Lynn Vavreck, and Martin Cohen, "The Mass Media and the Public's Assessments of Presidential Candidates, 1952–2000," *Journal of Politics* 69 (2007): 1160–75.
55. Iyengar, *Is Anyone Responsible?*, 56.
56. Ibid.
57. Lesa Hatley Major, "The Mediating Role of Emotions in the Relation-

ship between Framing and Attribution of Responsibility for Health Problems," *Journalism and Mass Communication Quarterly* 88 (2011): 502–22.

58. Matthew V. Storin, "While America Slept: Coverage of Terrorism from 1993 to September 11, 2001," Working Paper 2002-7, Shorenstein Center, Spring 2002, http://shorensteincenter.org/wp-content/uploads/2012/03/2002_07_storin.pdf.

59. Remark by Richard Holbrooke at a Shorenstein Center brown-bag lunch, October 4, 2001.

60. Iyengar, *Is Anyone Responsible?*, 140.

61. Nicholas Lemann, "Research Chat: Nicholas Lemann on Journalism, Scholarship, and More Informed Reporting," Journalist's Resource, June 20, 2012, http://journalistsresource.org/reference/research/nicholas-lemann-journalism-scholarship-reporting.

62. J. S. Brown et al., "Situated Cognition and the Culture of Learning," *Educational Researcher* 18 (1989): 32–41, cited in Michelle K. McGinn and Wolff-Michael Roth, "Reviewed work(s)," *Educational Researcher* 28 (1999): 14–24.

63. Lee S. Shulman, "Those Who Understand: Knowledge Growth in Teaching," *Educational Researcher* 15 (1986): 9. Described in Punya Mishra and Matthew J. Koehler, "Technological Pedagogical Content Knowledge," *Teachers College Record* 108 (2006): 1021.

64. Jean Lave and Etienne Wenger, *Situated Learning: Legitimate Peripheral Participation* (Cambridge, UK: Cambridge University Press, 1991), cited in Lynette Sheridan Burns, "Teaching Journalism as Decision-Making Best Practice in Journalism Education: An International Web Conference," March 25–April 7, 2001.

65. Steve Coll, "Research Chat: Steve Coll of *The New Yorker* and the New America Foundation," Journalist's Resource, June 20, 2012, http://journalistsresource.org/reference/research/research-chat-steve-coll-new-yorker-new-america-foundation.

66. Tom Rosenstiel, *The Beat Goes On* (New York: Twentieth Century Fund, 1994), 16, quoted in Rosen, *What Are Journalists For?* 290.

67. Anderson et al., "Post-Industrial Journalism."

68. Harry C. Boyte, *Civic Agency and the Politics of Knowledge*, Kettering Foundation, April 3, 2009.

69. Shulman, "Those Who Understand," 9.

70. Quoted in Donica Mensing, "Rethinking [Again] the Future of Journalism Education," *Journalism Studies* 11 (2010): 514.

71. Emery, *The Press and America* (1962), 735.
72. Quoted in Scheuer, *The Big Picture*, 132.
73. Quoted in W. David Sloan and Lisa Mullikin Parcell, *American Journalism: History, Principles, Practices* (Jefferson, NC: McFarland, 2002), 82.
74. Scheuer, *The Big Picture*, 133.
75. "Planning for Curricular Change in Journalism Education," 5.
76. Cherian George, "Beyond Professionalization," *Journalism and Mass Communication Educator* 66 (2011): 259.
77. Robert Steiner, "In Toronto, We're Dumping the J-School Model to Produce a New Kind of Reporter," *Nieman Journalism Lab*, October 16, 2012, www.niemanlab.org/2012/10/robert-steiner-in-toronto-were-dumping-the-j-school-model-to-produce-a-new-kind-of-reporter/.
78. "New Curriculum Project," unpublished and undated report, Columbia University Graduate School of Journalism, New York.
79. Alex Jones, "Forward," in "A Report on the Carnegie-Knight Initiative on the Future of Journalism Education," Shorenstein Center, 2011, 1.
80. Quoted in Wolfgang Donsbach and Tom Fiedler, "Journalism School Curriculum Enrichment: A Mid-Term Report of the Carnegie-Knight Initiative on the Future of Journalism Education," Shorenstein Center, October 2008, 2.
81. Ibid., 3.
82. Ibid., 2.
83. See Leonard Downie, Jr., and Robert G. Kaiser, *The News about the News: American Journalism in Peril* (New York: Vintage, 2003).
84. Lemann, "Research Chat."
85. Anderson et al., "Post-Industrial Journalism," 93.
86. Robin Blom and Lucinda D. Davenport, "Searching for the Core of Journalism Education," *Journalism and Mass Communication Educator* 67 (2012): 79.
87. The unpublished survey was conducted by the Shorenstein Center in 2008.
88. See, for example, Chris Argyris, "Teaching Smart People How to Learn," *Harvard Business Review* 69 (1991): 99–109.
89. Quoted in Jones, "Forward," 3.
90. Quoted in Giles, "Universities Teach Journalists Valuable Lessons."

91. Wilson Lowrey, George L. Daniels, and Lee B. Becker, "Predictors of Convergence Curricula in Journalism and Mass Communication Programs," *Journalism and Mass Communication Educator* 60 (2005): 31–46.
92. Jones, "Forward," 4.
93. Mitchell Stephens, "Beyond News: The Case for Wisdom Journalism," Discussion Paper D-53, Shorenstein Center, June 2009, 24, http://shorensteincenter.org/wp-content/uploads/2012/03/d53_stephens.pdf.
94. Quoted in Katie Koch, "Academia, Meet the Press," *Harvard Gazette*, March 28, 2012, http://news.harvard.edu/gazette/story/2012/03/academia-meet-the-press/.
95. Quoted in Andrew Phelps, "From White Paper to Newspaper," *Nieman Journalism Lab*, November 21, 2011, www.niemanlab.org/2011/11/from-white-paper-to-newspaper-making-academia-more-accessible-to-journalists/.
96. Quoted in Koch, "Academia, Meet the Press."
97. Anderson et al., "Post-Industrial Journalism."
98. Quoted in Meyer, *The Vanishing Newspaper*, 233.

FIVE

The Audience Problem

1. Lippmann, *Public Opinion*, 223–24.
2. Thomas Jefferson, letter to Virginia legislator Charles Yancey, January 6, 1816, accessible at http://oll.libertyfund.org/?option=com_staticxt&staticfile=show.php%3Ftitle=807&chapter=88152&layout=html&Itemid=27.
3. *New York Times Co. v. United States*, 403 U.S. 713 (1971), http://caselaw.lp.findlaw.com/cgi-bin/getcase.pl?court=us&vol=403&invol=713.
4. See Michael Schudson, *The Power of News* (Cambridge, MA: Harvard University Press, 1995), 199.
5. Matthew Gentzkow, Edward L. Glaeser, and Claudia Goldin, "The Rise of the Fourth Estate," in *Corruption and Reform: Lessons from America's Economic History*, ed. Edward L. Glaeser and Claudia Goldin

(Cambridge, MA: National Bureau of Economic Research, 2006), 187–230.

6. V. O. Key, Jr., *Public Opinion and American Democracy* (New York: Knopf, 1961), 388; see also Paul Starr, *The Creation of the Media* (New York: Basic Books, 2004).
7. See David T. Z. Mindich, *Just the Facts: How "Objectivity" Came to Define American Journalism* (New York: New York University Press, 2000).
8. Frank Bruni, *Ambling into History: The Unlikely Odyssey of George W. Bush* (New York: HarperCollins, 2002), 101.
9. Cited in Graber, *Processing Politics*, 184.
10. See, for example, Charles Layton, "State of the American Newspaper. What Do People Really Want?," *American Journalism Review*, March 1999, www.ajr.org/Article.asp?id=3271.
11. Doris Graber, *Processing the News* (New York: Longman, 1984), 103–5.
12. Delroy L. Paulhus and Douglas B. Reid, "Enhancement and Denial in Socially Desirable Responding," *Journal of Personality and Social Psychology* 60 (1991): 307–17.
13. See, for example, Layton, "State of the American Newspaper."
14. Michael J. Robinson, "Two Decades of American News Preferences," parts 1 and 2, Pew Research Center for the People and the Press, 2007, www.pewresearch.org/2007/08/15/two-decades-of-american-news-preferences/. The discussion on the pages that follow is derived from Robinson's assessment.
15. Patterson, "Doing Well and Doing Good," 6–7.
16. Michael J. Robinson, "Two Decades of American News Preferences, Part 1: Analyzing What News the Public Follows—and Doesn't Follow," Pew Research Center for the People and the Press, 2007, 9, http://pewresearch.org/files/old-assets/pdf/NewsInterest1986-2007.pdf.
17. Ibid.
18. Patterson, *The Mass Media Election*, 86–89; Graber, *Processing Politics*, 203–6.
19. Shanto Iyengar, Helmut Norpoth, and Kyu S. Hahn, "Consumer Demand for Election News: The Horserace Sells," *Journal of Politics* 66 (2004): 174.
20. Ibid.
21. Graber, *Processing the News* (1988), 206.
22. "The Invisible Primary—Invisible No Longer," Pew Research Cen-

ter's Project for Excellence in Journalism, October 29, 2007, 8, www.journalism.org/node/8187.

23. Quoted in Hamby, "Did Twitter Kill the Boys on the Bus?," 28.
24. W. Lance Bennett, "Political Communication and Democratic Governance," in *Democracy in the Twenty-First Century*, ed. Peter Nardulli, draft manuscript. See also Susan Herbst, *Reading Public Opinion: How Political Actors View the Democratic Process* (Chicago: University of Chicago Press, 1998); Jamieson and Waldman, *The Press Effect*, 168.
25. Quoted in Hamby, "Did Twitter Kill the Boys on the Bus?," 26.
26. See, for example, David E. Sanger, "Obama Nuclear Agenda Only Gets Harder after Treaty," *New York Times*, December 21, 2010, www.nytimes.com/2010/12/22/us/politics/22assess.html?_r=0.
27. Jay Rosen, PressThink blog, April 12, 2009.
28. Patterson, *Out of Order*, 60–65.
29. Tom Wicker, "The Role of the Media—Informing or Influencing the Electorate?," paper presented at NBC Forum, Washington, D.C., March 1977, 1–2.
30. Hamby, "Did Twitter Kill the Boys on the Bus?," 27.
31. Ibid., 67.
32. Pamela J. Shoemaker, Timothy P. Vos, and Stephen D. Reese, "Journalists as Gatekeepers," in *The Handbook of Journalism Studies*, ed. K. Wahl-Jorgensen and T. Hanitzsch (New York: Routledge, 2009).
33. Dagnes, *Politics on Demand*, 30.
34. Pincus, "Newspaper Narcissism."
35. Levy, "Disdaining the News."
36. Graber, *On Media*, 30.
37. Ibid., 22.
38. Quoted in Jib Fowles, *Why Viewers Watch* (Newbury Park, CA: Sage, 1992), 163. The study was Mark Levy's doctoral dissertation at Columbia University, New York.
39. Robinson, "Two Decades of American News Preferences, Part 1," 19.
40. Pete Hamill, *News Is a Verb* (New York: Ballantine, 1998), 49.
41. Gerry Philipsen, "Speaking as a Communal Resource in Four Cultures," *International and Intercultural Communication Annual*, 1989, 79–92.
42. See, for example, Cornelia Brantner, Katharina Lobinger, and Irmgard Wetzstein, "Effects of Visual Framing on Emotional Responses and Evaluations of News Stories about the Gaza Conflict, 2009," *Journalism and Mass Communication Quarterly* 88 (2011): 523–40.

43. Robinson, "Two Decades of American News Preferences, Part 1," 9.
44. Ibid., 11.
45. Jacquielynn Floyd, "When Horse Races Go Too Far Astray," *Dallas Morning News*, August 30, 2004, 1B.
46. Rosenstiel et al., *We Interrupt This Newscast*, 101.
47. "What Americans Learned from the Media about the Health Care Debate," Pew Research Center's Project for Excellence in Journalism, June 19, 2012, www.journalism.org/commentary_backgrounder/how_media_has_covered_health_care_debate.
48. Cappella and Jamieson, "News Frames, Political Cynicism, and Media Cynicism," 71.
49. Patterson, *The Mass Media Election*, 86, 89.
50. Graber, *Processing the News* (1984), 203, 206.
51. See, for example, Adam Nagourney, "Broad Gun Control Efforts Introduced in Wake of Shooting," *New York Times*, December 18, 2012, www.nytimes.com/2012/12/19/us/states-leaders-proposing-steps-to-control-guns.html?_r=0.
52. "How the Media Covered the Gulf Oil Spill Disaster," press release, Pew Research Center's Project for Excellence in Journalism, August 25, 2010.
53. David Buckingham, "News Media, Political Socialization and Popular Citizenship: Towards a New Agenda," *Critical Studies in Mass Communication* 14 (1997): 344–66; Graber, *Processing Politics*, 134.
54. Robinson, "Two Decades of American News Preferences, Part 1," 12.
55. Ibid., 8.
56. Graber, *Processing the News* (1984), 105.
57. Christine F. Rideout, "News Coverage and Talk Shows in the 1992 Presidential Campaign," *PS: Political Science and Politics* 26 (1993): 712–16.
58. Pincus, "Newspaper Narcissism."
59. Popkin, *The Reasoning Voter*; Benjamin I. Page and Robert Y. Shapiro, *The Rational Public* (Chicago: University of Chicago Press, 1992).
60. Kovach and Rosenstiel, *The Elements of Journalism* (2007), 221–22.
61. Rosenstiel et al., *We Interrupt This Newscast*, 9.
62. Meyer, *The Vanishing Newspaper*, 2.
63. Ibid., 82.
64. Jeffrey A. Dvorkin, "It's About Time: Have NPR Reports Become Too Short?," Organization of News Ombudsmen, November 7, 2002,

http://newsombudsmen.org/columns/its-about-time-have-npr-reports-become-too-short.

65. "The Invisible Primary," 8.
66. Richard Adler, "News Cities: The Next Generation of Healthy Informed Communities," Report of the 2010 Aspen Institute Forum on Communications and Society, Aspen Institute, Queenstown, MD, May 10, 2011, 46.
67. Michael P. McCauley, *NPR: The Trials and Triumphs of National Public Radio* (New York: Columbia University Press, 2005), 79.
68. "Americans Show Signs of Leaving a News Outlet, Citing Less Information," Pew Research Center's Project for Excellence in Journalism, March 18, 2013, http://stateofthemedia.org/2013/special-reports-landing-page/citing-reduced-quality-many-americans-abandon-news-outlets/.
69. "Understanding the Participatory News Consumer," Pew Research Center's Internet and American Life Project, March 1, 2010, www.pewinternet.org/Press-Releases/2010/Online-News.aspx.
70. Tom Rosenstiel et al., *We Interrupt This Newscast*, 185.
71. Clay Shirky, remark made at twenty-fifth anniversary seminar of the Shorenstein Center, October 14, 2011.
72. Jim VandeHei, remark made at twenty-fifth anniversary seminar of the Shorenstein Center, October 15, 2011.
73. Adam Moss, remark made at twenty-fifth anniversary seminar of the Shorenstein Center, October 14, 2011.
74. Ibid.
75. Vivek Kundra, remark made at twenty-fifth anniversary seminar of the Shorenstein Center, October 14, 2011.
76. Rosenstiel et al., *We Interrupt This Newscast*, 185–86.
77. Anderson et al., "Post-Industrial Journalism."
78. Ibid.
79. Stephens, "Beyond News," 10.
80. Ibid., 25.
81. Patterson, "Doing Well and Doing Good," 7.
82. Jakob Nielsen, "Search Engines as Leeches on the Web," Jakob Nielsen's Alertbox, October 31, 2012, www.nngroup.com/articles/search-engines-as-leeches-on-the-web/; see also Jakob Nielsen, *Designing Web Usability* (Indianapolis, IN: New Riders, 1999).
83. Meyer, *The Vanishing Newspaper*, 2.

84. See, for example, John Maltby, Liza Day, Lynn E. McCutcheon, Raphael Gillett, James Houran, and Diane D. Ashe, "Personality and Coping: A Context for Examining Celebrity Worship and Mental Health," *British Journal of Psychology* 95 (2004): 411–29.
85. Quoted in McCartney, "News Lite," 19–21.
86. Matthew Carleton Ehrlich, "The Journalism of Outrageousness," *Journalism and Communication Monographs* 155 (February 1996).
87. Deborah Potter and Walter Gantz, "Bringing People Back to Local TV," NewsLab survey, 2000.
88. Ladd, *Why Americans Hate the Media and How It Matters*, 126.
89. Stroud, *Niche News*.
90. Richard Maisel, "The Decline of Mass Media," *Public Opinion Quarterly* 37 (1973): 159–70.
91. Meyer, *The Vanishing Newspaper*, 82.
92. Rosenstiel et al., *We Interrupt This Newscast*, 49.
93. Quoted in "The State of the News Media 2013: Overview," Pew Research Center's Project for Excellence in Journalism.
94. Graber, *Processing the News* (1988), 129.
95. Timothy E. Cook, *Governing with the News* (Chicago: University of Chicago Press, 1998), 173.
96. Cited in Jones, *Losing the News*, 203.
97. See Lippmann, *Public Opinion*, 37–40.
98. Rosen, *What Are Journalists For?*, 295.

SIX

The Democracy Problem

1. Lippmann, *Public Opinion*, 19.
2. Bruce Bimber, *Information and American Democracy: Technology in the Evolution of Political Power* (New York: Cambridge University Press, 2003), 34.
3. See, for example, W. Russell Neuman, ed., *Media, Technology, and Society: Theories of Media Evolution* (Ann Arbor: University of Michigan Press, 2010).
4. Frank Luther Mott, *American Journalism: A History, 1690–1960* (New York: Macmillan, 1962), 122–23, 220–27.

5. Emery, *The Press and America* (1962), 515–16.
6. William H. Young and Nancy K. Young, *The 1930s* (Westport, CT: Greenwood, 2002), 163.
7. Robinson, "Public Affairs Television and the Growth of Political Malaise."
8. Martin J. Wattenberg, *Is Voting for Young People?* (New York: Pearson Longman, 2008), 32.
9. The preradio news figure is the author's estimate based on the adult population and newspaper circulation in the 1920s.
10. Thomas E. Patterson, "Young People and News," Shorenstein Center, July 2007, 22, www.hks.harvard.edu/presspol/research/carnegie-knight/young_people_and_news_2007.pdf.
11. Patterson, "Doing Well and Doing Good," 13.
12. Victoria J. Rideout, Ulla G. Foehr, Donald F. Roberts, and Mollyann Brodie, "Kids and Media at the New Millennium," Kaiser Family Foundation Report, Menlo Park, CA, 1999, 12.
13. Patterson, "Doing Well and Doing Good," 13.
14. Wattenberg, *Is Voting for Young People?*, 32.
15. Ibid.
16. "Americans Spending More Time Following the News," 43.
17. Patterson, "Young People and News," 12–14.
18. Ibid., 11; Hindman, *The Myth of Digital Democracy*, 131.
19. Hindman, *The Myth of Digital Democracy*, 68.
20. "In Changing News Landscape, Even Television Is Vulnerable," Pew Research Center for the People and the Press, September 12, 2012, www.people-press.org/2012/09/27/section-1-watching-reading-and-listening-to-the-news-3/.
21. Joseph Turow, *Breaking Up America* (Chicago: University of Chicago Press, 1997), 2.
22. See Pew Research Center surveys, 1994–2012.
23. "Americans Spending More Time Following the News," 43.
24. Todd Gitlin, *Media Unlimited* (New York: Henry Holt, 2002), 5–6.
25. See Robert Putnam, *Bowling Alone* (New York: Simon & Schuster, 2000).
26. See William Powers, *Hamlet's BlackBerry* (New York: HarperCollins, 2010); Gitlin, *Media Unlimited*.
27. Marshall McLuhan, *Understanding Media* (Cambridge, MA: MIT Press, 1964), xi.
28. Samantha Murphy, "Afraid of Losing Your Cell Phone? You May Have

Nomophobia Like Half the Population," Mashable Tech, February 21, 2012, http://mashable.com/2012/02/21/nomophobia/.

29. Quoted in Steve Lohr, "The Smartphone's Rapid Rise from Gadget to Tool to Necessity," *New York Times*, June 10, 2009, B1.

30. Quoted in Cara Feinberg, "The Mediatrician," *Harvard Magazine*, November/December 2011, 52.

31. Amanda Lenhart, "Teens, Smartphones, and Texting," Pew Research Center's Internet and American Life Project, March 19, 2012, http://pewinternet.org/Reports/2012/Teens-and-smartphones.aspx.

32. See Kevin G. Barnhurst and Catherine A. Steele, "Image Bite News: The Coverage of Elections on U.S. Television, 1968–1992," *Harvard International Journal of Press/Politics* 2 (1997): 40–58.

33. Ibid., 42.

34. "Internet Sapping Broadcast News Audience," Pew Research Center for the People and the Press, June 11, 2000, www.people-press.org/2000/06/11/section-iv-attitudes-toward-the-news/.

35. Bauerlein, *The Dumbest Generation*, 45.

36. "Key News Audiences Now Blend Online and Traditional Sources," Pew Research Center for the People and the Press, August 17, 2008, www.people-press.org/2008/08/17/key-news-audiences-now-blend-online-and-traditional-sources/.

37. Mickie Edwardson, Kurt Kent, and Maeve McConnell, "Television News Information Gain: Videotext versus a Talking Head," *Journal of Broadcasting and Electronic Media* 29 (1985): 367–85.

38. Jonathan S. Morris and Richard Forgette, "News Grazers, Television News, Political Knowledge, and Engagement," *Harvard International Journal of Press/Politics* 12 (2007): 91–107.

39. "Interview: Sherry Turkle," *Frontline*, February 2, 2010; see also Sherry Turkle, *Alone Together* (New York: Basic Books, 2011).

40. Doris A. Graber, "Seeing Is Remembering," *Journal of Communication* 40 (1990): 134–55.

41. Herbert A. Simon, "Designing Organizations for an Information-Rich World," in Martin Greenberger, *Computers, Communication, and the Public Interest* (Baltimore: Johns Hopkins University Press, 1971), 40–41.

42. "Five-Minute Memory," November 27, 2008. The study was conducted by behavioral psychologists and commissioned by Lloyds TSB for purposes of determining marketing strategies.

43. Herbert H. Hyman and Paul B. Sheatsley, "Some Reasons Why Information Campaigns Fail," *Public Opinion Quarterly* 11 (1947): 412.
44. Prior, *Post-Broadcast Democracy*, 83; see also Ackerman and Fishkin, *Deliberation Day*, 5; Keeter and Zukin, *Uninformed Choice*; Delli Carpini and Keeter, *What Americans Know about Politics and Why It Matters*; Bauerlein, *The Dumbest Generation*, 235.
45. See Edward Jay Epstein, *News from Nowhere* (New York: Vintage, 1974); Maxwell E. McCombs and Donald L. Shaw, "The Evolution of Agenda-Setting Research: Twenty-Five Years in the Marketplace of Ideas," *Journal of Communication* 43 (1993): 58–67.
46. See Patterson and McClure, *The Unseeing Eye*.
47. Shanto Iyengar, "The Flow of Information in the Digital Age," Political Communication Report, October 2011, www.politicalcommunication.org/newsletter_21_3_iyengar.html.
48. Colin Leys, *Market-Driven Politics* (London: Verso, 2001), 150.
49. Karl W. Deutsch, "Communication Theory and Social Science," *American Journal of Orthopsychiatry* 22 (1952): 469–83.
50. Eric J. Johnson and Lisa Zaval, "Some People's Climate Beliefs Shift with Weather: Study Shows Malleability on a Long-Term Question," Earth Institute, Columbia University, New York, April 6, 2011, www.earth.columbia.edu/articles/view/2794; Lee Dye, "Global Warming and the Pollsters: Who's Right?," ABC News, June 16, 2010, http://abcnews.go.com/Technology/DyeHard/global-warming-polls-climate-change/story?id=10921583#.T_yQO5HpcjA.
51. See, for example, Benkler, *The Wealth of Networks*.
52. Bruce A. Williams and Michael X. Delli Carpini, *After Broadcast News* (New York: Cambridge University Press, 2011), 88.
53. See, for example, Gillmor, *We the Media*.
54. Williams and Delli Carpini, *After Broadcast News*, 89.
55. Singer, "The Journalist in the Network," 76.
56. Scott Gant, *We're All Journalists Now* (New York: Free Press, 2007).
57. Quoted in William Cole, ed., *The Most of A. J. Liebling* (New York: Simon & Schuster, 1963), 7.
58. Mary Lou Fulton, quoted in Mark Glaser, "The New Voices: Hyperlocal Citizen Media Sites Want You (to Write)!," *Online Journalism Review*, USC Annenberg, November 17, 2004.
59. There are times when crowd judgments are superior even to those of professional analysts. See James Surowiecki, *The Wisdom of Crowds* (New York: Doubleday, 2004).

60. Anderson et al., "Post-Industrial Journalism," 1.
61. Serena Carpenter, "How Online Citizen Journalism Publications and Online Newspapers Utilize the Objective Standard and Rely on External Sources," *Journalism and Mass Communication Quarterly* 85 (2008): 533–50.
62. Hindman, *The Myth of Digital Democracy*, 101.
63. Ibid., 90–91.
64. Ibid., 60–61.
65. Tom Grubisich, "Grassroots Journalism: Actual Content vs. Shining Idea," *Online Journalism Review*, USC Annenberg, October 6, 2005, www.ojr.org/ojr/stories/051006/.
66. Graber, *On Media*, 52.
67. D. Travers Scott, "Pundits in Muckrakers' Clothing," in *Blogging, Citizenship, and the Future of Media*, ed. Mark Tremayne (New York: Routledge, 2007), 39; Michael Keren, *Blogosphere: The New Political Arena* (Lanham, MD: Lexington, 2006).
68. William P. Eveland, Jr., and Ivan Dylko, "Reading Political Blogs in the 2004 Election Campaign," in Tremayne, *Blogging, Citizenship, and the Future of Media*, 108; see also Thomas J. Johnson and Barbara K. Kaye, "Wag the Blog," *Journalism and Mass Communication Quarterly* 81 (2004): 622–42.
69. Carpenter, "How Online Citizen Journalism."
70. Graber, *On Media*, 52.
71. W. Russell Neuman, "New Media—New Research Paradigm?," Political Communication Report, October 2011, www.politicalcommunication.org/newsletter_21_3_neuman.html.
72. Williams and Delli Carpini, *After Broadcast News*, 124.
73. John Dewey, *The Public and Its Problems* (New York: Holt, 1927), 142.
74. Ibid., 213.
75. Dewey has been cited by Jay Rosen, Jeff Jarvis, and others as the foundational theorist of citizen journalism.
76. Jeff Jarvis, *What Would Google Do?*, reprint ed. (New York: HarperBusiness, 2011), 245.
77. Jamieson and Waldman, *The Press Effect*, 12.
78. Graber, *On Media*, 52.
79. Williams and Delli Carpini, *After Broadcast News*, 311.
80. See Rosen, *What Are Journalists For?*
81. John Hartley, "Journalism as a Human Right," in *Global Journal-*

ism Research, ed. Martin Löffelholz and David Weaver (Malden, MA: Blackwell, 2008): 43.

82. David S. Broder, "Press Should Level with the Readers," *Washington Post*, June 9, 1979.
83. Dennis and Merritt, *Media Debates*, 156.
84. Klein, "Unpopular Mandate."
85. Lippmann, *Public Opinion*, 202.
86. See, for example, Delli Carpini and Keeter, *What Americans Know about Politics*.
87. Maureen Dowd, "Toilet Paper Barricades," *New York Times*, August 12, 2009.
88. Bruce Ackerman, "*The Daily Show* and *The Colbert Report* in a Changing Information Environment: Should 'Fake News' Be Held to Real Standards?," in *Will the Last Reporter Please Turn Out the Lights*, ed. Robert McChesney and Victor Pickard (New York: New Press, 2011), 301.
89. Quoted in Boyte, "Civic Agency and the Politics of Knowledge," 9.

INDEX